A Journal of Arts, Literature and Social Commentary

2012 • Number 6

Stone Canoe, a Journal of Arts, Literature and Social Commentary, is published annually by Syracuse University. Address all correspondence to *Stone Canoe,* 700 University Avenue, Syracuse, New York 13244-2530. E-mail: *stonecanoe@uc.syr.edu.* Phone: 315-443-3225/4165. Fax: 315-443-4174. Web: *stonecanoejournal.org.*

Stone Canoe showcases the work of a diverse mix of emerging and well-established artists and writers with ties to Upstate New York. In so doing, the journal supports Syracuse University's ongoing commitment to creative community partnerships, and seeks to promote greater awareness of the cultural and intellectual richness of the region.

Stone Canoe considers for inclusion previously unpublished short fiction, creative nonfiction, short plays, poems, essays, and works of visual art in any medium. Unsolicited submissions are welcome from March 1 through July 31 of each year. Submissions must be sent via our web page, and must include a short biographical statement and contact information. Complete submission instructions and forms are available at *stonecanoejournal.org/submission.*

There is no additional fee required to be considered for one of our seven prizes in various categories. Details about each are provided on our web site.

Stone Canoe is set in Bembo, a trademark font of the Monotype Corporation, based on a typeface designed by Francesco Griffo in 1495.

Stone Canoe 6 is available for purchase in print or e-book format through our web site, *stonecanoejournal.org.* The print version is $20 and the e-book version is $10. The print version may also be ordered by sending a check to *Stone Canoe,* 700 University Avenue, Syracuse, New York, 13244-2530. The educational rate for classroom use is $12, and past issues are $15.

Stone Canoe 6 is also available at Syracuse University Bookstores, Follett's Orange Bookstore, Barnes and Noble, and *Amazon.com,* as well as at other regional bookstores and at a growing number of other arts venues.

ISSN: 1934-9963 ISBN: 978-0-9791944-9-8

Stone Canoe is a proud member of the Council of Literary Magazines and Presses.

Peter T. Bennett, *Tag #14,* aluminum, 7"x6"x1 ½", 2011

About the Cover

Peter T. Bennett, *Tag #14,* aluminum, 7"x6"x1 ½", 2011 (detail)

Aluminum has a vast cultural and industrial history with many established narratives, rich with possibilities. It is quite possibly the 20th century's first truly modern material.

The *Tin Types,* 2010-11, was initiated in response to my desire to move my previous drawings into a more physical material and to explore thematic subject matter that paper would not support. At that time I had access to a large quantity of salvaged aluminum ductwork and believed it would provide the results I was looking for. Early in the developmental phase, the drawing process changed dramatically to serve the demands of the material. Inevitably, however, the issues of mechanical technique gave way to questions of content and intent.

Tag #14 is part of a series of small works, 7"x 6"x 1 ½", that began to address some of the fundamental questions about process and content. Does the material inform the content? Does the expressive nature of content change as size and proportion change? How does scaling down alter the viewer's relationship/response to the work? Can the reduction in size objectify the piece? Does the potency of an image change as this editing process occurs? These and other questions about subject matter, intent, and process continue to shape my internal dialogue. Aluminum provides numerous properties that build into the *Tin Types* Series content, meaning, and a continuing challenge.

Peter T. Bennett

Peter T. Bennett was born in 1946 in Syracuse, New York, and lived in Fayetteville, New York, until 1962. His first art classes were community-based programs offered in the '50s through the old Everson Museum. He currently lives and works in Maine.

His Tin Types, 2010-11, *are a direct response to move his ongoing series of drawings,* The Artists, *into a more tactile and substantial medium. Many of the same historical narratives that continue to inform his drawings have become more focused and immediate in the aluminum.*

Acknowledgements

Stone Canoe Number 6 is dedicated to Larry Levis, an influential and highly original American poet who studied with Philip Booth and Donald Justice at Syracuse University in the late '60s/early '70s. His sudden death of a heart attack at age 49 was, in the words of Philip Levine, current U.S. Poet Laureate and Larry's first mentor, "a staggering loss for our poetry, but what he left was a major achievement that will enrich our lives." Larry published five books in his lifetime; a sixth book, *Elegy,* edited by Levine, was published after his death. In these pages we offer three essays about Larry by writers who knew him well, followed by a sampling of his poetry.

Special thanks to the following people for their contribution to the successful launch of *Stone Canoe* 6:

Judy Barringer, Director, Constance Saltonstall Foundation for the Arts, and the entire Saltonstall Board

Peter Blanck, Chairman, Burton Blatt Institute, Syracuse University, and creator of the *SC* Burton Blatt Institute Prize for Arts Leadership

Lorraine Branham, Dean, S.I. Newhouse School of Public Communications, Syracuse University, and creator of the *SC* S.I. Newhouse School Prize for Creative Nonfiction

Nancy Cantor, Chancellor and President, Syracuse University

Gregory Donovan, Professor of English at Virginia Commonwealth University and editor of the online journal *Blackbird*

Rob Enslin, Communications Manager, The College of Arts and Sciences, Syracuse University

Hedy and Michael Fawcett, creators of the *SC* Prize for Visual Arts

Allen and Nirelle Galson, creators of the *SC* Prize for Fiction

Bea González, Dean, University College of Syracuse University and creator of the *SC* Prize for Poetry

Andrew Havenhand, Director, XL Projects Gallery, the College of Visual and Performing Arts, Syracuse University

Tom Huff, sculptor and creator of the *Stone Canoe* carvings

Gregg Lambert, Dean's Professor and Founding Director of the Humanities Center, Syracuse University

Doran Larson, Associate Professor, Hamilton College

Trish Lowney, Executive Director, Office of Sponsored Programs, Syracuse University

Robert Zuckerman, Senior Program Officer, and Christine Leahy, Program Officer, NYSCA Literature Programs

Dirk Sonneborn, Executive Director, and Heidi Holtz, Director of Research and Projects, The Gifford Foundation.

Laura J. Steinberg, Dean, the L.C. Smith College of Engineering and Computer Science, and creator of the L.C. Smith Prize for Engineering and Technology Writing

Stone Canoe is pleased to have the following **Constance Saltonstall** alumni represented in the current issue: Betsy Andrews, Mary Gilliland, David Lloyd, Bushra Rehman, and Thom Ward.

Thanks as always to the ***Stone Canoe*** **Advisory Board** for their wise counsel and support:
Omanii Abdullah-Grace, Judy Barringer, Peter Blanck, Carole Brzozowski, Michael Burkard, Carol Charles, William Delavan, Stephen Dunn, Arthur Flowers, Wendy Gonyea, Kenneth Hine, Johanna Keller, Christopher Kennedy, Robin Wall Kimmerer, David Lloyd, David MacDonald, Pamela McLaughlin, Philip Memmer, Elizabeth O'Rourke, Minnie Bruce Pratt, Maria Russell, Eileen Strempel, Suzanne Thorin, Silvio Torres-Saillant, John von Bergen, Kheli Willetts, and Marion Wilson.

Thanks to Dean Ann Clarke of Syracuse University's College of Visual and Performing Arts for once again offering the College's **XL Projects Gallery** as the site for our *Stone Canoe* 6 art exhibition.

Thanks to a remarkable team of editors, who are listed on the title page.

Thanks to our loyal sponsors, without whom *Stone Canoe Number 6* would not be possible. See their individual pages in the back of the book, and on our web site.

Finally, many thanks to the University College staff who worked on this issue for their unending patience in the face of this demanding project.

"The Poem You Asked For," from *Wrecking Crew,* by Larry Levis, c 1972, and from *The Selected Levis,* by Larry Levis, selected by David St. John, c 2000, is reprinted by permission of the University of Pittsburgh Press.

"The Two Trees" from *Elegy* by Larry Levis, c 1997, and from *The Selected Levis,* by Larry Levis, selected by David St. John, c 2000, is reprinted by permission of the University of Pittsburgh Press.

Stephen Dunn's essay, "Larry Levis in Syracuse," was previously published in *Blackbird.*

Photograph of Larry Levis on page 37 courtesy of Erin Seals.

Stone Canoe is supported in part by a grant from **NYSCA**.

The 2012 *Stone Canoe* Prizes

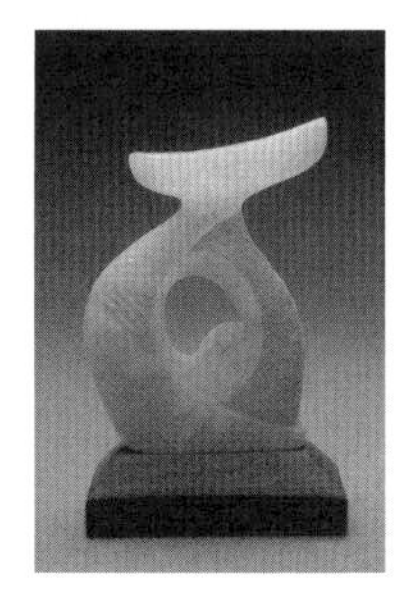

Tom Huff
Stone Canoe,
white alabaster,
2006

Stone Canoe awards yearly prizes for exemplary work submitted to the journal by emerging writers or artists in various categories. Submission of a single work of creative nonfiction, technology writing, short fiction, three poems, or three works of visual art in any medium will qualify for consideration in the respective genres. No additional fee or application is required.

An additional prize, the **Burton Blatt Institute Prize for Arts Leadership**, is awarded each year to an individual who exemplifies the value of inclusiveness within the arts community.

All prize winners receive $500 and an original alabaster stone canoe carving by Tom Huff.

The **2012 S.I. Newhouse School Prize for Creative Nonfiction** is awarded to **Tina Post** for her essay "Fight and Flight: The Near Room."

The **2012 Allen and Nirelle Galson Prize for Fiction** is awarded to **Jennifer R. Adams** for her story "Penn Station."

The **2012 Bea González Prize for Poetry** is awarded to **Bridget Meeds** for her poem "Everybody Down."

The **2012 Hedy and Michael Fawcett Prize for Visual Arts** is awarded to **Alexandria Smith** for her drawings "swing lo, swing high," and "untitled histories."

The **2012 L.C. Smith Prize for Engineering and Technology Writing** is awarded to **Brian Rautio** for his essay "Boffins, Tech, and RADAR, Oh My!"

The **2012 Burton Blatt Institute Prize for Arts Leadership** is awarded to filmmaker **Sharon Greytak** for her entire body of work and its importance to the international arts community.

We congratulate the winners and thank the creators of these prizes for their generous support.

Announcing a New *Stone Canoe* Writing Prize

Beginning in 2013, the Institute for Veterans and Military Families (IVMF) at Syracuse University will award the **Institute for Veterans and Military Families Prize for Written Work by a Veteran.**

The prize will be awarded annually to a U.S. veteran for a previously unpublished short story, essay, creative nonfiction piece, or poem (or series of up to three poems). The subject matter of the written piece may be about veteran or military family issues, but it is not a requirement.

The prize is an unsolicited award, and the selection will be made by *Stone Canoe* jurors, in consultation with IVMF staff. The two visiting jurors chosen so far for the new prize are Anthony Swofford, Gulf War veteran and author of the acclaimed book, *Jarhead,* and Brian Turner, Iraq veteran and prizewinning poet. The prizewinner will receive an award certificate, a $500 monetary prize, and a small alabaster stone canoe carving by noted Native American sculptor Tom Huff.

The prize will be awarded at the annual *Stone Canoe* publication launch celebration, held in January of 2013. As with the other 2013 *Stone Canoe* prizes, the submission period will be March through August 2012.

Launched in 2011 by founding partners Syracuse University and JPMorgan Chase & Co., the Institute for Veterans and Military Families is the first national center in higher education focused on the social, economic, education and policy issues impacting veterans and their families post-service. Through the pillars of educational programming, employment, and actionable research, the Institute provides in-depth analysis of the challenges facing the veteran community, captures best practices, and serves as a forum to facilitate new partnerships and strong relationships among the many individuals and organizations committed to making a difference for this community.

The 2012 Gifford Foundation High School Arts Prizes

This year, *Stone Canoe* is again publishing the work of four students from the Syracuse City High Schools who have been awarded prizes for their work in the categories of poetry, fiction, nonfiction, and visual arts. Each winner receives an award certificate from *Stone Canoe* and a $500 monetary prize, courtesy of the Gifford Foundation.

• • •

The **Gifford Foundation Arts Prize for Poetry** is awarded to **Jeanie Nguyen**, a senior at Nottingham High School, for her poems "Human" and "Vietnam, June 1982."

The **Gifford Foundation Arts Prize for Fiction** is awarded to **Brianne Wood**, a junior at Nottingham High School, for her story "When There's No Tomorrow."

The **Gifford Foundation Arts Prize for Nonfiction** is awarded to **Mykolaj Suchý**, a freshman at Nottingham High School, for his essay "Ukraine."

The **Gifford Foundation Arts Prize for Visual Arts** is awarded to **Jimmy Ellerbe**, a senior at Corcoran High School, for his drawing "Still Life with African Mask."

Congratulations to all the winners and thanks once again to the Gifford Foundation for funding these prizes.

"The world is but a canvas
to the imagination."
-Henry David Thoreau
OF THE PEOPLE PEACEABLY TO

DRAMA

FICTION

VISUAL ARTS

POETRY

TECHNOLOGY

NONFICTION

MOVING IMAGES (SC 6 ONLINE)

See *www.stonecanoejournal.com* for complete Moving Images section and for additional poems, stories, and essays. Individual contributors to *SC 6 Online* are listed in the "contributors" section beginning on page 400.

Editor's Notes

Ballast and Blast

Welcome to the sixth annual issue of *Stone Canoe.* We are still afloat, still negotiating the rapids, still striving for that optimum combination of "ballast and blast" that Michael Martone once described as the distinguishing feature of our publication.

Once again, the journal is available in print and in e-book form, and as an added bonus there is a fresh collection of stories and poems in the "SC Online" section of our web site, *www.stonecanoejournal.org.* This year our web site will also offer more rich media, such as audio and video clips from some of our poets and musicians, and links to films such as *My Story in a Late Style of Fire,* Michele Poulos's recently completed film biography of poet Larry Levis, and *Not My Life,* Robert Bilheimer's riveting new documentary on the evils of human trafficking. We are also proud to unveil our second annual web-based "Moving Image" section, which includes an extensive interview with Mr. Bilheimer and several other important essays and interviews related to the subject of video and film.

Beginning with this issue, we are also including sections on music writing and engineering and technology writing, and we are awarding our first prize in the latter category, a gift from Syracuse University's L.C. Smith College of Computer Science and Technology. This brings our total number of *Stone Canoe* prizes to ten, including four designed specifically for Syracuse city high school students, and the ten winners for 2012 bring us fresh evidence of the creative energy that flourishes in our midst.

Jennifer R. Adams, winner of our fiction prize and currently a lecturer in English at Cornell, has worked as a journalist in Philadelphia and an ESL teacher in Rome, Italy. Another Ithaca resident is our poetry prizewinner, Bridget Meeds, a graduate of Ithaca College and West Genesee High School in Syracuse. Tina Post, our nonfiction prizewinner, lives with her family in a "ramshackle farmhouse" in Auburn. The winner of our visual arts prize, Alexandria Smith, is a Brooklyn-based artist with degrees from Syracuse, NYU, and Parsons, and has taught middle school in Harlem. Brian Rautio, the engineering and technology writing prizewinner, is a Ph.D. candidate in electrical engineering at Syracuse; the arts leadership prizewinner, Sharon Greytak, is a distinguished New York-based filmmaker who also teaches at Syracuse.

I am particularly impressed with the Gifford Foundation high school prize winners this year. Jeanie Nguyen skillfully evokes a scene from her native Vietnam in just a few lines of poetry. Mykolaj Suchý demonstrates a sense of narrative control well beyond his years in his wonderful essay about connecting with his extended family in Ukraine. Brianne Wood's short story is a lesson in how to handle a sensitive topic with a skillfully restrained combination of dialogue and interior monologue, and Jimmy Ellerbe's charcoal drawing shows signs of a maturing artistic talent with a bright future.

With each issue it seems that our extended community grows larger. More and more of our contributors, though originally from this region, now live and work elsewhere; yet, as one artist put it, their work is often "grounded in the Upstate experience." Contributions to *Stone Canoe 6* have come to us from Connecticut, Florida, Missouri, Rhode Island, South Carolina, Texas, and Mexico. Tony Trischka and Eliot Fisk, two Syracuse natives, have lived, taught, and performed throughout the world, but, as their interviews attest, they are highly conscious of their roots, and return to their hometown as often as possible, to give concerts, master classes, and workshops.

This year's 150 contributors are notable for their diversity in other ways as well. Many of course are well-established writers or artists, and some are just beginning their careers. There is a lawyer who writes and produces plays, a law professor who writes poems, a retired state senator who translates German poetry, and a retired surgeon and research scientist who has discovered a second career as a writer. There are faculty and staff from thirteen regional colleges and universities, teachers from public and private high schools throughout the country, workers in poverty programs, and an inmate from a correctional institution.

Our newly-established writing prize for veterans, sponsored by the Institute for Veterans and Military Families at Syracuse University, will undoubtedly attract submissions from even further afield, and we are confident that an increased presence of veterans in our pages will enrich the publication in important new ways. The panel of jurors we have assembled so far for this prize are combat veterans as well as prizewinning authors: Anthony Swofford and Brian Turner.

Ultimately, each issue of *Stone Canoe* is a product of the collective taste and judgment of our editors, and we are grateful to have had the privilege of working with such a distinguished group for issue Number 6. They come to us from Colgate University, Cornell University, Hamilton College, Pratt/Munson-Williams-Proctor Arts Institute, Syracuse University, from within the Syracuse community, and, in one case, from California, and they have in common a heartfelt belief in the importance of nurturing the next generation of artists and writers and musicians, who will then bring their own mix of ballast and blast to the cultural life of our extended Upstate New York community.

Robert Colley
Editor, *Stone Canoe*
Syracuse, New York
December 2011

Visiting Editors' Notes

As poetry editor of *Stone Canoe 6* I do this: I put my pig on a leash and we go out in Central New York and hunt for the rare and pungent thing that is the new poem. I don't know if I'll find the buried treasure of a truffle in the warm pile of submissions or I'll find the button stage of a poisonous mushroom. They look a lot alike. I'm always looking for something "with the aura and authenticity of an archeological find," as Seamus Heaney says, which means the poems I encounter are really very old; they come from the ancient impulse of making feeling into word sounds like the blues or like the click, whistle and bird song of the first African poems. They shape the psyche on our way to death like the old poems. But they are also very new, bright shiny objects that are unearthed from the news in the blaze of glory and are delicious in texture and delightful in form. The best ones I find are continuously inviting us into their interiors. They shimmer or resist the easy formulations. They have come from a pang; so they have transformed some hurt, Emily Dickinson style. They often have concision, surprise, volatility, and intimacy about them. Or, if not concision, a "curious puffing," like Stevens says, that makes us bend down and listen to the blab and will undo us with their labials and gutterals. I find in many of these poems a kind of speech, like that of a "metaphysician in the dark, twanging." I'm not making any claims for the importance, just the fact of their oddness and their "umami," as the Japanese say, their deliciousness.

Bruce Smith
Poetry Editor

In the last issue of *Stone Canoe* we "called" for poetry to honor the memory of Lucille Clifton, the late, great poet of Upstate New York to whom that issue was dedicated, and received so many wonderful poems that we created a special overflow digital section in the online version of *Stone Canoe.* For this current print issue, we have included those vibrant poems, which are thick with details of what it means to live and love, work and worry and struggle, deep in our regional life—from an ear that's "half a heart" to the way of *"el español in Siricusa";* from the woman who talks to Hitchcock to

African American educator Prudence Crandall as a little girl like "a nail"; from venturing to ferry along the stony edge of Assiniki—Seneca Lake—to writing poetry on a prescription pad in an empty waiting room.

Minnie Bruce Pratt
Poetry Editor

Keep me interested.
Break my heart.

That's what I tell creative writing students on the first day of every semester, and that's what I was looking for when I began sifting through dozens of creative nonfiction submissions in late summer. What you have before you, in *Stone Canoe 6,* is here because I couldn't put it down after the first sentence. Because I couldn't forget it after the last.

Now that my work is finished, I feel like a kid gloating over the marbles she won on the playground: steelies and aggies and mint candy swirls; shooters and peewees. How many there are! How lovely each one is! And how different from all the rest! How rich I feel when they click against each other in my palm! If I had to give one up, which would it... No way!

In the pages before you now, Michael M. Meguid, a retired surgeon, writes movingly of appendectomies he has performed—not all of them in the sterile conditions of the OR. Natalia Rachel Singer flirts with the lines between prose, poetry, and visual art. And Tina Post, winner of the S.I. Newhouse Prize for Creative Nonfiction, fuses reportage with memoir to explore race and violence in late-20th-century America.

Check out the online companion to *Stone Canoe* for a spooky memoir, by D.S. Sulaitis; lyrical notes toward a definition of beauty, by Becca McArthur; and a piece of reportage, by Kiki Koroshetz, that will change the way you think about the single mother in line in front of you at Walmart.

What a privilege it's been to curate these works. Individually and collectively, they fill me with awe. Also, with humility. Mostly they make me want to roll up my sleeves and get back to work, making worlds out of words.

"The good piece of writing startles the reader back into Life," says Joy Williams, in "Why I Write." Also, this: "Good writing never soothes or comforts. It is no prescription, neither is it diversionary, although it can and should enchant while it explodes in the reader's face."

Light a fire and curl up in a comfortable chair with the creative nonfiction in this issue. Slide a hassock under your feet. Fix yourself a mug of Earl Grey or a glass of Jameson's on the rocks. Be prepared to learn new things. (Dan Roche's essay, "Facilitating," is about how an autistic man frees the poetry inside him.) Be prepared to relearn some things you used to know. (In Renate Wildermuth's memoir, "The King of Crumbs," her parents show love and annoyance in the same breath.) I promise you'll laugh. I promise you'll be enchanted. Your heart might get broken, but you'll survive. Most likely, you'll be startled back into Life.

Jennifer Brice
Creative Nonfiction Editor

Of the one hundred plus stories that were submitted for this issue of *Stone Canoe,* about twenty made it to a second reading. They were all stories with fresh, odd, striking language, a sure hold on their fictional world, and a sense, it seemed to me, of urgency, of things that just needed to be told. And that need, that urgency, held up through a third reading. From the late-night obsessive, father, husband, and home owner, stalking his house and yard, raging over a neighbor's cat shit, to Stephen Marion's funny and horrific feel for East Tennessee, both its land and people—each and all of these stories had the quality of a telephone ringing in the night, and a voice at the other end that was whispering, humming, racing, pausing. I had to listen. And these stories had to be published.

Paul Cody
Fiction Editor

One of the things a good playwright is able to do is show us who we are as a society, as a culture, as a nation, right now. From my dramaturg's desk, I can tell you that many of our young and emerging playwrights are responding to our nation's current and expanding season of economic difficulty with dramas about good people navigating bad times. But for me, topicality alone holds neither the stage nor my deepest attention when reading a play.

At the center of the plays I find most satisfying are characters in whom, no matter their situation or station in life, I recognize something of myself or my neighbors, good, bad and ugly; characters who dream, struggle, falter and go on; characters transfigured by the times in which they live. I like it when a play explores an important issue of our time by dramatizing that issue within the intimacy of a family, community, or group.

The illegal and legal immigrants (many of them U.S. citizens) who labor as migrant farmworkers in this nation's food-producing fields work under gathering clouds of suspicion and—I don't think it's too strong to say—contempt, the result of increasingly strict, perhaps even racist, immigration laws. In his full-length drama, *Fallow,* excerpted here, Kenneth Lin asks dramatic questions of social relevance and currency: What happens when a young, well-heeled, idealistic, white Cornell University student chooses to become a migrant worker? Who does he become as the sun under which he toils tans his skin, coloring him indistinguishable from the Mexicans he works with in the fields? What is the meaning of his death? And can shared fear, loss, and grief give birth to necessary communion between those separated by class and race?

"I'm wasting my time," said the late American dramatist Lanford Wilson, "if my plays don't make comment on contemporary society." According to the FBI, the number of anti-Mexico hate crimes (many against migrant farmworkers) has soared by 35 percent since 2003. And since 2003 California (a setting in the play), which has the nation's largest Mexican and Mexican American population, has seen the number of hate crimes against Mexicans nearly double.

This is where we are, right now, as a nation. Thank goodness Kenneth Lin is watching.

Kyle Bass
Drama Editor

The top three essays in this category were chosen based on five criteria: their high level of technical knowledge and accuracy; their personal appeal to the reader; their creativity and wit; the knowledge they impart to the reader, and the passion for engineering and science that is an obvious, innate part of their composition. Tom Moran's personal essay, "Pointing to the Moon: An Engineer's Path," is a moving account of a life devoted to aerospace engineering, highlighted by a suspenseful account of the Surveyor 7 moon landing. Taking a different approach, Andrew Martin's eye-opening yet easygoing essay, "Everyday Engineering," uses gentle instruction to show how engineers touch seemingly basic aspects of our lives on a daily basis, from getting to work to eating soup for lunch. Finally, the winning essay, "Boffins, Tech and RADAR, Oh My!" by Brian Rautio, provides an insightful look at the historic change in the public image of engineers, presented with admirable economy and considerable warmth. All three are excellent examples of a little-known truth: Engineers write with the same keen focus and elegance of thought that allows them to solve the most intricate puzzles of science and technology.

Megan Davidson and Jerry Heller
Technology Editors

The inaugural music section of *Stone Canoe* focuses on two virtuoso performers from the same generation who felt the need to live through music. They spent their formative years in Syracuse public schools during the foment of the late '60s and '70s. Both have popularized their instruments and broken through boundaries by arranging, composing and inspiring many new works. They grew up in nurturing families that encouraged, but did not press them unduly, to become performers. Tony Trischka says the banjo chose him. Eliot Fisk was given both a banjo and a guitar, and the guitar spoke more clearly to him. These interviews with two distinguished musicians will make for fascinating reading.

Neva Pilgrim and Steven Stucky
Music Editors

As collaborators in this endeavor, we began our role in selecting art works for the 2012 edition of *Stone Canoe* with conversations about what our particular experiences and insight might bring to the present volume. As we began to consider the submissions for the visual art section of the book, we looked to the many works of art to suggest a theme, and coupled with our own experience of active participation in the visual arts as residents and practitioners in Central New York for many years, diversity became the focus for our task. As a result we have been driven by a desire to present the surprisingly rich and varied cultural production in the visual arts in this region.

It is the many opportunities for artists to study in the region, in excellent art programs in public and private educational institutions, along with an extraordinary level of support for the arts that make Central New York a place of opportunity for artists. We think of the region as unique in its influx of artists from all over the world, taking part in artist residencies, exhibition opportunities, and artist projects. In our selections for the book, we included artists who have taken advantage of the affordability and opportunities for artists to center their creative lives in the region, and others who came here for opportunity and experience, and have since moved on to other places.

We have chosen work of the highest quality from a broad range of media and practices, including traditional forms such as canvas painting and carved sculpture, to examples of artworks that question the boundaries of media and expectations of what constitutes a work of visual art. Along with representations of artworks we include a version of a complete artwork with the contribution of the collaborative team of Bartow + Metzgar. The text and layout of this team's submission is the artwork and the documentation of the project, "Stratimentation, Investigations of a Metaphoric Landscape." We have included traditional forms of art photography, in the poetic and conceptually complex images of Marna Bell, along with the work of Wilka Roig, that document performative gestures, and are photographic works at the same time.

In the selection of artists, we have a diverse range of career levels from young emerging artists such as Alex Smith, with her personal and racially charged drawings, to artists with nationally and internationally recognized careers such as Lori Nix, whose nontraditional approach to photographic work is attracting international attention. We were able to choose works from an intergenerational group of artists, from a variety of racial and ethnic experiences, and educational backgrounds.

As the first co-editors of the visual arts section of the *Stone Canoe,* we focused on making some changes to the format of the book that we feel enhance the experience of the artwork. These include segregating the images from the literary submissions so as to avoid unintended associations with the written works. The visual arts selections are in a stand-alone section of the journal for the first time.

This volume includes a smaller group of selected artists, a compromise we accepted in order to include a short artist statement along with the images, giving the audience a better understanding of each artist's intention. We tried to include a sample of a broad range of artistic activities, and with these limitations in mind, many strong submissions were necessarily excluded from the final selection.

Finally, we very much appreciate the submission of Peter T. Bennett, whose contribution became the cover for the 2012 edition of *Stone Canoe 6*. In an era of e-books, as the "object-ness" of the book begins to dissolve, the obsessively constructed metal book cover by this artist serves as a metaphor of the value of the physical form of the book.

Yvonne Buchanan and Dorene Quinn
Visual Arts Editors

Despite hard times in virtually all arts and cultural work, it's encouraging to me as an Upstate New Yorker that *Stone Canoe* endures and has even been able to launch new sections and expand its web site presence. It was my great pleasure to edit the journal's first Moving Images section last year and to continue that role for this issue. "Moving Images" of course references our aim to cover the broad range of film, video, and animation art forms that have significant roots and seminal practitioners in our region, as well as global reach.

Although you're reading this in the print edition of *Stone Canoe* and can find the titles and contributors' bios in these pages too, the essays comprising Moving Images appear entirely online. Because *Stone Canoe* isn't yet widely known for this subject, this strategy offers our writers potentially greater exposure and a slightly more forgiving deadline, since many of the pieces in this section arise from summer and fall events and interviews tied to a regional cinema calendar at some odds with *Stone Canoe*'s own production timetable.

Two essays come out of summer projects whose gestation lengthened into fall. SUNY Oswego scholar Patricia Clark considers what happens when black musical forms are appropriated in largely white feature films. Animation enthusiast Kevin Martin Kern spent his summer in Bologna, Italy, studying film preservation at the hands of the masters of *Il Cinema Ritrovato*. Now an archivist for a major Hollywood studio, he pronounces Bologna a life-changing experience.

Three pieces come out of major fall film festivals. Frank Ready considers how celebrity filtered his experience at September's Toronto International Film Festival. Andrew Johnson had to wait till October to conclude work on his profile of Israeli filmmaker Dani Menkin, two of whose films screened at the Syracuse International Film Festival (SYRFILM). Both these young critics are finishing the Goldring Arts Journalism master's program in the Newhouse School (full disclosure: I'm also a Goldring alum).

Over its eight years, SYRFILM has become a well-regarded and widely respected festival in the world of international independent cinema, drawing entries from thirty countries and enjoying repeat visits from a growing number of filmmakers. I profile three of those—Haim Bouzaglo of Israel, Milcho Manchevski of Macedonia, and Rob Nilsson of the Bay Area—whose relationships with Syracuse have deepened and flourished.

SYRFILM arises from Syracuse University's Department of Transmedia in the College of Visual and Performing Arts—named last summer as one of the top 25 film studies programs in the world—and Owen Shapiro directs both. Several years ago award-winning experimental filmmaker Sharon Greytak joined that faculty. I also offer a profile of her work, focusing on her latest feature, *Archeology of a Woman,* starring Sally Kirkland, whose post-production she completed while commuting each week between Manhattan and Syracuse through much of the fall semester. (Greytak is also the recipient of *Stone Canoe's* Burton Blatt Institute Arts Leadership Prize this year.)

Finally, there's a profile of documentary filmmaker Robert Bilheimer, whose exploration of global human trafficking, *Not My Life,* premiered on CNN International in late October. Bilheimer joins us in Syracuse in early February for a screening of this film, a collaboration between *Stone Canoe* and the Newhouse School. Special thanks to *Stone Canoe* executive editor Bob Colley for suggesting this piece.

And here's a trailer for coming attractions: This year you can keep going back to *stonecanoejournal.org,* as the journal formalizes what already started happening last year in more piecemeal fashion. We haven't a name for it yet, but whether it's the "mid-year supplement" or the "quarterly special," look later this spring for pieces as varied as SYRFILM's Chinese filmmakers and photographer Alec Soth's retrospective at the Everson Museum, to name just two planned projects.

Nancy Keefe Rhodes
Moving Images Editor

Larry Levis, Poet (1946-1996): An Appreciation

Born in Fresno, California, Larry Levis earned his B.A. from the California State University at Fresno, where he studied with the current U.S. Poet Laureate, Philip Levine, who later called him "the most gifted and determined student I've ever had the good fortune to have in one of my classes." He later got his M.A. degree at Syracuse University and his Ph.D. from the University of Iowa, and in his relatively short lifetime published five remarkable books of poems and a collection of stories. A posthumous book, *Elegy,* was edited by Philip Levine and published in 1997. His many awards included the Lamont Prize and the United States Award from the International Poetry Forum. His sudden death at age 49, said David St. John, "sent a shock wave through the ranks of American poetry. " Levis's impact on other poets may be summed up by Ray Gonzalez who said in the *Bloomsbury Review:* "If I could describe everything poets want their poems to do, regardless of their style and intentions, I would turn to Levis's poetry, once again, and not say a word."

Larry Levis

Levis's time at Syracuse University was brief, but his Upstate legacy lives on in the form of the Larry Levis Memorial Internship Program, a collaboration between the University's Graduate Creative Writing Program and *BOA Editions,* a highly regarded literary press in the neighboring city of Rochester.

The three essays included here will hopefully give the reader not familiar with Levis's work a strong sense of who he was, and how important he was to those around him as well as to the world of poetry in general. Stephen Dunn remembers his time with Larry in graduate school in Syracuse; Greg Donovan, his friend and colleague at Virginia Commonwealth University, recalls his final years there; and Michele Poulos discusses her just-completed documentary on Levis called *My Life in a Late Style of Fire.*

The poems that follow, selected from four of Levis's books, offer a glimpse of the range of poetic styles at his command, and will hopefully guide the reader toward a deeper exploration of his complete body of work.

–Robert Colley

Stephen Dunn

Larry Levis in Syracuse

Only four would-be poets were admitted into Syracuse University's graduate writing program in 1969. Actually there were five of us, but one was Larry Levis, who was a poet. Larry was 22, fresh out of Fresno and already with pedigree, having studied with Philip Levine and Robert Mezey. I was 29, relatively new to poetry (I had been a history major as an undergraduate and hadn't been to a school in many years), fresh from a year of living and trying to write in Spain. Though I may have had some ability, there seemed an enormous initial gap between me and the other admittees, especially Larry. Larry seemed full-blown, perhaps even an original.

I think we were able to become friends—from my side of the equation—because Larry was immensely likable and apparently devoid of ego. But also because I felt no competitiveness toward him, as I did toward some of the others. He already had a voice; he was in another category. He was tall, gangly, off the farm. And attractive; his overall manner and carriage, not to mention his mustache, made him James Dean leaning toward Burt Reynolds. My wife liked him (women were always drawn to Larry), and he was frequently a visitor at our apartment. Until his second or third Fellowship check arrived—sometime after Syracuse winter had commenced—the warmest clothing he owned was a dungaree jacket and a rubber raincoat. He was our Californian, and some of us even confused his drawl, his slow delivery and curious accent, as Southern Californian. We were wrong; it was peculiarly Levisonian.

We had come to study with Philip Booth, Donald Justice, W.D. Snodgrass, George P. Elliott, arguably the best group of writer-teachers that existed at the time. In Philip Booth's small workshop that first semester in 1969, I kept silent most of the time. There was a very brilliant Fellowship student (I'll not name him) from the South who held forth every class. None of us was articulate, certainly not Larry, whose speech was hesitant, at worst sprinkled with "you knows," a kind of punctuation for him, sometimes annoying, like "like" these days. The brilliant student's poems, however, were convoluted. We soon learned that his brilliance, his apparent brilliance, was overly convoluted too. Much elaboration and ranginess, little touching down. In a month or so, it was clear who was the most interesting and able poet. Booth clearly knew. When that year Larry won The Academy of American Poets Award for best poem, no one was surprised.

It took longer to realize that Larry was a good thinker as well. Together, we took a course called *The Modern Imagination* from William Wasserstrom, a formidable and curmudgeonly professor. In it, among other books, we read *The Tin Drum,* several Beckett plays, Konrad Lorenz' *On Aggression,* Huizinga's *Homo Ludens,* a wonderful and eclectic range of texts. Larry and I were the only creative writers in the class; the rest were scholars, Ph.D. candidates. Wasserstrom had little patience with students whose analytical skills weren't sharp. He had no patience with the unprepared or the foolish. Frequently he'd stop a student in mid-sentence, cut him off. But an amazing thing started to happen by mid-semester. Larry would start to speak, again slowly, lots of "you knows" and "sort ofs," and Wasserstrom let him speak. By this time professor and class had learned that if you gave Larry some room, some slack, that the end of his drift or sentence was going to click in, that he was going to say something very smart. Any other student verging on the inarticulate would be (and was) interrupted. Larry had more acute things to say than anyone in class, especially, as I remember, about Beckett.

In our second year at Syracuse, Larry, with the help of Don Justice's translation class, was turning to the Latin American and French poets that would prove so important to his work. Neruda, Reverdy, Baudelaire, Follain, Vallejo. He found models in them and others for how to blend his politics with his aesthetics. It was 1970. Larry's politics were more than fashionably leftist; they arose of something essentially proletarian in his make up. The war and Nixon preoccupied many of us, and Larry in particular. It seems comic to say so, but if he hadn't been such a gentle man he might have been a violent one.

One Christmas break, he returned from California with a beautiful woman, Barbara. He had only casually mentioned her to us, but here she was, his wife. They'd just gotten married. She was his first wife, and the one dearest to us. Many good times together, pot and booze oiling the laughter. He was a husband now, and to bring in more money he took a job at a steel mill. Hard work, but work that wholly fit Larry's romance of himself as a man of the people, a worker. On the back of his precocious first book, *Wrecking Crew,* he listed steelworker as one of his former occupations.

His best and often extraordinary poems were, of course, ahead of him. But in those two years at Syracuse the seeds of them were present. For reasons I'm not entirely sure of, we drifted apart in the late eighties. Each of us had come far as poets, the only two Syracusans from that era to do so, but we also lived far apart and had cut out different paths for ourselves. I wished to see him again, and not long after I invited him to read at my college. I felt instantly close to him, and I think he felt the same toward me. Five months later he'd be dead. What I'll remember about him, beyond the poems, were his special brand of humor and his infinite sweetness.

Gregory Donovan

The Care and Feeding of a Dead Poet

"All this was a mission."
—Rainer Maria Rilke, *Duino Elegies*

Irony is cheap—one of several reasons why it's so common, in all senses of the word, in contemporary life and art. Irony allows a cool withdrawal with a shrug at the very moment when inconvenient truths emerge or strong emotions arise that would force us to stand up to them. Ironies are the wetted tongs we use to hold red-hot iron away from us, as I'm doing in the title of this essay. Irony too often is used by immature writers as a way of avoiding having to say what they think or believe—they can leave it up to the reader. Yet irony is an imperfect escape, and at times we may use it precisely to invoke that imperfection, offering it as a sneaking admission that this is something we can't easily bear. Plath uses irony in that ironic way in her often misunderstood "Daddy," where the irony is so extreme and acidic that it becomes self-accusation, self-mockery. Irony may proceed from, but isn't the same as, confusion or embarrassment or amazement or awe. It may be indigenous to jokes, but really, it's not the equal of humor. When a friend dies, we may be conscious of any number of sweet absurdities or ugly truths, and find ourselves painfully stumbling over the ridiculous, but it's no longer time for flip recitals of irony, which can only unveil our commonplace cowardice in the face of death. Contemplated death, like birth, is grand—inescapably powerful, absolute, profound. It cannot be questioned or appealed, cannot be tricked or reversed. And so there isn't much room for irony in the elegiac. When your friend dies, and the friend is a poet, and a great poet at that, there isn't a proper place for irony in the natural urge toward elegy. All too often, of course, we might feel that the community of poets takes up their flourishing pens all too readily and publish all too quickly their poems of elegy. It can feel as if the impulse has been tainted by ambition or greed or callousness: "My friend died, but at least I got a poem out of it." This dark suspicion, ripe material for the practice of irony, is balanced by the simple fact that whenever a poet faces trouble and hurt, what else can be done but to make a poem in response? Or is keeping silent really the only appropriate tribute? And if so, for how long? We find ourselves caught on these horns.

The man could write like fire. That is the first and the foremost, and the final, word. That is what he was doing on the day that he died—he was deep in the throes of it, lost in his work. He was on a temporary leave taken to finish a collection of poetry—and in fact, that is precisely what I am doing myself at this moment that I write. That isn't irony—it's connection. Larry Levis was my friend and my colleague, and it came to me to be one of the people who discovered him dead in his home on Church Hill in Richmond, Virginia, on May 8, 1996. A student had called to say that his mail was piling up on his porch: something was wrong. Instantly, I recollected, amidst the cascade of increasing dread, that he had been missed recently at the reading of one of his thesis students, that we had made excuses for him, that we had elected to leave him alone with his pressing work which we knew he was close to finishing. But something was wrong, and we could feel it. Another of Larry's close friends, Mary Flinn, had called to ask if I would go check out his house, to see if perhaps he had left unexpectedly on a sudden trip. Yes, we told ourselves, that must be it. I drove to his place, armed with a screwdriver and hammer, determined to break in and answer all questions. But when I arrived, I saw that Mary had already called the police, and they had contacted the fire department. Firemen were preparing to break down the front door and I asked them not to do that—perhaps he was actually simply out of town. (I also knew who would be asked to fix the door; as with many of my writer friends, Larry knew that I was handy—that I'd been a painter and carpenter and could even do a little plumbing—and that fact was often used against me.) The firemen climbed up onto the porch roof and broke one of the second story windows to gain entrance. They came out immediately and said he was there, with faces that said this was bad news, the worst. By that time, Mary Flinn had driven over and we both sat down, collapsed, really, onto a small concrete wall before his house, stricken. Our disbelief turned to a kind of bizarre hilarity mixed with horror when we saw his body being bumped down the stairs—he was a big, tall man—wrapped in a black body bag marked with the words "Robinson's Removal Service." The black absurdity was far too strong to be mere irony, and the stark reality was nearly flattening.

At that moment, a mission was imparted.

In the weeks that followed, disbelief mixed with the uncanny as friends reported Larry walking through doorways just ahead of them or making costumed appearances in dreams. It was said he could be seen or felt as a haunting presence in the house he loved so well, and those stories continue to be told even now. It is hard to accept when such a fully awake and alive person—such a strong personality and memorable presence and unmistakable voice—is obliterated in an instant. None of us in his community of friends and students could well handle that impossibility. We all looked for something to do. At first, in whatever ways I could, I helped his sister Sheila Brady, the landscape architect who had always seemed to understand her brother so well, who was dealing with the immediate aftermath of Larry's death. Then I got on a plane and flew to Fresno. It was something I felt was necessary for me to do. I spoke at length with Phil and Franny Levine, and I visited with Larry's brother and sister there, and talked with others among his friends. I drove out to the Levis family place in Parlier, which they always call "the ranch," surrounded by acres of orchards and vineyards, the unmistakable dusty scenery of the Central Valley of California which so often appears in his work, and I spent an afternoon sitting there on the back porch with his mother, softly talking intermittently as each of us handed to the other something that Larry had written which we thought the other might enjoy reading. The most difficult visit was with Larry's son, Nick, who had joined his family in Fresno, devastated by his loss. What was there to say? Yet in each case, I wanted his family and friends to know that despite the fact that Larry had died alone, his body undiscovered for days, it would have been quite inaccurate for anyone to think that circumstance gave evidence that his life in Richmond had been isolated or dark. Larry was surrounded by friends who genuinely cared about him and enjoyed his frequent company there, especially among the visual arts community. He often spoke of how much he loved his charming house in historic Church Hill (where Patrick Henry had given his famous liberty or death speech and Edgar Allan Poe's mother was buried). Despite some tribulations, Larry was observably happy in his life in Richmond, and clearly enjoyed living in a place that had a palpable, complicated past which could be mined for poetry. His friends were leaving him alone to finish his book, never imagining that he was, as he wrote, completing the last act of his life. On that fateful day, after his body was taken away, when I entered the front bedroom of his house where he liked to write on an architect's drafting table he had set up, there was a draft of a poem there, marked up with revisions, and his fountain pen lay with cap open on top of it, as if he had just stepped away a moment, intending to return.

So it turned out to be something natural and necessary, and not ironic, that I would become involved in keeping alive the memory of a beloved poet and in praising the undiminished value of his work. Many among my friends and acquaintances have found themselves in that same position, and while they might pretend to laugh at their situation ironically, I suspect that is not how it feels. In fact, for me, in this case, that particular turn of events feels, well, fated. When I first met Larry Levis, during the time I was attempting to hire him to come to Virginia (I had flown to Utah for a whitewater rafting trip organized by Pam Houston), we soon realized as we talked that we had experienced an unusual symmetry, each of us having spent time in many of the same places but never at the same time—Missouri, Utah, even Fresno, California—as well as sharing many of the same poet friends and heroes. When we told a story to each other, we often knew the exact person, or the exact spot, featured in it. I had heard stories about Larry from friends in those places long before I ever met him. There had been other unusual congruities as well.

The first time I heard Levis read from his work was at an Association of Writers & Writing Programs conference in Pittsburgh. Larry stood there, tall with black hair and moustache, California-cool in his black shirt printed with palm leaves—you've probably seen the photo—slouching over his work and reading in the somewhat mumbling, nearly private yet highly effective voice he used, one which gave each audience member the sense he was speaking directly to them, individually—or perhaps it was more as if they were having the privilege of entering a man's private, highly articulate, stringently honest inner musings, an intense conversation with himself unexpectedly overheard. The poems were brilliant, and the experience was stunning. Long after the reading had ended and everyone had left the room, I was still sitting in my chair, considering, sorting, taking it all in. I was quite surprised when a small group of people walked up to me—they must have been far in the back of the room as he read—and each of them said, rather shyly, how much they had enjoyed the reading and thanked me for it. For a moment I had no idea what to do or what had happened. I really couldn't believe there was any possibility that anyone could mistake me for the man who had just read, a man who, as everyone liked to say, both with affection and sometimes resentment, was "tall, dark and handsome." Those things I am not. But in an instant I calculated that, if I did tell these gentle people of their rather silly mistake, the embarrassment might be the most memorable thing they would carry away with them from the experience, spoiling it forever. So, really without thinking it out or having a plan, I nodded my head and thanked them graciously, and told them of my gratitude for their interest in my work. They went away happy. Later, when I told Larry that story, I joked with him that I was a better Larry Levis than he was, since I was good enough to stay around to thank my audience and hang out with them. He agreed, and said, laughing, that he should probably send me out on tour to do his readings for him and that would keep all his fans happy.

One of the first formal activities associated with remembering Levis in which I was involved came that November following his death, when several of us in Richmond organized a memorial service to which many of Larry's best friends were invited. A number of those in attendance were asked to read a favorite poem of Larry's and I chose "Slow Child with a Book of Birds," a poem which over the years I have often given to my students in creative writing courses as a model—which is another way, and a most important one, of passing along a poet's legacy.

Five years after Larry's death, the October/November 2001 issue of *The Writer's Chronicle* (the AWP journal) ran an article focused on the use of metaphor in two of America's great contemporary poets, now both gone: "Two Roads Diverged in a Wood: Character, Metaphor, & Destiny in the Work of William Matthews & Larry Levis" by Tony Hoagland. Hoagland sketches several contrasts between the two: Matthews as a poet of consciousness versus Levis as a poet of ecstatic vision; Matthews as a poet of integration and perspective, a "discursive musician" in whose work attention-grabbing metaphors became subordinate to the use of sophisticated diction and etymology, vs. Levis as a poet whose metaphors and imagery evolved from the context of a familiar '60s American surrealism into a more explosive and escapist use of both, finally coming to a more mature and sustained use of "radical metaphor." Hoagland suggested that the "radical metaphor," while perhaps still operating within the framework of narrative, nevertheless moves beyond the conventional use of metaphor as a device for suggesting equivalences between unlike things into metaphor as "an encounter which either illuminates or incinerates the seeker," one which "is both a departure and an arrival, both otherworldly and shockingly present"—that is, pyrotechnic metaphor used for its own sake.

While I enjoy the characteristically intelligent and valuable insight Hoagland displays in that article, it does express some ideas about Larry Levis and his work with which I would disagree. I don't see quite the same poet that Hoagland sees in Levis, although I know that Hoagland's praise reflects the manner in which Levis's work is often, and in certain ways deservedly, celebrated. I'm in agreement utterly with Hoagland's citing Levis's "eruptions of imaginative energy"—no doubt about that one. But the emphasis on the ungrounded metaphor as an end in itself in Levis's work—that's where I might part company with Hoagland.

In part my departure arises from actual conversations I had with Larry. Our conversations often floated around in the world of jazz, and once, as we were talking, I invoked the example of John Coltrane, who, it was said, felt that jazz would lose its way if it completely lost contact with its roots in the blues, which led to both of us coming to an agreement about a related idea, which is (I have to paraphrase): no matter how deliciously and wildly and amazingly inventive a poem might become, if it completely loses touch with life as it is actually lived, it can't be fully valued by a reader. Levis's work was itself beautifully and memorably inventive, often taking unexpected turns and bringing together unexpected and even seemingly dissonant combinations of materials. But it always stays in contact with elements that can move us with the power of recognition. Or, as Coltrane, that wild inventor himself said, "All a musician can do is to get closer to the sources of nature, and so feel that he is in communion with the natural laws."

The other thing that Hoagland's description in his essay seems to miss for me, both as reader and friend to the poet, is the emotional strength, clarity, and generosity in the work of Larry Levis—something we might call *heart*. How can that be overlooked? His writing consistently expresses an abiding affection for the lost, the ignored, the abused, the confused. His enormous generosity was always coupled, yes, with a strong intellect and a dazzling inventive capacity. But in the great work of his later career, the invention was always harnessed in the service of something large.

As you can see from my discussion of his poetry, it's not solely my affection for the man that makes it easy and natural for me to be involved with carrying forward his memory. The poetry itself would be justification enough, and if you read it with attention, you will ultimately read it with admiration. In fact, that is exactly what I have found—that his work is enjoying an ever-increasing readership, most especially including large numbers of younger poets, who repeatedly have told me that they find in his work an inspiration that brought them to poetry in the first place or that keeps them going and growing in the art. Just last week I went to a party attended by a number of young poets and I found myself standing in the kitchen, telling stories about Larry Levis, because it was my privilege to have known him, and because they so clearly wanted to hear those stories. Each year I also help to judge the annual Larry Levis Reading Prize competition, which is generously sponsored by his family, and each year it's my job to invoke the memory of Larry Levis by telling a story about him, or revealing some aspect of his writing process which I discovered when I helped to go through and arrange the poems he left behind on his computer when he died (none of which he had dated), or by taking a close look at one of his poems and its backgrounds. I was given a gift in having had the chance to know the man, to sit with him and talk over dinner or a glass of wine. I pass that gift along if I can.

If Levis was a poet of elegies, as the titles of his final poems suggest, nevertheless his form of elegy was a particularly life-affirming rather than death-obsessed creation. Which brings us to Rilke, whose complexity and radical linguistic ingenuity and steady circling around that ultimately zeroes in on the profound in his longer poems remind me of the tactics used by Larry Levis in his. In the first of his *Duino Elegies,* Rilke soon begins to seek various ways to provoke the reader. First, he tries being profoundly frightening ("Each and every angel is terrifying"), then, he gets sarcastic, suggesting that if you "Throw the emptiness in your arms out/ there into the spaces we inhale" perhaps then "the birds/ will sense the air expanding with a more profound flight" (my translation). In other words, your big-time sorrowful angst is really for the birds. But Rilke goes on to construct a different sort of challenge:

> Yes, the springtimes needed you, it's true. Many stars changed
> for you, so you would notice. A wave nearby
> heaved itself up in those days gone by, or else,
> as you were passing by an opened window,
> a violin gave itself. All this was a mission.
> But did you accomplish it?

The day I discovered that Larry Levis had died, like it or not, I was given a mission. I have also sensed in myself and in others that question: Did you accomplish it? And worse, there is the question of whether the whole enterprise of remembering a fellow poet has something inescapably ironic about it. But I don't believe that the praise of one poet involves the diminishment of another. The real competition in poetry is not with one another, but with oneself. There is no shame or embarrassment in taking up that mission of remembrance. The care we give to the poetry we value is also a mission, perhaps because poetry itself is holy, just as "the ankle of a horse is holy," to quote Levis, and that mission is indeed a sacred one. Faced with such a mission, it is always tempting to scoff or toss off a witty evasion, much harder to stifle the temptation. In the true elegy, the difficult work of difficult recollection, there is no room for cheap irony. Or if you do use it, it better hurt.

Michele Poulos

My Story in a Late Style of Fire: A Documentary Film Exploring the Work and Life of Larry Levis

It began with a dream. I remember waking early that February morning in my cabin in Richmond, Virginia. It was 2010. There were patches of snow on the ground; the peacocks were nestled in the barn down the hill. I didn't awake with a particular image in mind as often happens with dreams. This time, I awoke with a voice resounding in my head: *You will make a documentary film about Larry Levis.*

The idea of making a documentary film seemed laughable: I hadn't picked up a video camera since I'd graduated from New York University's film school eighteen years earlier. And yet, the notion never went away, and I began to set about finding ways to make the implausible possible.

A year and a half later, my film crew and I have completed filming approximately 40 hours of raw footage for *My Story in a Late Style of Fire,* a feature-length documentary film exploring the work and life of poet Larry Levis. I estimate that we are halfway through production. When Levis died at age forty-nine in Richmond, Virginia, he was employed as a professor at Virginia Commonwealth University, teaching in their M.F.A. in Creative Writing program. He had published five well-received books of poetry, a collection of stories, and numerous essays. Among his awards, Levis had won three fellowships in poetry from the National Endowment for the Arts, a Fulbright Fellowship, and a Guggenheim Fellowship. His work also appeared in *American Poetry Review, The Southern Review, Field,* and *The New Yorker,* as well as in other magazines. Many poets have told me that they love the work of Larry Levis, and since his death, his reputation and influence have steadily continued to grow among a varied and increasingly widespread audience. The film reveals Levis from multiple perspectives, including responses by a diverse group of writers who judge that his work is of lasting and great importance, such as Pulitzer Prize winner Charles Wright, Guggenheim Fellow David Wojahn, National Book Award finalist Kathleen Graber, senior editor of *Blackbird* Gregory Donovan, and many others, including both the young and the well-established.

The structure of the film is framed around oral history interviews with his surviving family members, colleagues, students, girlfriends, ex-wives, and his many friends. Threading the interviews together are family photographs, family videos, and his poems, many of them read by a younger generation of poets, such as the critically acclaimed Joshua Poteat. Accompanying his poems will be visually artistic scenes designed to compliment his words. These portions of the film will be somewhat impressionistic and provide the audience with a visual "breather," or relief. The goals for the film are twofold: on the one hand, to accurately present the facts about Levis's life, exploring how and why it has influenced the literary community, while on the other to engage some of the greatest poets alive in lively and penetrating discussions, through the frame of Levis's work, about the historical and cultural connections of his poetry.

Some of the questions that the documentary will address are: How did Levis mature as a poet from his first book to his last? What about his work inspires such devotion not only from poets, but even from a more general readership? How did he feel about living in Virginia and was location an influence in his work? And the larger questions: What has been his impact not only on Virginia but also on the national writing community? How has contemporary poetry changed because of him? Why does the general public think poetry is inaccessible? Especially toward the end of his life, yet throughout his career, Levis focused on the elegy, writing that "[t]he elegist, if his art is to be authentic, must also die, imaginatively at least, with his subject."

It's my intention that the film will serve a variety of audiences. First, there is the immediate literary community in Virginia. Virginia Commonwealth University's Cabell Library has recently acquired the letters of Levis and is working toward creating a permanent display of some of his personal items and papers. Scholars, writers, and enthusiasts of writing will not only have access to many of his personal items, but will have access to, for example, the correspondence between himself and his mentor Philip Levine, who recently became the nation's poet laureate. This means that the Cabell Library has the potential to become an important center for studies on the author's life and work, and the Library's collection is featured in the documentary, including footage of VCU graduate poetry students making use of the Levis Collection.

Second, it will serve an audience interested in the South and Southern Writing. At the end of his life Levis had become a writer at work in the South, creating poems and essays that often examined the people, places, and events of the South. For many, although the term "Southern Writing" is as elusive as it is controversial, its themes of family, centrality of race, love of the land, and vivid characters are qualities that draw a large audience.

Finally, the film will of course serve the broader national and international literary community and beyond. Because Levis's work continues to inspire succeeding generations of poets and writers, it is important to honor his contribution. Viewers will be interested to hear some of the greatest writers writing today offer insights into his work. We'll hear from family members as well. Levis struggled with various addictions and was married three times—his life experiences often found their way into his writing. It is important to examine his life as well as his art, and the literary community will benefit from seeing the intersection of the two.

If readers are interested in tracking the film's progress, they can visit the Facebook page at *www.facebook.com/mystoryinalatestyleoffire*. And if anyone would like to contact me directly about the film, they may reach me by visiting my web site, *www.michelepoulos.com*.

Larry Levis

FROM *WRECKING CREW* (1972)

The Poem You Asked For

My poem would eat nothing.
I tried giving it water
but it said no,

worrying me.
Day after day,
I held it up to the light,

Turning it over,
but it only pressed its lips
more tightly together.

It grew sullen, like a toad
through with being teased.
I offered it all my money,

My clothes, my car with a full tank.
But the poem stared at the floor.
Finally I cupped it in

my hands, and carried it gently
out into the soft air, into the
evening traffic, wondering how

to end things between us.
For now it had begun breathing,
putting on more and

more hard rings of flesh.
And the poem demanded the food,
It drank up all the water,

beat me and took my money,
tore the faded clothes
off my back,

said Shit,
and walked slowly away,
slicking its hair down.

Said it was going
over to your place.

FROM *THE AFTERLIFE* (1977)

In a Country

My love and I are inventing a country, which we
can already see taking shape, as if wheels were
passing through yellow mud. But there is a problem: if we put a river in the country, it will thaw
and begin flooding. If we put the river on the border, there will be trouble. If we forget about the
river, there will be no way out. There is already a
sky over that country, waiting for clouds or smoke.
Birds have flown into it, too. Each evening more
trees fill with their eyes, and what they see we can
never erase.

One day it was snowing heavily, and again we were
lying in bed, watching our country: we could
make out the wide river for the first time, blue and
moving. We seemed to be getting closer; we saw
our wheel tracks leading into it and curving out
of sight behind us. It looked like the land we had
left, some smoke in the distance, but I wasn't sure.
There were birds calling. The creaking of our
wheels. And as we entered that country, it felt as if
someone was touching our bare shoulders, lightly,
for the last time.

FROM *THE DOLLMAKER'S GHOST* (1981)

To a Wall of Flame in a Steel Mill, Syracuse, New York, 1969

Except under the cool shadows of pines,
The snow is already thawing
Along this road...
Such sun, and wind.
I think my father longed to disappear
While driving through this place once,
In 1957.
Beside him, my mother slept in a gray dress
While his thoughts moved like the shadow
Of a cloud over houses,
And he was seized, suddenly, by his own shyness,
By his desire to be grass,
And simplified.
Was it brought on
By the road, or the snow, or the sky
With nothing in it?
He kept sweating and wiping his face
Until it passed,
And I never knew.
But in the long journey away from my father,
I took only his silences, his indifference
To misfortune, rain, stones, music, and grief.
Now, I can sleep beside this road
If I have to,
Even while the stars pale and go out,
And it is day.
And if I can keep secrets for years,
The way a stone retains a warmth from the sun,
It is because men like us
Own nothing, really.

I remember, once,
In the steel mill where I worked,
Someone opened the door of the furnace
And I glanced in at the simple,
Quick and blank erasure the flames made of iron,
Of everything on earth.
It was reverence I felt then, and did not know why.
I do not know even now why my father
Lived out his one life
Farming two hundred acres of gray Malaga vines
And peach trees twisted
By winter. They lived, I think,
Because his hatred of them was entire,
And wordless.
I still think of him staring into this road
Twenty years ago,
While his hands gripped the wheel harder,
And his wish to be no one made his body tremble,
Like the touch
Of a woman he could not see,
Her fingers drifting up his spine in silence
Until his loneliness was perfect,
And she let him go—
Her laughter turning into these sheets of black
And glassy ice that dislodge themselves
And ride slowly out,
Onto the thawing river.

FROM *ELEGY* (1997)

The Two Trees

My name in Latin is light to carry & victorious.
I'd read late in the library, then
Walk out past the stacks, rows, aisles

Of books, where the memoirs of battles slowly gave way
To case histories of molestation & abuse.

The black windows looked out onto the black lawn.

• • •

Friends, in the middle of this life, I was embraced
By failure. It clung to me & did not let go.
When I ran, brother limitation raced.

Beside me like a shadow. Have you never
Felt like this, everyone you know,

Turning, the more they talked, into...

Acquaintances? So many strong opinions!

And when I tried to speak—
Someone always interrupting. My head ached.
And I would walk home in the blackness of winter.

I still had two friends, but they were trees.
One was a box elder, the other a horse chestnut.

I used to stop on my way home & talk to each

Of them. The three of us lived in Utah then, though
We never learned why, me, *acer negundo,* & the other
One, whose name I can never remember.

"Everything I have done has come to nothing.
It is not even worth mocking," I would tell them
And then I would look up into their limbs & see
How they were covered in ice. "You do not even
Have a car anymore," one of them would answer.

All their limbs glistening above me,
No light was as cold or clear.

I got over it, but I was never the same,

Hearing the snow change to rain & the wind swirl,
And the gull's cry, that it could not fly out of.

In time, in a few months, I could walk beneath
Both trees without bothering to look up
Anymore, neither at the one

Whose leaves & trunk were being slowly colonized by
Birds again, nor at the other, sleepier, more slender

One, that seemed frail, but was really

Oblivious to everything. Simply oblivious to it,
With the pale leaves climbing one side of it,
An obscure sheen in them,

And the other side, for some reason, black bare,
The same, almost irresistible, carved indifference

In the shape of its limbs

As if someone's cries for help
Had been muffled by them once, concealed there,

Her white flesh just underneath the slowly peeling bark

—while the joggers swerved around me & I stared—

Still tempting me to step in, find her,

And possess her completely.

Edward Ruchalski

Keeping Us Afloat: A Closer Look at Paul Simon's Song "So Beautiful or So What"*

On first hearing, "So Beautiful or So What" appears to be a simple strophic pop song consisting of three repetitions of the following: two verses followed by a refrain (or AAB repeated three times). And it is just that: a song in which the verses set the mood or scene by giving descriptive information, while the refrain functions as a respite or pause, allowing the listener to reflect on that information.

The song begins with an African-tinged blues riff played lightly and yet with exhilarated energy on electric guitar, doubled by resonator. The resulting combination, and the way in which the two instruments are panned, creates a subtle effect—similar to a slap echo. After the fourth repetition, an acoustic guitar responds with a brisk, descending melody that overlaps with the original riff to create a web of sound. At the same time, it's as if the ghost of John Lee Hooker has just snuck up on the front porch to deliver the news. But when Simon begins to sing over the riff, his story is much less self-absorbed. He's not singing about wandering, money, work, or even sex. Nor does he seem to be playing a character who is in dire straits. Rather, it is as if he is simply thinking to himself out loud, without being overly confessional, or cryptic. In some ways, Simon is exploring the common expression, "Is the glass half empty or half full?"—a theme that dates back in our popular tradition to the old hillbilly classic, "Keep On the Sunny Side."

Structurally, this first verse (and all the verses that follow) takes on a microscopic form of the larger song (AAB). The first two lines describe an activity, while the last line, functioning as a refrain, reflects on the possible outcome of this activity. Each line is sung over four measures in 4/4 meter and over the same chord. The first two lines rhyme, while the third is a slant rhyme. The verse is basically blues in its oldest form: 12-bar. However, Simon deviates from the conventional form (a three line stanza, in which the second line is a repetition of the first) by continuing to give us more information in the second line.

*From Paul Simon's new release, *So Beautiful or So What* (Hear Music, 2011)

Here is the first verse of Paul Simon's "So Beautiful or So What":

(A) I'm going to make a chicken gumbo
Toss some sausage in the pot
(A') I'm going to flavor it with okra
Cayenne pepper to make it hot
(B) You know life is what we make of it
So beautiful or so what

A traditional 12-bar approach to Simon's first verse would be as follows:

(A) I'm going to make a chicken gumbo
Toss some sausage in the pot
(A) I'm going to make a chicken gumbo
Toss some sausage in the pot
(B) You know life is what we make of it
So beautiful or so what

Following the first verse, the riff, along with the acoustic guitar melody, is repeated twice before Simon begins singing the second verse. There is a sense of community in the interplay between the instruments: a feeling that we are all in this together. There is no lone bluesman or soloist, here.

The second verse is a variation of the first, and functions musically in exactly the same way. The only major difference is the lyrics within the A sections, which again place Simon in a domestic setting. This time, however, through a bedtime story, he is determined to educate his children, to make them aware of a simple philosophy so that they will have some tools in order to shape their lives accordingly. Simon emphasizes the question "Will it have a happy ending? Maybe yeah; maybe not" by striking crotales on the second beat of the first measure—exactly when he sings the word "have," as if to stress this idea of having a choice in how we experience and behave, or how we possess our own emotional lives; how we may shape an experience by our own perspective, be it in a negative or positive light. The choice is ours.

Immediately following the second verse is the refrain, in which Simon contemplates while singing, "So beautiful, so beautiful, so what." Here, the lyrical form turns to the conventional AAB blues form. But with so few words and over a shorter period of time (eight bars instead of twelve), the song feels far removed from the blues. It is here that the texture finally changes. The guitars fall out, leaving the ghostly sound of the glockenspiel, Simon's own backing vocals, and a simple childlike flute melody that pops in like a bird song. The emptiness of the texture has a peaceful, dreamlike quality almost suggesting a paradise, as if Simon is leaning towards the positive or "so beautiful" possibility for existence.

At this point in the song, the form (AAB) has been heard once. Following this, there will be no more structural additions, no chorus—no surprises. The form will simply repeat twice more. Lyrically, Simon has what it takes to keep us listening. He's a great storyteller, perfectly balancing serious subjects with concern and humor. His unaffected approach to singing—along with his clear articulation, precise phrasing, and wonderful sense of pitch—is refreshing, and rarely found in popular performances.

For me, it is the subtle, unusual touches of color carefully added here and there that keep the song afloat. These additions help to enhance and shape the mood of the song. The light, swift cymbal roll just before Simon begins the second verse, along with the strange, descending, chromatic glockenspiel melody, suggests both the "raindrop in a bucket," and "a coin dropped in a slot" to which Simon compares himself. The *saz* (a Turkish stringed instrument), meanwhile, seems to be the little devil standing on Simon's left shoulder, taunting and nagging him. Its haunting sound becomes more prominent towards the end of the song as the lyrics get darker. It even seems to mock Simon, appearing whenever he mentions something unpleasant.

Most interesting is the vocal harmony that appears only twice in the song when Simon doubles his own voice an octave lower on "Ain't it strange the way we're ignorant." It is as if Simon is underlining the text, making it clear to the listener what human quality leads to negativity, unhappiness, and destruction. But Simon is still musing, never preachy or condescending. In the refrain that follows, the flute now plays an octave lower than it did in the previous refrain, as if it too has been influenced by the harmony, or dark turn that the singer has taken. These sweeteners don't feel out of place or artificial. They feel organic, as if the music is rolling down a hill, gaining mass by collecting objects in its path.

In addition, the drummer keeps time in an unusual way, mostly without cymbals, but with plenty of bass drum: a sound of wood, not skin. I imagine a moving train, or the wheels of some ancient machine that has been ticking since the beginning of time. But at the same time, these drums help to ground the riff. The music never feels out of control.

As the song progresses, Simon drifts away from talking about the "I" and begins to talk about the insignificance of the self. The song steps out of the safety of the home and into the world that seems vacant and hostile. It's as if he is thinking about how our actions, or our inactions, in the home may affect how we interact and connect, or don't connect, with the rest of society. The song ends with the riff playing through the refrain as if there is no longer a heavenly place in the song to go to. Simon continues to sing, dropping the "so what" and leaving us with only "so beautiful," as the final refrain fades into silence.

Eliot Fisk and Tony Trischka: Local Kids Make Good

Steven Stucky and Neva Pilgrim, *Stone Canoe's* music editors and distinguished musicians in their own right, talked this past fall with virtuoso string instrumentalists Eliot Fisk and Tony Trischka, both Syracuse prodigies who have gone on to achieve worldwide acclaim as masters of their respective instruments, the guitar and the banjo.

After graduating from Jamesville Dewitt High School, Eliot Fisk went on to study at Yale, and later formed the Guitar Department at the Yale School of Music. He was the last pupil of Andrés Segovia, who described him as belonging "in the top line of our artistic world." He is known internationally as a master of the classical guitar repertoire, as well as for his collaborations with other musicians in such styles as classical, jazz and world music. Many of his recordings have entered the Billboard charts as best sellers. Eliot is currently on the faculty at the Universität Mozarteum in Salzburg, Austria, where he teaches in five different languages, and at the New England Conservatory of Music. He is also founder of the Boston GuitarFest, an annual "cross-disciplinary extravaganza," and is known for taking classical music into unusual venues, such as schools, senior centers, and prisons. He currently maintains homes in Boston, Salzburg, and Granada, Spain.

Tony Trischka is considered by many to be the most influential banjo player in the roots music world, and has been described by the *New York Times* as "the godfather of what is sometimes called new acoustic music." He is a graduate of Nottingham High School and Syracuse University, where his father was a professor of physics. After forming several popular local groups, he began to get broader recognition and ended up touring with such bluegrass legends as Bill Monroe and Earl Scruggs. He now plays for huge audiences in the U.S. and abroad, and has gained fame as a bandleader, film musician, radio star, and teacher. On his award-winning 2007 album, *Double Banjo Bluegrass Spectacular,* he duets with many star players, including Scruggs, Steve Martin, and his star student, the renowned Béla Fleck. His 2008 recording *Territory* features duets with an even broader range of musicians, and explores the full panorama of banjo tunings and traditions. Tony is a master of the bluegrass style, but he is also known for stretching the traditional banjo repertoire in his collaborations with such diverse partners as Ornette Colman, Bruce Springsteen, the Wichita State University Percussion Ensemble, and the National Radio Orchestra of Korea. He is the producer of Steve Martin's 2011 album, *Rare Bird Alert,* featuring Paul McCartney.

Despite daunting international commitments, both Eliot and Tony remain true to their Upstate New York roots, returning periodically for recitals, lectures, and master classes within the community. Both came back to town in March 2011: Eliot and his wife, acclaimed guitarist Ziara Meneses, performed with the Syracuse symphony, and Tony returned for an intimate Folkus Project concert at the Syracuse Westcott Community Center.

–Robert Colley

Steven Stucky

A Conversation with Eliot Fisk

Steven Stucky: Eliot, welcome back to Boston. On which side of the Atlantic are you mostly living these days?

Eliot Fisk: I've been based in America for about the last ten years. I have a very good class at the Mozarteum in Salzburg, and a very good class here at the New England Conservatory, and both are very international. The two systems affect people differently. In higher education, the American system is unparalleled because of our long tradition of free speech, and free debate. The one thing we've really succeeded in doing in this country is keeping a free marketplace of ideas just popping. You can start something from zero, like Neva Pilgrim did with the Society for New Music in Syracuse, or like I did with my little guitar festival in Boston called the Boston GuitarFest, and from zero you can build something up as long as you have the persistence. You can take a little dream, or a big dream, and you've got a better chance of realizing it. In Europe, if it doesn't fit the preconceived niche in society, you're locked out. A lot of American composers, some really good ones, have been locked out of Europe unless they happen to write in a certain style that fits whatever *ism* the European classical music establishment thinks is "in" right now. For example, the tyranny of the Berio-Boulez-Stockhausen triumvirate was funny, because the *next* "ism" that they accepted, amazingly, was minimalism. It was a definable thing, a genuine *ism*, so they accepted that as New Music. Meanwhile some of the so-called postmodernist Americans who I think are doing some great things don't get performed over there.

The differences are fascinating: it's a case study in the advantages and disadvantages of government support of the arts, and having something of a niche for classical music in the society. My school in Europe is supported almost entirely by the government. The New England Conservatory fights for its life every year. But then here we have a livelier exchange of ideas, and more of a tradition of people talking to each other. I appreciate the American dynamism and the European solidity.

I think America has much greater potential, as yet unrealized. We have to do a much better job figuring out how to have an impact. I actually think that the musicians have done a great job, but many of the arts administrators have not been able to make the right kinds of connections to sell the high quality of what we classical musicians try to do. These two lives I lead, one in Europe and one here, show all kinds of possible directions one could go in trying to solve that conundrum. I think it's perhaps the biggest problem there is in the world of art right now. The internet is, as the Germans would say, a *Tummelplatz der Mittelmässigkeit*—"playground of mediocrity"—a great big moving river that carries all boats on it. In one way, there's tremendous potential that we're just beginning to figure out. You can go to YouTube and hear Rubinstein, hear Kissin, hear Schiff. Everybody is there, all mixed together. That's a lot of static.

SS: The potential is enormous. But at the same time the leveling, the uncritical democratization that says everything is just another channel to be surfed, and all channels are created equal...

EF: That's exactly what I mean. We've been hearing that the American audience for classical music is only old people, but we've been hearing that for twenty years. In America you see some things dying, and some things growing. New things popping up where there was nothing, and other things dying where there used to be something. Look at the LA Phil, look at San Francisco. Look at Michael Tilson Thomas, Esa-Pekka Salonen, Dudamel, Marin Alsop down in Baltimore, JoAnn Falletta up in Buffalo. These charismatic people are part of the solution, and they offer some pretty exciting examples of how things can work.

But one problem is the heavy emphasis on soloists. For instrumentalists so much depends on the competition system—a system that's set up to penalize creativity and risk taking, and to reward conventionality. Imagine if in big business the people with new ideas were shot down. But that's how classical music has worked for a long time. There's a certain dehumanization. They want the person who can play 150 dates a year, and come out like a little machine every night and just do it right. Especially in the '70s and '80s a lot of bad decisions were made. They just went after the bottom line instead of trying to find the special sparkling people and getting to them early and being proactive; we marketed and cheapened and therefore dumbed down the product. Eventually you start to see the consequences. We came to resemble the pigs at the end of *Animal Farm:* We were supposed to be something exceptional, something different—supposed to be idealistic, not about the bottom line. And we were supposed to be truly democratic and not just *Tafelmusik* for the moneyed elite. Not enough of us did that kind of revolutionary work to go out and create new audiences. Day in, day out, it's not glamorous. It's a lot of afterschool programs. It's trying to find an American version of *El Sistema;* it's banging on a lot of doors. We haven't taught students to fight us, to resist us. We haven't pushed the students hard enough to be their own person and come in with challenging ideas. There hasn't been enough thinking outside the box.

I think the great exception is the composers, who have been doing wonderful things, and whom we all should have gotten behind much earlier. There should be a much greater flow of contemporary music into the curriculum. Even at New England Conservatory we still have too many people just practicing their Brahms and Rachmaninov eight hours a day.

What if we educators decided that 5 percent of our graduating class every year was going to be revolutionary arts administrators? Just 5 percent! Or what if we made it our priority over the next 25 years to attack de facto racial segregation in the classical music audience? What would happen if somebody really tried to do that? First of all, we'd get a flood of new ideas into the classical music world, and a whole new audience. We don't even have Latinos in our audience, let alone African Americans. Musicians don't want it that way; nobody wants that. It's just another reflection of certain deep-seated societal problems. Nobody's even talking about any of a host of ideas that could turn classical music upside down. So let 95 percent of the graduating class of every conservatory keep doing what they're doing, but let's at least try to have 5 percent of them be arts revolutionaries, really shape things up, have some real dialectic between theory and practice.

SS: Are you able to push your students in the way you're describing?

EF: I tell every one of them that if this doesn't transform your life and mine, both of us will have failed. Each person has a unique set of talents. You want to steer them to develop musical talents, of course, but also nonmusical talents.

SS: Eliot, do you have a theory about yourself? What is it in your background that made you the unusually passionate, articulate, innovation-driven artist you turned out to be?

EF: Well, first of all, you and I were born in America. "Born in the USA" has a lot to do with it, where the inquiring mind is really valued. I had the great advantage of having a very brilliant father, a real live wire. That was a huge thing. My mother was a pillar of strength, an amazing person with a capacity to work hard and follow through. And then I had a brother who passed away about five or six years ago, who had Down Syndrome. I think with us artists something happens to us. We're blessed (and cursed) with this incapacity to be Panglossian about the world. We *don't* think it's the best of all possible worlds, and we're bothered by things that aren't just, aren't right, aren't as good as they could be. As Americans we come into the world with a tremendous idealistic sense of promise as embodied in our Constitution and Bill of Rights. The frequent contrast between those heights and the depths of our quotidian existence, when things are going horribly against what should be our guiding principles, is painful. To some extent I was predestined through my parents to feel these contrasts and be concerned about them. What really put it over the top was this experience of having a Down Syndrome brother. Not so much the fact of his condition—that was sad, of course, hard to deal with—but the lack of decent facilities to care for such a person in the America of the early 1960s and into the 1970s. You ran right into the big American problem: if you've got lots of money you can get all kinds of health care. But if not, then you're forced to use public institutions, which might be good or not, depending on the state. We were living in Philly, and the state institution where we put my brother was just horrible. We moved to New York State, which had high taxes and a lot of corruption in Albany, but I tell you, in the '70s, '80s, '90s (I don't know about now) they sure took care of people with handicaps. My brother was slowly melded into the New York State system and ended up in a wonderful group home in Jamesville, outside Syracuse. He was cared for so lovingly and wonderfully by those employees of the State of New York, and that made a huge difference. So, for me, I think the subject was more related to the lack of good care, which we couldn't afford in the early years. And then the trauma of having to make the diagnostic decision after a while that he really couldn't continue living at home. We just didn't have the facilities to care for him, to educate him. Caring for him was just wearing my mother to the bone, even with her prodigious energies. As a family, we made this agonizing decision, and we would go and pick him up on the weekends. So we had this psychic wound that would open and close, open and close, constantly.

Another interesting thing about people is that we can choose. Christ, or Martin Luther King, or Socrates, or Gandhi—any of these people could have escaped their ultimate fate. Dr. King didn't have to take on the whole encrusted racist system; he could have just been a nice preacher and not bothered anybody. But he couldn't do that. And Christ also didn't necessarily have to sacrifice himself. Socrates was offered the chance to get away. Gandhi could have gone on being a lawyer. But they all somehow felt that they had to do this. In a much lesser way, I guess, with music, it felt like it chose you; it was something you had to do. It was for me a way of dealing with the suffering. But also I think, as a human being, there's a difference between feeling physical pain (say, cutting your finger), and suffering, which has a deeper, perhaps spiritual dimension. Allowing yourself to feel is a uniquely human quality (as far as we know). But there are those human beings who block it off, don't let it touch them, become for whatever reason, fear perhaps, closed off. And there are people who can't help feeling. We artists are people who can't help feeling. And you have to put that feeling somewhere. Music is a positive, wonderful way of dealing with these feelings. For me, the messages from great composers can make life rich, can make it infinite in possibility.

With the guitar we really get into the question of meaning. A composer can write something, very legitimately, but the instrument might not want to do it. So they have to change this or that, or even rewrite a passage. There are so many ways of changing things to try and get at what a composer was really after. I love working with non-guitarist composers, because they always push you to go beyond what seems possible. It's endlessly fascinating. And then when you go to perform the piece on stage, of course, it's a whole other thing, projecting that to new listeners who have never heard the piece before. How do you communicate that? That's the great duty, responsibility, and thrill of being the performer—when you get it right. And in the moment of playing, to have those occasional moments of grace where you can transcend yourself.

SS: One of the great rewards to the composer is when a great performer—even accidentally—discovers something new in a piece. Then that becomes, in a sense, part of the piece.

EF: That kind of attitude is, I think, wonderfully American. There are a few Europeans who might agree. Berio was wonderfully flexible, with the *Sequenza.* He was really great. But some others are more deterministic: it's got to be that way or no way. There is that strain in European composition, though I think it's lessening.

SS: You've said that music chose you. How early did that happen?

EF: It happened very slowly. Nobody in my family was a musician, though my parents had classical records. Again, it was through my brother, indirectly, because my mother said, "Well, one thing we can do as a family, we can get a guitar and strum and sing songs." So, when I was seven, my father came home with a very cheap guitar and a banjo. They were terrible instruments, but I kind of started then. I got sick of the banjo after a while, so I went to the guitar with self-instruction books. Three months later I was still fiddling around with this [instrument], and I remember my mother asking me, "Would you like lessons?" To me this seemed unthinkable! Who could afford music lessons? That sounded to me like the ultimate luxury. But of course I said yes. My parents were members of the Quaker meeting in the Philadelphia area, and a member of our meeting happened to be the principal bass player in Ormandy's Philadelphia Orchestra, Roger Scott. My parents asked him what to do, and Roger said, "Well, if he's going to study guitar it had better be classical, because if he can do that he can do anything," which of course is not true. My parents found a man who had attended a few of Segovia's classes at the Accademia Musicale Chigiana in Siena, Italy, and he became my first guitar teacher. Then, when I was ten or eleven, my father had a sabbatical in the southern Swedish city of Lund for ten months. I was put into a Swedish school. I didn't speak any Swedish, so that was tough. People were nice to me, but I was lonely. Everything was new, back then much more so than it would be now. That was 1965 or '66, when different parts of the world seemed much more separate than now. So I started to practice. I didn't have anything else to do. They found a teacher for me there, and by the end of that year I had gotten serious with the guitar. When we came back my father thought maybe it was time to get a better instrument. I was in a guitar store in Philly trying out guitars, and the people in the store said, "Get him to William Viola." He was an engineer at IBM and a self-taught guitarist who gave lessons on Saturdays at the store. He was a very disciplined, extraordinary man, extremely intelligent, who had taught himself the Segovia way of playing from Segovia's records. He was a real task master. He really pushed me for the next two years. The only time I had any really good, basic guitar instruction was from him. After two years with him, we moved to Syracuse. There wasn't anybody to teach me in Syracuse, so I was just going to high school like a normal kid and kind of teaching myself from records. Then, starting about my sophomore year, I went to Aspen to study with Oscar Ghiglia for four or five weeks of the summer. That opened a lot of windows for me. Then I went to Yale, because I wanted a liberal arts school with a good music department. By that time I was totally bitten by the bug. I knew that's what I wanted to do, probably by the age of about fourteen or fifteen. Again, my parents weren't pushing me; it was really something I decided. As you know, in America you really have to do it all yourself. That has advantages and disadvantages. Nowadays, there's a lot more pedagogy. I would have had a lot easier time of it in a lot of ways, but that's the way things were back then. There was really a lot of "teach yourself." I met Segovia while I was in college. That was hugely important for me, and he became a mentor. He's been my inspiration. Meeting him was really beautiful. I was nineteen; he was eighty-one. I'd see him once or twice a year. When he'd come to New York, I'd go down and play for him. He was very gracious to me, very supportive, right up to the end of his life.

SS: Did the fact that you had to be self-taught at some periods and you sort of bounced around leave any marks on your technique and your teaching? Is there something unconventional about your playing for that reason?

EF: I think so. I got interested in Baroque keyboard music by Froberger and Bach and those kinds of composers. To do on one guitar what two hands could do on the harpsichord—that was a huge challenge. And then at Yale I also started to work with Ralph Kirkpatrick, the great harpsichordist. He was a pitiless teacher. He didn't understand why a guitar couldn't do just as well as a harpsichord in this extremely difficult music. He was a great teacher for me, a wonderful inspiration. And then at Yale I became very close friends with Robert Beaser, who composed the first big piece that was written for me called *Canti Notturni,* that was in a non-tonal language and had a lot of complex rhythms—things I had never really encountered before. That piece was a huge nudge forward. And through Bobby I got more tuned in to contemporary music in general. And then little by little I met a lot of other composer friends and was able to commission works by a lot of other people that became really important to me. So that's really how it happened.

Neva Pilgrim

A Conversation with Tony Trischka

Neva Pilgrim: What first captivated you about music and when did you decide to make it your career?

Tony Trischka: I can remember from a very early age that music itself grabbed me. I went to a movie, *Man without a Star* with Kirk Douglas—I must have been 7 or 8 at the time, and the music bowled me over. We also had Beethoven's 9th Symphony in the house, and I loved it. I also loved folk music, e.g. Pete Seeger and the Weavers. I was a "red diaper baby" and can say that today, although then people were afraid to say such things because of McCarthyism.

I took piano and flute lessons, but that didn't really excite me. I composed my first piece, a protest song, at age 12 or 13 during the Civil Rights movement. I wrote a few of those around that time. Then, about 1965 or so, I started composing banjo pieces. Since then most of my compositions have been almost entirely instrumental. The last year or so I started writing some songs based on the Civil War—not trying to write in the period style, but trying to write music the way I would write it on Civil War themes. It's really been a great experience.

Growing up I listened to Bob Dylan, then heard the Kingston Trio play *Charlie and the MTA,* in which Dave Guard played a banjo solo and I thought, "I have to do this." Around that time I went to a Hootenanny at Syracuse University and heard a banjoist playing bluegrass style, and that was it, I was gone.

You asked when I decided to become a musician—I never did. I always was a musician. In fact my very first paying gig was playing at the University Club in Syracuse—$15 for 15 minutes at the age of 14—pretty good pay. From then on I kept playing all through the rest of my time at Nottingham High School and at college.

I attended Syracuse University as a Fine Arts major. That was during the Vietnam War protests—1970—the year of the strike, and I never finished the paper for the last three credits until 18 years later. Looking back, I would have done it a lot differently today. It would have been helpful for me to have music theory and composition, perhaps even a business course. It would have been helpful to have some technical knowledge at my fingertips.

NP: Who encouraged you to keep going?

TT: My parents bought me my first banjo, then when I was craving a better banjo, they bought that for me. But they didn't encourage me to have a career in music—it was more like "follow your heart." They also never said "go get a real job." Now I'm the father of a drummer, and encouraging my son to do something else to make a living [laughs].

NP: After graduation you started touring, or did you do some teaching as well?

TT: I had been playing and just kept playing, and it carried on. I never looked back. As I think about it now, I actually started teaching back in 1970. This woman asked me to teach her banjo, and when I told her I didn't teach, she said, "That's OK, I won't pay you." She was my first student and also an SU student. Now I have my own online banjo school.

NP: How did you manage to get jobs after SU?

TT: For a long time, up through 1990, I always played with various bands, and for the most part the business head in the band got the jobs. After 1990 I started doing my own thing more of the time. I think it was in the late 1990s that my electric band played at Jazz Fest.

NP: Do you feel privileged that you've made a living at what you love?

TT: I can't even begin to tell you how privileged I feel to make a living at what I love doing. Years ago I somewhat took it for granted. I remember while living in New York City I was taking a cab to the airport to fly to Helsinki for a festival. He asked if I was excited about going, and I said, "I've been to Europe several times. So I'm looking forward to it, but I'm not excited." And he got really angry with me. I started realizing at that point that I am so, so lucky.

NP: You mean to meet and engage lots of interesting people throughout the world?

TT: Absolutely. I'd have to fall all over myself to tell you how lucky I've been.

NP: Do you consider yourself a risk-taker, or have you more or less gone with the flow?

TT: Early on in my career I was a risktaker, but not as much now. When I first started, the music that was out there for the banjo generally stayed within certain parameters. My musical tastes ran from '60s folk music, Brian Wilson, to the Beatles, Zappa, and Miles Davis. I loved Ives, Schönberg, modern jazz, and so forth. In my first album I adapted those sensibilities to the banjo. I always had some kind of strange sounds in there. I would add a little synthesizer to one and a little saxophone on another. So, yes, early on I was definitely stretching boundaries. I tried to write what I felt, what I heard. So I would get some pretty scathing reviews in the traditional bluegrass magazines. But now a lot of those battles have been won.

NP: There are more banjo players now than when you were growing up?

TT: Yes, I think so. I have hundreds of new banjo players on my online school. Béla Fleck, who started studying with me when he was 15, just premiered his banjo concerto with the National symphony. It was a 35 minute piece of serious music. He's taking this all the way out there. I was in Nashville a couple of weeks ago when he played. We're still very close friends.

NP: It seems that you're always developing future projects. Do you just dream these up or do they develop out of collaborations with others?

TT: Sometimes by accident, sometimes from an idea I have, and sometimes from playing with others. One thing I'm really excited about is a documentary, *Give Me the Banjo.* It will air Nov. 4 on PBS. Marc Fields is the documentarian, and I'm the music director. It's been in the works for about eight years now. Some people think the banjo is just a hee-haw hillbilly kind of instrument, but this documentary traces it to its African roots, its whole social history that reflects modern times.

There was this festival in Ireland and our guitar player/singer couldn't make it because his daughter was ill, so we did this trio and ended up hiring musicians there, and it worked out great. Sometimes you have to just go with what's handed you and make something out of it—to improvise.

NP: Did the Syracuse environment contribute anything to your development? Or were you just who you were and it wouldn't have mattered where you grew up.

TT: Wow, that's a tough question. Those grey days could get pretty depressing in mid-February. But Syracuse—the city itself—has powerful memories for me, since I lived there until I was 23. That probably got in there at some level. And those crisp fall days walking to Archbold Stadium for football games with my dad. That's all very redolent. Also, for the opportunities people gave me, and continue to give me, the support I felt. I remember playing at Captain Mac's Clam Shack on Erie Boulevard. It was my regular stomping ground. Syracuse is still close to my heart—both the city and Syracuse University. The places I played. In closing, I can say that after all the traveling and playing I've done, and it's a cliché, but it's true... it still amazes me that music crosses all boundaries and brings people together. I recall when I was in the Czech Republic, then Communist Czechoslovakia, and we played for 30,000 people. There were secret police everywhere, but the people braved all that and came to hear the music. That was absolutely my best tour.

Betsy Andrews

MORNING IS A HALF-BAKED BIRD, A WATER-POET'S NONSENSE, A NEWSCAST HULLED LIKE COCONUTS

morning is a half-baked bird, a water-poet's nonsense, a newscast hulled like
  coconuts,
a swindle in the cartographic conscience—how half a hundred atlas makers
stroke the climes and bow the lakes and twang the vegetation
but neglect to thrum the dented drum of the grubbed and rubbled mountain,
where a list of furry woodland critters subject to evacuation
on a signpost by the impoundment ditch serves as "habitat reclamation"
at the overburdened gash that keeps the lights on in distant states,
the Appalachian faucets running orange;
at the far end of this page, there's a wood rat who loves pretty things
he's scrounging in our flyrock for shotgun shells and shards of glass to carry to
  his burrow
in the center, there's a fleet of D-9 dozers chewing furrows in the skyline
where the mountain used to be; and the sea?
it's in the margins here—its teeny-tiny winglike fins folded in

TO SOUND LIKE ITSELF IS WHAT WATER WANTS, TO LOOK LIKE ITSELF, TO FEEL WET

to sound like itself is what water wants, to look like itself, to feel wet
walloped by cinderblock, spars and bottles, the wanting-locked water lay down
the wanting-locked water lay down its lustre, it lay down its lustre and stank
the wanting-locked water stank without lustre, it stank without lustre and we
cut it with knives; we cut it with scissors, the wanting-locked water, we cut it
with radars, we ginned it; the wanting-locked water was ginned and engined,
we engined and cinch-lipped and quicksilvered water; the water was baited
with nixies and bogles, it was looted of moon, it was piss-and-spit crooked;
the water engaged in protective reactions—it limped, it wore bright orange pants
the wanting-locked water was orange with panting, it was orange and panting,
it stank. "I want a clean cup," interrupted the Hatter: "let's all move one place on."
One place on, the octopus burrowed into a crevice of the Duotex blow-up boat,
by the recessed valve between the self-bailing floor and the thermobonded
bouyancy tube, the octopus burrowed, slender and orange, the wonderpus
burrowed, thinking, "this is coral, it's rock crack, it's shell"; its slot-box eyes
clanging like bells on hillocks, its ginger arms stroking; the sun beat down, the
stories were told of the last of the last of the last Martian race,
with bodies like mazes and three beating hearts; the day went on day,
the sun turned away, the octopus turned a Duotex grey, and, finally,
from the captain's fingers it slipped, dipping its quill in its damning pot and
scribbling rage at the lot of us on the illuminated page of the ocean, fuck you
in the name of the tide pools and shrimp haunts; to eat is what the octopus wants,
its excitable beak, its gifted locomotion, what the octopus wants is to live

THE MORNING IS A VEXING, IT IS CHAMBER-SWEEP AND QUARREL

the morning is a vexing, it is chamber-sweep and quarrel,
quickening fruit for the water-thieves, vacationers mugging the coral
the morning is a shell-drift, an addle-egg, a purse
bursting with subsidized removals; a welter heap, an ash pot, a curse
upon the harbor, its beige-on-beige huskings, its loss;
as a matter of public policy, it's a stink-broth bewitched at the cost
of the fledglings, the hatchlings, the sanderlings, the crabs
the morning is shelter-throat, it's shake-foot and scabs
from a night wheeling 10,000 valves beneath the streets
while the doped city slumbers upon its thirst-keep
the morning is a taking, it's a 60-mile plunder,
sticky sweet spot for the dead-zone cats clawing holes down under
the morning is a double-down on the secrets at the bottom,
it is by-kill, it is *has-to-be,* it is industry, it's a sodden
living for "the living," by which we mean Man
the morning is a vexing; it is catch-as-catch-can

Aimée Baker

Dustland Fairytale
(Deanna Michelle Merryfield, 13, missing since July 22, 1990)

Inside the car she slides against corsages of cigarette smoke and their foxed skin. The one with star-clustered lips kisses her wrist flesh, the blue of veins. She plans a revelation of pierced skin. Holes safety pin deep, rubbed warm with India ink.

They pull through the ruts of the trailer park, the murmur of dust behind them. Door creaking and footsteps the only dark sounds. At her uncle's she traces hearts on her twin's window, two unmirrored halves. Tapping on the glass she spells out, "I miss you," hopes her sister hears the words in her dreams.

She slides back, silvered hairs catching on the seat. In the plum-tinctured night her twin sleeps. And she, in that husk of metal, the sallow burn of vodka in her throat.

Carroll Beauvais

Do Not Say the Earth Doesn't Love Us

These strangers on the beach
range the shades of the cosmos:
moonlight, red clay,

pink beet, deep bronze.
Wiry bundles of nerves and veins
draped in skin, ivied
by Lycra patches.

All these flimsy layers we want to cover,
we want to uncover. The human form
remains translucent.

With all the direction of a plastic bag,
wrinkled and holey, I've drifted back
to this shore, involuntarily seeking
some sick shadow
of the moon-faced ghost
that orchestrates the ebb and flow
of my solitary grief.

Can you hear the song of the waves
that is not a song but a low growl,
a baring of foam and fangs
against the miserable earth?

This thief earth
that woos you with beach
and drink, laughter that rises
with cigarette smoke
from adored and familiar faces
under the umbrella,

before death's mouth
engulfs you
into that impenetrable sleep.

I say, No. Give them back.

I say, Come and get me.

Bruce Bennett

INCARCERATION

LAST WORDS

September 19, 2009 *The New York Times*

....What follows are quotations taken from inmates' last statements in Texas. The statements [were] delivered before family members, relatives of victims, friends and the press....

"Nothing I can say can change the past."

"I would like to say goodbye."

"I wish I could die more than once to tell you how sorry I am."

"I don't think the world will be a better or safer place without me."

"I would like to say goodbye."

"I am taking it like a man."

"I don't think the world will be a better or safer place without me."

"I couldn't do a life sentence."

"I am taking it like a man."

"For everybody incarcerated, keep your heads up."

"I couldn't do a life sentence."

"I can't take it back."

"For everybody incarcerated, keep your heads up."

"All my life I have been locked up."

"I can't take it back."

"Cathy, you know I never meant to hurt you."

"All my life I have been locked up."

"I want to tell my mom that I love her."

"Cathy, you know I never meant to hurt you."

"I can't take it back."

"I want to tell my mom that I love her."

"I wish I could die more than once to tell you how sorry I am."

"All my life I have been locked up."

"Nothing I can say can change the past."

Diann Blakely

Malted Milk Blues: Duet with Robert Johnson #12

Black women wet-nursed Thomas Jefferson,
A fact omitted from the Constitution

Like his red hair, his debts in Old Virginia.
I got a funny funny feeling, he'd say,

Or would have if it weren't the Age of Reason,
When God, whose clockwork universe still ran

With little fuss, blessed his home, Monticello.
Keep drinkin' malted milk to drive my blues

Away, they weren't yet singing in the quarters,
Where Sally Hemings combed her long black hair

And loved or hated him each time he touched
Her breasts. *There must be spooks around my bed,*

Her four red-headed children didn't sing,
Not yet. They stood on the porch, listening

As bloodhounds trailed a scent, as winter stirred
And stirred snow-covered leaves. And soon Nat Turner,

Who knelt just down the road, would watch as blood
Dripped on parched corn. *I'm talkin' out my head,*

He didn't sing when he wrote his confession.
Black women wet-nursed Thomas Jefferson;

His prayer-drunk, fellow Coloniser built
Our James estate with columns pale as milk,

As bones or ghosts, with bricks as red as blood.
A funny feeling, hair risin' on my head

As my heirloom clock ticks: I'm overdrawn
And smoking, awful for my constitution,

Six generations removed from black nipples,
More from my forebear's wealth. O Tom and Sal

And *spooks around my bed.* What cures the past?
My bones sing O ask bloodhounds O ask Nat.

Stones in My Passway: Duet with Robert Johnson #14

Imagine four months' worth of vomitus and sweat,
  Piss, blood, hard starveling feces
Clotted on chain-mangled skin; the moans, and curses spat
  At gods whose heads turn from these seas;

Imagine buckets of stale water slapped on your flesh,
  Its sores disguised with tar, as you
Step toward the auction block and voices rise to lash
  Harsh consonants on air perfumed

With more sweat, and tobacco. My forefather's white columns
  Backdrop the next part of this story,
And though passed centuries make him distant as Adam,
  There's a deafening echo or three

And change still jingling in ancestral bids, and hearts.
  O native currency. O shame—
He freed some for Liberia, gave some false starts
  In Alabama, a move now blamed

For my bad lungs and psychopharmeceuticals
  When his nephews turned emigré.
If blame's just gossip, forgiveness takes two souls,
  And song: *I got stones in my passway*

And my road seems dark as night. As dark as that road
  Down which shackled forebears were cast
In your first story. In my first story. O back we'll go,
  Replaying marches of the past

To Virginia plantations, to deeper Souths,
   And...just how far can I follow?
I*'ve got pains in my heart,* strummed fury curls your mouth
   Though Jesus loves me, this I know

Pains in my heart. May I begin again, please, for us;
   God and the Devil bid on song
To survive story every time. But the right chorus?—
   DoReMi...no. O wrong, wrong, wrong.

John Colasacco

Immortals

Wagner was on his deathbed.

Phone calls kept coming, and very often I was the one to answer them.

Once, he sat up in bed, shook with rage, and threatened to tell me something that I would not believe.

Kit Frick

The Fixes

Shadow puppets in the cold room. Shadows taking shape, taking dark-wall hearts: the fixes.   We blame the weather for our infinite sadness. The very human weather. It wears a ragged belly. It wears its lungs pinned to its sleeve: the fixes.   We say crazy. We say woman. We say I was built with four hearts, I'm sorry, I'm sorry. We say it in the too-bright restaurant. We say it with bile in our throats: the fixes.   Bright footfalls on the cobbled street. Our feet. Our perfect new shoes. The way we feel elevated, a beacon, primed to be noticed, the human pound of hearts beneath every coat, the rise and fall of buttons like eyes, how they fix on our faces, our swinging step, our possibilities, infinite, dividing to multiply, a great rush of birds against the brilliant sky—the fixes.   This is what we say to feel. This is what we say.

Beckian Fritz Goldberg

ANNIHILATION

I was writing about the city when it occurred to me
I was writing about nuclear annihilation and as I was writing
about nuclear annihilation it occurred to me I was writing about
you. Then it occurred to me it was the distance before the city then,
desert where the electric power station rose sparkling like a jungle gym
constellation. I'd sometimes park the car and listen to it
buzz in all the stillness and pure black sky. I was listening
to nuclear annihilation. It occurred to me as I was writing about
the city which was really about nuclear annihilation which was really
about you is that there is where nowhere began: I'd ridden out of the city
with the boy and the barbed wire and chain link around the station
was bordered with citrus exploding white blossoms that bedded the air
with their female honey and we laid down a blanket but he would only go
so far, and I did not know why. I didn't know how to ask, and I could see
the end coming: the lights, some red, some gold, on the towers
of the plant glowing like its own city. I
never lay so bare again. And all around the hum of annihilation
even before they built the nuclear plant further out from the city
where I was no longer writing: In the grapefruit tree the little rasp
of a black cardinal. The sound of cars waltzing on the road. Late sky,
the pink of the skin under skin. Some gray blue
like the uniform of someone you can't quite remember. Or of
whom you should not speak past seventeen.

The Rose I Send Myself

That rose is as sad as leaving the beach. Blowsy and sagging. All towels. The whole world is suddenly dogless. In this way sadness is the most particular.

Things to do when a rose comes up from nowhere: call your mother, mourn, admit it, don't, & step out in the cool night. It can be a stranger's face. A scent. It comes up like a thought you don't know you're having until it's between your teeth.

Dancing ensues. The first pink dips the water. The rose is attached to no other memory, it is alone. That's why it must belong to childhood. It must be something I kept to myself.

The end of summer, lipstick long on the napkin. To be humble and surrender is all it thinks about, that rose. All head. The last umbrella stuck in the sand.

An image can ruin you. An image can doom you. The eye's much bigger than the heart. Why pretend memory has something to teach us, that wilting evangelist...

Tara Helfman

For John

From the bedside tapedeck
Thomas urged you rage,
but I begged you surrender.

Measured lines of morphine calm
bloomed from your throat,
carnivorous flowers
on a living death mask.

Oh, poor Lazarus,
the miracle will not take,
for poems capture;
they don't create.

Anna Journey

Tooth Fairy Pillow

I'd like to continue
where we left off,
like that light rain in the dogwood, or that voice

swooning after static. In the childhood
house there's a cabinet where the eyes

of potatoes go on
with their deep, mutant reach—dark-
keepers, those tubers

rooted in the gaze. There's a way
back, I know, through the twin bed's

shallow frame. There's a way
back to the life

where my blond nightstand holds

a square pillow trimmed
in eyelet lace: white

with a yellow plaid pocket
in its center. Before bed I'd tuck a tooth

inside and wake
to find in its place a folded dollar. Let's move on
from right there, and, by the way, where

are my teeth? By now
you've snatched a whole set. Tell me,

is that sound
their clacking? I'd like to carry on

the exchange. My trade: six hangnails

for one cry from the childhood
tabby—he'll arrive,

years gone, on the bed, he'll step light
as meringue in his black-
tipped fur. Here's

my final offer: one fistful of red
hair snipped for every afternoon

of sipping
mint tea with my grandfather returned.
My thumb tip

for a screened porch, that dry wind
through the dahlias. I'll crawl

inside in my whole skin
shrunk down

to the size of a pocket. Let's start again
that burlesque as these potatoes shed their eyes

in my sink—blind offering. When I hit

the light switch and climb

the loose stairs toward sleep, I'll listen
for your late-night step, your white

necklace rattle.

Walnut Filled with Black Dresses

Of course there are lunatics
loose in the cottonwoods, the blonde counselors
hiss around the campfire. A nearby asylum

purrs with halogen lanterns
by the lake. I sleep near
the banana spider's shimmy, since the other girls

chose their cots first. My carrot-colored sleeping
bag flares its hot acrylic. I walk
to the latrine at night with another girl,

who ditches me, taking
the flashlight. I sprint the whole way back
to the tent on the pitch-slurred path, listen

for the lunatics' whisper, the cicadas'
sudden upshift. Bodies everywhere. In the morning,
craft time: the teens pass out halves

of walnut shells with the yellow meat
scooped out. A pair of hot-glued
cotton balls with plastic eyes will make

koala babies in cradles. In real life
the marsupial's claws can undo a girl
down to the copper

jut of each kidney. When I ooze
hot glue into the shell, it dries
to the fiberous black folds

dividing the bowl until all I see is a walnut
filled with black dresses. My friend,
Vicky, breaks her leg,

leaves camp early. For days I jump
off a rotten cottonwood log,
and each time

I flinch before hitting
bone. Besides, there are lunatics
loose in the woods who've shucked

bodies of cicadas and run, who've left one
crackling topaz skin grafted
to a cottonwood's side. When their voices rise,

the husks shake like the dead's
old jewelry. When they fall, they're empty lockets
stalling where the face goes.

Nancy Kang

Paroled

no peyote, no burnt offering, no grass
his fingers with daggers of sunlight between them,
no softly blurred tattoo, downed with coarse hair
to be caressed, say, by the monumental mittens
of a home state, with frowns and grins made ancient
as arches in eroding crimson stone

that time away
a small sliver, a toenail crescent, a catfish antenna,
a coin trampled underfoot like so
many used straws, candy wrappers, and
an elastic wreathed with hair
pulled out with a whipping motion
vertigo on a state fair ride

resurrection plants,
bloom in the desert: at the first drops of dew
they sprout and spread, eager limbs mimicking
mammalian heat, not the popping and sliding of
bones and limbs, but green veins
and glass beads in transit
from one cell to another

but always enclosed in walls
to keep the moisture in, the other life out.

Gina Keicher

To Build a Bee Box

The night was billiards and bets, pool hall girls in sequins drinking scotch, men clutching rocks glasses like stick shifts until the beekeeper arrived in his helmet. There was no place for him to sit with his bee box beside him, so he set it in a corner. Four drunk men rapped the box with their pool cues. The beekeeper pulled the veil to his helmet over his face as the bar became a hive of spilled liquor and dashing. When he became tired, the beekeeper took the box and left without re-collecting the bees. From under the pool table, you and I saw his feet removed three inches off the floor, how they hung on the air to the entryway. You said I couldn't be allergic to ghost bees and poured water over the raised, pink spots on my legs. The stuff effervesced upon contact with my knees and shins. Back home, we emptied our pockets onto the dresser to find fistfuls of stingers where there used to be change. The tiny needles glittered across the room for the long part of the night we remained awake. We stared across the dark at their brilliance, wondered what bees ejected this kind of gleam, and whether or not the bartender stayed overtime to sweep the floor of all those furred bodies, the legs still curled into the black and yellow striped bellies, poised as if still in flight.

Ivy Kleinbart

What World
for Robert Creeley

The air grew
fur and felt
walked through
where I wandered,

into errant violence,
as if coming
from some place
whole. It didn't

happen in degrees.
A switch went on
and I found myself
lit up, hideous.

What's persistence.
What perception
deep enough to
bother a lifetime, risk

alone, for what, no
choice, maybe
one chance a day,
sifting. What

in the world
(or beyond) is simple.
Every word, like a
face riddled with sockets

looks you in your
good eye, wants
desperately to dance
and dance in certain air,

where love gives
form to hope.

David Lloyd

Lessons in Geography

I. Childhood

The turquoise parrot squawks in five languages
while the monkeys pirouette and gran plié.

Each night a new species of butterfly unwraps its wings.

Each day someone discovers a cure for cancer.

My friends the ants have erected a hill with many mansions.
They haul in crumbs for my breakfast,
and I sip God's nectar from their lips.

It's true what parents say,
that the world is endless and beautiful,
but not as beautiful as me.

II. Adolescence

A lunar landscape.
White mountains. Black craters.
Nothing offers, nothing stirs
on a Saturday afternoon.

High above the body
a great blue and green orb turns and yearns
like a far from home, home,
a beaker where life breeds.

Beyond the void, voices
whisper my name.
Bones skitter over crusts.
Starlight warms the eyes.

III. Adulthood

Let there be light! I command—
and TV shines its multitudinous mirrors.

Let there be dark! I command—
and a finger flicks a switch.

But there's grumbling in the plumbing.
An ache in my left knee.
The children have abandoned me
for other children's charms.

Go forth! I command my armies,
arrayed across the yard.
Re-conquer the world!

But like the Macedonians at Hyphasis,
they're squatting, they're tired,
they're frightened by elephants,
and can only imagine
what they already know.

IV. Old Age

Beyond the rippling air: three palm trees
where shades congregate.

Your grandmother rolls out dough on a stone slab.

My father turns a page.

My mother ladles water from a bucket to a cup.

Wait for me, I say.
I'm thirsty, and need to drink.

Thomas McGraw

Mud

We move out in rain
To a range six miles
Through low pine scrub
And it's pissing down
So heavy that brigade
Decides on the cattle cars
For the ass end
Of the day
But the CO knows
No cattle car's going
To haul your ass off
A battlefield unless
You're in a bag
So we fall in
And march stiff
Into the rain
Which hasn't let up
Now that it's dark
We don't go cross
Lots but stick
To a dirt path
Now mud soup
I got light feet
I didn't want to spend
All night cleaning
Mud off my boots
So I step on top
Of the mud instead
Of in it
When we muster
At Company HQ
Two hours later
Top checks me out
    What the fuck
    Mac ain't your feet
    Got no tops

Bridget Meeds

Everybody Down

This is the first song Jim ever heard. A bird came into his house and frightened his father. A black cat refused to eat from his hand. A seed grew into a plant, a leaf, a fruit and he picked and ate it. Into his garden the sun shone and the rain fell. He went to school with the sea. He offered his mother one hundred dollars to leave his father but she refused. He straddled his motorbike—his quiet motorbike—and rode away, a small man in black shimmering in the heat rising from the road.

Philip Memmer

Psalm

Because you are always ceasing
to be, and then ceasing
to cease to be,

both at once, always, like a house
burning as it is built,
the floor smoking

as the roofers nail down shingles,
the carpenter gasping
as he frames walls

in the reek. Because the embers
are the new white wood, and
the cool nails scorch

his hands. Because the bubble boils
centered in the level.
Because the char

sends leaves. Does he know you will live
forever in this house
he will never

finish? Or that from his hammer's
handle, a blackbird sings?
Because the eggs

hatch in ashes. Because the young
take flight in flames. Because
for the thousandth

first time, his mother gives to him
your name, and buries him
in your suit. It

was his father's. It will be his
only son's. She smiles to
remember it:

the last time she saw you, whistling
as you planed the boards, as
you burned alive.

Devon J. Moore

Patricide

When I ask my father,
who is pieces of bone and ash
in the green ceramic urn
on the bookshelf by my bed,
to forgive me for not killing him,

I say, I'm ready now, to kill you.

I ask his permission to reassemble his body,
to recreate his tendons, muscles, and bones out of dust,
to pull him out of the white-hot flames
of the funeral home's furnace,
lift his ninety-pound body out
of the cardboard box coffin,
and carry him home.

I say, Let's rewind time,

when I lay him out on the pale blue-flowered sheets
of his hospice bed, a womb of mattress and metal,
the morphine drip and feeding tube reattach,
snaking like an umbilical cord into the crescent
incision three inches above his navel.
I put my hand on his rice-paper-thin skin
and feel for a heartbeat. He is a fifty-six-year-old dead fetus.

I say, I can't kill you, you're already dead.

And then there is a pulse,
his last slow, labored breath
exhaled and inhaled in reverse.
I want to wear the stench of his rotten gums
like perfume, his life-breath is so welcome.

I say, Let me bathe you one last time,

and I anoint him with Johnson's baby wash
on a soft pink washcloth. I had almost forgotten
the angular contours of the bones beneath his face,
and how I thought there was no more difference
between flesh and bone, his skin was so translucent.
Beneath the warm soft touch he coos.

I say, I wanted so much to please you.

I bathe his neck and his beating chest
with the heat of the pink cloth.
The tiny capillaries beneath his skin unfurl
their life-filled sails. I had almost forgotten
the way his stomach bile had erupted
through the hole in his abdomen, corroding away
the soft stomach flesh. Although I am gentle,
he whimpers. I remember why I am here.

I say, Take me back to a time before the pain,

and the abscesses on his backside fill in with flesh,
the burn from the stomach acid shrinks,
and the tiny black tumors uncoil themselves
from around his nerve roots, unclamping,
retreating, vertebra by vertebra,
to the smooth pink flesh of his throat.
He opens his eyes and looks at me.

He says, I had a dream I was driving in my green Mustang and
you were there.

And I use my father's pocketknife to sever
the thick plastic feeding tube from its distended pouch.
The brown-tinted milky liquid flows over my fingers
and down my forearm; it drips
from my elbow and pools
on the carpet beneath his bed.

He says, Remember when you were a kid and I took you to the ocean.
You sat in the wet sand, digging holes with your hands,
looking for a shell that echoed.

I secure the little, red-plastic stopper
into the bottom of a morphine filled syringe.

He says, You wanted to take the sound of the ocean home with you,
but more water would come and fill in the spaces you had made.

I say, there was always more sand,
always another wave.

Beyond the sound of the waves
and the hollow of an urn,
I listen to the holes in the skin,
in the face, in the arm, in the heart,
in the space of his voice, losing his voice now,
this is the sound grief makes, not much at all.

Nicola Morris

Foster Home at Pevensey Bay, England

for my brother, Peter

They switched my mother.
Gave me my brother.
Oops. Misplaced mother.

Quiet. Don't ask. It's rude.
No-one will explain. Food,
a bed, school. What more
do you need? My need roars
at night, awake. I adore

my brother but, still, to lose
a mother? It's a big mistake.
I collect shells in a cake tin, forget
which name I live in today.

But yes. My brother Peter's
birthday. Forget the beaches
the shells, the stones
under the pier. I held him, fed him
loved him the best I knew how.

We waited for her love
to return, belly unswollen
her flash of smile rolling
us into the present.

Give us her safe hands. We prevent
our own destruction, my brother and I
as best we can. He's the fly
with me bird, the stay with me family.

Happy birthday, brother. Your birth
was my good fortune. My gift
from our slip off the map. My lift
from solitude to family. My luck.

Jeanie Nguyen

Human

I am
a mess of
supple, pink meat,
not any different from
the bloody packages
you buy at supermarkets.

Miles of red and blue veins
meshed together like
piles of wires that you find
behind a high-tech machine.

Fragile bones thrown into a
Velvety sack of skin.

My flesh rips,
Skin versus paper,
Paper wins.

My veins can burst open,
The bruise blossoming on my leg
Is evidence of this.

My bones break.
Push me a little too hard,
And the ivory pieces
Might shatter.

I am not invincible
I pretend to be.

Vietnam, June 1982

The green fields stretch for miles,
Broken only by murky brown water where the fisherman sets up his nets,
Rice paddies filled with local women slaving in the sweltering sun,
And dusty roads a playground for children
My mother is one of them.
I see her, a girl of eleven,
Playing with twigs and rocks,
Dressed in pants that display her filthy ankles,
Bones showing through her thin shirt.
I wonder when was the last time she had a meal.
But, hair the color of milk chocolate,
Big brown eyes,
Pale skin,
So unlike the other children.
"*Bui doi!* Dust of life! *Con lai!* Half breed!"
The other kids yell out to her,
And I see the broken look on her face.
It's not her fault her mother had fallen in love with a white man.

I follow and watch her run into her home, barely a home,
A small boat, a misshapen, floating mess of wood and cloth,
Swaying on top of a brown river.
I wonder what she would think if she looked up and saw me watching,
A teenage girl that looks so much like her.

I listen to her soft cries,
Cries that melt into the sounds of the river.

What if I go to her?
Sit her down on the bank of the river
And show her my brown hair, brown eyes,
Pale skin?
What if I tell her,
In my mediocre Vietnamese,
That she is beautiful,
That she will one day have everything she ever wanted,
That she will be loved?
Would she hear me?

Jesse Nissim

Impossible Feat

Dear Mister B—You have a calf like a totem or poured milk. You have brute thickness woven into your scaffold. Seamless animal. In color photos you're lovely as a single lady in a smart hat; arrivals still unfold under your hairline. Here's a brief list of the things that stand between us: corner crack on the ceiling; blistery winter in the practice room, once warm; the steam. These gatekeepers demarcate your unencumbered world. World without gravity or boundary.

Mister B—(later)—I'm hanging like a cow's ribcage in a meat cooler, dark red calcifying white. You have your cumberbund of Texas bluebells, a spine to navigate cities like a snake. I wonder if you'd mind, since you're stopping through anyway, would you rate me (from one to ten). I think you will find I'm quite remarkable.

Mister B—(much later)—Tether me to the ethereal. I'm addicted. Tilt me gently on a slab of glass. Look through your machine. Tell me what the audience will see.

Self-Named Body

The body's body, the body-as-doctor.

Body as solitary confinement, body as guard; criminal, convicted body.

Pawnshop body, barter body, body of secondhand effort.

Impossible body, psychic, extraordinary.

The body of seeing through, body of a million eyes, body that looks with all its faculties.

There is a body I keep things in
Backed against pink
An endless drawer I've left open
Around the apartment
The voices of her [ ]
The banner of her [ ]
The tree of her [ ]
The texts of her [ ]

Familiar body, known body, family.

Impenetrable body. Liar.

Body outside of gravity, body as stranger, body as thrown object.
(Breaker of windows) Body as compromise, as warning, as promise.

Body-memory. Physical structure: house, driveway, mailbox, location.
(What is the body's address?)

Body of contact, keeper of contracts.

The collective body, body of information, the incompetent collective [ ].

The missing body: scapegoat, sacrificial, mythic.

The body effectively present but not visible.

Nate Pritts

Color Or No Color

Four days in a row, I woke up before the birds.
The color of the quiet was so expectant,
precise, as when first you kiss the curl swaying

in front of you & then you kiss the girl
attached. There's logic inherent
in the morning's dull hush. Once

my eyes opened onto fog & I doubted myself
so much I practically went back to sleep about it.
Days later, it was only the racket of a cardinal

that forced me back into myself, the brilliant
noontime sunshine reminding me that sometimes
one needs to look dramatically away. There are

moments of extreme emotion followed by
other moments that are much less extreme.
Where's the logic in that? There's a spot

no bigger than a fingertip on the inside of your wrist
that needs touching. What happens
is that suddenly so much noise doesn't matter.

Ed Tato

Bandwidth

Wind buffets the half-opened window,
and tires hum and rumble,
as AC/DC battles Elton John
for the space at 101.3:
a few riffs of Hell's Bells,
then a chorus of Candle in the Wind.

You press seek, to find The Christmas Two-Step,
then Thomas Aquinas up two on Archbishop McQuaid,
to find a man whispering about end-times Israelites
while highbeams in the rear view mirror blind you.

They pass with the passing
of the semi you somehow hadn't seen,
and when you're tucked in behind him,
a nice distance from the back of his rig,
you press seek again,
to find cowboy rap and death metal rap,
to find an evangelist you don't understand at all—
you're just drawn by the beats he keeps
as he keeps repeating,
iglesias, Jesu Christe, dinero.

His rhythmic charisma distracts you,
and you've lost the truck and all the other traffic
but find a full three minutes of Thunderstruck
before the radio cuts out completely,
before the road bends from the headlights
and dips and outruns them,
and the rain starts to fall.

James Bradley Wells

Orphic Winters

> *It all depends upon your desire. A naked intention directed to God, and himself alone, is wholly sufficient.*
>
> —*The Cloud of Unknowing*

What curse is more metamorphic
than to be unbeloved? In states
of deprivation, there is the chance
that insight dilates and sharpens,
punches through to the grist
engrained in the mill of things.
Branches of treetops stripped
of leaves back in Fall become
low-hanging clouds composed
of doves' bones. Winter's mood whetted
by desiccation floods over the gray day.
Snowflakes alight like a flock
of doves with flaming wings
come down to teach a universal
language. What more utterly
than emptiness grows the soul's
amplitude, if to be
unbeloved leaves only to love?

Rainer Maria Rilke

Der Panther
Im Jardin Des Plantes, Paris

Sein Blick ist vom Vorübergehn der Stäbe
so müd geworden, daß er nichts mehr hält.
Ihm ist, als ob es tausend Stäbe gäbe
und hinter tausend Stäben keine Welt.

Der weiche Gang geschmeidig starker Schritte,
der sich im allerkleinsten Kreise dreht,
ist wie ein Tanz von Kraft um eine Mitte,
in der betäubt ein großer Wille steht.

Nur manchmal schiebt der Vorhang der Pupille
sich lautlos auf-. Dann geht ein Bild hinein,
geht durch der Glieder angespannte Stille-
und hört im Herzen auf zu sein.

Rainer Maria Rilke

The Panther

His look from peering through the bars
Has become so tired that it holds nothing more.
To him, it is as if there were thousands of bars,
And behind these thousands, no world.

The easy motion of his strong and supple stride,
Which turns about itself in ever smaller circles,
Is like a dance of strength around a center point,
Where a great will stands, stunned.

Only occasionally he pushes up the eyelid covering the pupil,
Quietly, then a picture is seen from within,
Going through his limbs, tautly still,
And stopping at the heart of his being.

Translated from the German by Jerome Wilson

Rainer Maria Rilke

Einsmkeit

Die Einsamkeit ist wie ein Regen.
Sie steigt vom Meer den Abenden entgegen;
von Ebenen, die fern sind und entlegen,
geht sie zum Himmel, der sie immer hat.
Und erst vom Himmel fällt sie auf die Stadt.

Regnet hernieder in den Zwitterstunden,
wenn sich nach Morgen wenden alle Gassen,
und wenn die Leiber, welche nichts gefunden,
enttäuscht und traurig voneinander lassen;
und wenn die Menschen, die einander hassen,
in einem Bett zusammen schlafen müssen:

dann geht die Einsamkeit mit dem Flüssen...

Rainer Maria Rilke

Loneliness

Loneliness is like a rain,
It climbs up from the sea to meet the evenings;
From plains, distant and remote,
It goes up to the sky, which it always has;
And only then from the sky does it fall on the city.

It rains down in the hours before dawn,
When all the streets are turned towards morning,
And when bodies, which have found nothing,
Disappointed and sad, let go of one another;
And when those, who hate each other,
Must in the same bed sleep together.

Then flows loneliness out with the rivers.

Translated from the German by Jerome Wilson

Kenneth Lin

FALLOW*

Cast of Characters

AARON Hayes (20) Well-heeled, young white man.

JANICE (early 40s) Waitress at a Perkins. Maine accent.

ELIZABETH Hazzard Hayes (late 40s) Well-heeled, white woman.

HAPPY Lugo (early 40s) Cheerful and bright entrepreneur.

Author's Note:

1. underlined text means that Aaron is writing. It takes him as long to say the text as it takes to write it.
2. "–" connecting words means that those words should run together as though they are one word.
3. "beat" is a short pause.

ACT ONE
SCENE I: A TINY AIRPORT/A LONELY TRUCK STOP

At rise: Mid-afternoon. It's hot and bright. ELIZABETH Hazzard Hayes (late 40s) a handsome woman sits at a bus stop at an airport. She wears a crisp new tourist's t-shirt. She has khakis on. Comfortable shoes. She has a pocketbook, and no luggage. Her wool sweater sits folded next to her in a bag from the airport gift store. She watches a car drive far away in the distance.

She has an 8" x 10" envelope in her lap. It's full of hand-written letters. It's addressed and there are a number of stamps on it from the "I Heart Milton Glaser"

* The full text of the play can be found at *www.endofscene.com*.

commemorative stamp collection. She reads one. It's written on a piece of paper that's been torn out from a spiral notebook. She chokes back a quiet sob.

LIGHTS DIM on her and RISE on...

AARON Hayes, (20) Elizabeth's Son. Handsome. No, beautiful. No, young. No, alive. He is dressed in a dirty Red Sox t-shirt and jeans. He doesn't wear socks. He writes a letter with a pencil in a spiral notebook. He stops writing and looks up.

AARON

May seventeenth. Blue Hill, Maine. Wild Blueberries.

Dear Mimsy,

He massages his writing hand. There is a blister on the palm. He resumes writing.

AARON (cont'd)

This is the fourth letter that I'm writing tonight and my hand hurts. I guess I don't write too much anymore. I type now. My hands don't remember how to do something as small as writing. I could send you an e-mail. There's an Internet cafe here. But, I know you like notes and I actually like the way this all feels.

He wrings his hands. Blister.

AARON (cont'd)

I'm in a truck stop and I'm sitting at a table at a Perkins, and I'm not wearing shoes.

He picks his feet off the ground and wiggles his toes.

AARON (cont'd)

I was sweeping dead bees out of the trailer and I stepped in some honey. So I decided to come in here without shoes. No one noticed.

He presses his feet to the carpet.

AARON (cont'd)

The carpet feels good under my feet. I was so hungry today.

He puts the pen down and fiddles with his blister.

JANICE (40s), the waitress at the Perkins, enters. She wears an apron around her waist.

JANICE

(Maine accent)

You know, you keep pulling at that blister and it's going to break, right?

AARON

I'm sorry?

JANICE

I've seen you messing with that thing all night.

AARON

I think I'm going to have to pull it off.

JANICE

Who told you that?

AARON

Well, that's what I saw people doing.

JANICE

You saw people yanking on their blisters like that.

AARON

Yeah.

JANICE

Who?

AARON

Uh, I don't know.

She takes some antiseptic wipes from her apron. She puts them in front of Aaron.

JANICE

From the first aid kit.

She unpins her name tag and wipes the pin with an antiseptic wipe. She takes out a lighter. (She's a smoker.) She puts the point underneath the flame.

JANICE (cont'd)

You can put a little hole in it and let it drain if it's bothering you, but you've got to leave the skin up there.

She holds the pin out to Aaron. He takes it.

JANICE (cont'd)

The skin's like a natural Band-Aid.

AARON

Really?

JANICE

My father was a doctor.

AARON

So is mine. (as in "We have something in common.")

JANICE

Well, you should know better then.

AARON

Just stick it in?

JANICE

Go ahead. But, heat it up again.

Aaron heats up the pin and sticks it in his blister. Fluid oozes out of the blister.

AARON

Whoa!

Janice hands him a napkin.

JANICE

That's right. Just push down the sides. Yeah. Like that.

She unwraps one of the wipes.

JANICE (cont'd)

Okay, clean it out.

AARON

Thanks.

Aaron wipes his hand. Janice takes a Band-Aid out of her apron and puts it in front of Aaron.

JANICE

If you pulled the skin off, your hands wouldn't be of any use to you tomorrow.

Aaron puts on the Band-Aid and Janice cleans her pin and puts it back on.

AARON

Thanks.

JANICE

You're welcome. You picking blueberries, hon?

AARON

I'm setting out beehives. They're a little awkward. Can't get a grip, so they rub.

JANICE

What do you mean, beehives?

Aaron points.

AARON

You see that truck out there?

JANICE

Which one?

AARON

The tractor-trailer.

JANICE

Mm.

AARON

The white one.

JANICE

(sees it)

Mm.

AARON

It was full of bees this morning. Our job is to bring bees to the fields so they can pollinate the crops.

JANICE

I always thought those were farm bees doing that.

AARON

No. The guy I work for travels all over the country, from growing season to growing season, all the way from Maine to California.

JANICE

Just to put bees out?

AARON

Bees can improve a harvest by thirty percent.

JANICE

What do you do with the honey?

AARON

Sell it, I think. I don't know. Today was my first day. But Jimmy, my boss, he says that the honey's going to be dark green, almost blue.

JANICE

I lived here all my life and never heard of such a thing.

AARON

He comes every year.

JANICE

Blue honey?

AARON

Well, I'll let you know if that's true in a week or so.

JANICE

You going with him all the way to California?

Beat.

AARON

Yeah. I think I'm going to.

JANICE

How old are you?

AARON

Twenty.

JANICE

What does your mother think about all this?

Beat.

AARON

She thinks it's a great adventure.

JANICE

That's what she says. Anyway, I like a man with calloused hands. You'll fill into them really nice.

AARON

Thanks.

JANICE

You want some ice cream, Mr. First Day?

AARON

Really?

JANICE

Yeah.

AARON

Sure.

JANICE

Chocolate okay? It's the newest.

AARON

Yeah. I like chocolate.

JANICE

Alrighty. Put your shoes on. My manager's coming in an hour to empty the drawer, okay?

AARON

Okay.

JANICE

Chocolate shake. Be right back.

She picks up the remains of the first aid and exits.

Aaron watches her go. Was he just let into some exclusive club?
Aaron resumes writing.

AARON

(excited)

Still, it feels good to be a part of something. We're all working so hard. Everybody helps each other. I'm a part of it and... everyone knows it. It's special.

Mimsy, I wanted to let you know that I'm not going back to Cornell in the fall. I know this was just supposed to be a summer job, but I'm really happy right now and I'm seeing amazing things. Cornell will always be there and Jimmy says he can use me. Dad won't understand, but I know you will and I hope that you will talk to him. Tell him I'm seeing a thousand amazing things a day right now. I might write an article about it, right? Who knows? I'll submit it to *The Atlantic.* I'm sorry this is the first letter you're getting this summer. I've been writing, but I haven't had a chance to get stamps. So, you'll get a bunch of these all at once. I hope you don't mind.

My best to Hommy and Humpa.

Your Beamish Boy,
Aaron - Late-Spring-Early-Summer.

P.S. Jimmy calls me "Ronnie." Just started calling me that. Did you and Dad ever think to call me that?

He tears the paper out of the spiral notebook. He puts it in an envelope and seals it. He addresses the envelope. He adds it to a stack of envelopes that is bound by a paperclip.

LIGHT OUT on Aaron

End of Scene

Seamless transition into:

SCENE II: A TINY AIRPORT

LIGHT comes back up on Elizabeth. She's still reading.

HAPPY Lugo (40s) enters. Mexican. He is dressed smartly in a shirt, vest, and tie. He carries a small cooler. He takes a Coke out of the cooler and presents it to Elizabeth.

HAPPY

(a Mexican accent)

You like a Coke?

ELIZABETH

What?

She folds the letter up and puts it away.

HAPPY

You look like you want a Coke.

ELIZABETH

Oh. No, thank you.

HAPPY

It's okay. I drive by. I see you look very hot. Like...

He fans himself with his hand.

HAPPY (cont'd)

You change your shirt.

ELIZABETH

Oh, the gift shop. Yeah.

HAPPY

You look like you want a Coke.

ELIZABETH

No, no. That's alright.

Happy wipes down the can with a clean, cloth napkin. He puts the Coke down next to her.

ELIZABETH (cont'd)

They ran out of rental cars. Can you imagine?

HAPPY

Small airport. It happens all the time.

ELIZABETH

I'm waiting for the bus.

HAPPY

Bus?

ELIZABETH
Yes. There's supposed to be a bus into town.

HAPPY
Not today. I don't think so.

ELIZABETH
Oh?

Happy looks at his watch.

HAPPY
Sunday, today. Today, no more.

ELIZABETH
I have a schedule.

Happy looks at the schedule. He points at the print.

HAPPY
"Monday to Friday." See?

He flips it over.

HAPPY (cont'd)
"Saturday and Sunday. Holidays." Today is Sunday.

ELIZABETH
Oh.

HAPPY
Where are you going? You can go with me.

ELIZABETH
What?

HAPPY

I'll take you. Where do you need to go?

ELIZABETH

Uh...(as "I'm not sure I want to go with you") I don't know.

HAPPY

I saw you here in the morning. Usually, I don't come here at this time. No more flights, in or out. But, I come back to see if you're okay. Come, I'm Happy. I take you where you need to go.

He extends his hand. Elizabeth shakes it, carefully.

ELIZABETH

You're happy?

HAPPY

My name is Happy.

ELIZABETH

Oh. Elizabeth.

HAPPY

Elizabeth. Elizabeth Taylor.

ELIZABETH

Right. Happy.

HAPPY

Queen Elizabeth. Look, see?

He points.

HAPPY (cont'd)

Over there. That is my taxi cab.

ELIZABETH

Yes.

HAPPY

Best cab anywhere! Very clean. I wash it every night.

ELIZABETH

I wasn't sure you were a taxi.

HAPPY

Gypsy cab. But, my cab is much safer than those medallion cabs. This model used to be for police cars. (making an introduction) Queen Elizabeth. Crown Victoria. And wait, wait...

Happy rushes off.

He returns with a binder. It's black with a big sticker of a smiley face on it. He hands it to Elizabeth.

HAPPY (cont'd)

Look.

Elizabeth opens the binder. There are about ten letters on business stationery. They are held in plastic sleeves.

ELIZABETH

Yes.

HAPPY

Whenever somebody takes my cab, I give them my business card and I say to them, "After you get home you think about your ride with me today. If it is the best taxi ride you ever had, please send me a letter so I can show the next person." The man I just dropped off. He's from Monsanto. You know Monsanto?

ELIZABETH

Only a little.

HAPPY

Big shot. He says he's going to write a letter. He uses me every time.

ELIZABETH

It's very impressive.

Happy opens the cooler.

HAPPY

If you no like Coke, I have Sprite, Ginger Ale, Diet Coke.

ELIZABETH

Mm.

HAPPY

If you want a hot drink, I have a thermos full of coffee my wife makes. I have hot water for tea and I have every kind of tea.

He points in the cooler.

HAPPY (cont'd)

I have also, horchata, sandwiches. Also my wife made it. Everything is no charge if I take you.

ELIZABETH

I—

HAPPY

Sorry, sandwiches I charge fifty-cents. But, is good meats.

Happy takes an iPod out of his pocket and begins to scroll through it.

HAPPY (cont'd)

I download every kind of music you like. What kind of music you like?

ELIZABETH

Hmm...

HAPPY

Name your favorite.

ELIZABETH

(no hesitation)

Fleetwood Mac.

He searches through the iPod.

HAPPY

I have.... Greatest Hits. Okay?

Beat.

ELIZABETH

Good enough. Let's go.

HAPPY

Yeah? Great. Okay. Where are you going?

ELIZABETH

San Bernardo.

HAPPY

San Bernardo...sixty dollars.

Elizabeth stands up.

ELIZABETH

Okay.

HAPPY

Why are you going to San Bernardo?

ELIZABETH

That's where the prison is, right?

HAPPY

Oh, yes. You have business at the prison?

ELIZABETH

Yes.

HAPPY

You?

ELIZABETH

I'm going to see the men who killed my son. And then I'm going to the juvenile detention center in Hancock, to see the boy they had with them. Are you ready?

Beat.

HAPPY

Yeah.

ELIZABETH

Let's go.

Elizabeth exits. Beat. Happy follows her out.

End of Scene.

Jennifer R. Adams

Penn Station

The balloon exploded in September, the cruelest month. Evening, wicker on fire, ten-foot wave of flames, seven men and women diving for their lives, the pilot dead. The farmhouse children made witnesses. Little elbows on the stainless lip of the kitchen sink, how they'd seen the red nylon in the sky, how they'd run out shrieking with the end of summer still freckled on their arms, blades of grass stuck between their toes, the earth cool and still cooling, bread still in their teeth, the thin chalk of milk still wet in their mouths. How their screams, those warm friendly screams, had met with the seven's, so incongruous—the childish joy, and then pain, fully-realized. Grown and hideous, that pain—and the children's noses suddenly keen like wild animals' to the singe of fire of flesh of hair of skin of quiet of dreams. How their innocence burned that afternoon, how it burned and it burned and it burned. And how I could do nothing but switch on the TV, the radio, be witness to the fucking-up of pure minds that asked for nothing but goodnight moon, but goodnight stars, but goodnight room, but goodnight noises everywhere.

I find myself cradled in my husband's box of a shower, sightless, eyes open to the white tiles, the chemical sour of shampoo in my mouth, slick over my chin and neck and chest. The water beating at my back, past my ass, down my thighs. My hands fumbled into a gesture of prayer, as if that is what hands do, naturally, in times like these. Curl up into themselves and pray. Pray to someone, for something. My head kicking at the corner.

My husband gone. Another conference in the dry hot middle of the country. A town dominated by cloudy rings of exurbs and air shows and dead main streets. He calls every night before going out to a chain restaurant and we speak of nothing. He tells me about forms, about selling forms, about the intricacies of forms. About the fine print of forms. How fine it is. He says, "Well then." And I say, "You'd better go." And he says "Yes. Yes." And I say, though I hesitate, I say, "You don't have to call tomorrow. You don't have to. You don't." And he says, "I know."

Before the balloon explodes, my lover meets me in front of Penn Station. This relationship, whatever it is, a twisted friendship, has been going on for over a year now. I don't have his number in my phone and forgot to bring it with me and I can't call him and he's late and we haven't picked a place to meet. I wait and wait outside by the taxi stand, the July sun setting past the steel and glass, the bright red and yellow and violet signs, the light switched and pulsing, pulsing, the same set of dirty men pungent with cologne circling and leering and beginning to hiss. I email him on my phone, *Where are you, please,* and wait. Again: *I don't belong here. I'm not kidding. This isn't funny.* I worry he's frightened himself, has guilt feelings, won't show, although this is his trip, a business trip. He's taken the train down from Boston. He's interviewing a screenwriter, a nonfiction writer, for a job. He's older than me but still young. He dresses like a child, the child his dead parents left behind, perpetually twenty-three—and he'll go to the interview in jeans and Converse sneakers and a bad limp from a skateboarding accident. He's married and I hate him and I love him, I love him madly. In the hotel room we don't have sex. We never have sex. We're silent and we coil into one another, still in our clothes, and we listen to one another's breath and we push our noses into one another's hair and skin and lips like animals, try to burn the odors into our memories. He tells me he wants to be with me, in an ideal world. I ask, what is that, an ideal world? He says, I want to leave but can't. He says, I don't know if you love me, I don't know if I trust you, and I say, I can't make you believe, I can't force your trust, and I run to the bathroom and lock myself in and heave and say, Oh god, Oh god, Oh god, what have you done? and put my face into the sink and flush cold water over the sorrow and the frustration and I come back out and we're silent again and we fall asleep like that, clothed and webbed together, pathetic, sad and yearning. Two lives half-lived.

When he leaves, he brings me to the station, leaves me in the interior. He's got a foot-long lock of my hair pressed into a book of poetry, he's got my underwear and stockings and bra stuffed into a bag he'll leave in his office. He's got everything but me, but my soul.

At the station, he buys me a donut covered in pink and orange sprinkles, watches me press my fingers into the dull chocolate skin, tear the cakey insides apart. We sit with our hideously happy donuts and don't eat them. He tries to make me laugh so I won't cry. He mimics my eyes, what he calls their doubled wildness. Doubles his own behind new glasses that I tease him about. But it just makes him look sad. I smile and he smiles back. His teeth are horrible, third world. He's an orphan, an only child, dead of kin, the limbs of his family tree shorn, the trunk razed. He's put his father in the grave, held his grandparents' ashes, nursed his mother until blood ribboned from her dead lungs to her lips.

A remainder, a remnant, broken. No one but his wife. He walks and believes tragedy to spool out behind him, messy and matted with pain. I should leave him be, leave them both be. His wife, she seems simple, good, pure-hearted. He takes care of her, I know this. I'm not sure if she's strong like I am. She's an outsider in the circle they exist in now, in his work, his life. A warm, small-town Texas girl in cold, intellectual Cambridge, the city of my birth.

I don't know if I'm good enough for him, good enough in my heart, if my intentions are good enough, although I worry about his own. Would I love him if he were ill and dying in ten years, bone-thin and yellow-skinned and as sick as his mother? I tell myself, yes, I would stay until he passed from the earth. I would let no one touch him but myself.

In the train station, he stares at me, stares and stares and stares, as if to cut me into his memory. He takes the train back to Boston. He takes the train first. We stand together, transfixed. The schedule board shuffles itself into order. The announcement. We hold one another. His face, unshaven, on my ear, in my hair. His body already turning from me, his feet like compass points drifting north, but his shoulders still square to my own, still mine. I reach for him again and he looks away and says *I have to go* and I say *No no no* and I hold his shoulders there with me, there before me, and I say *Kiss me* and he says *No, I'm getting all teary* and I say *Kiss me, please* and he only half-smiles, tragic, defeated and I grab him and kiss his mouth but he pulls me away and runs off and I can only hit him in the arm with my handbag, swing it until it barely touches the almond skin of his forearm and he looks back and laughs; it makes him laugh! And he turns and walks off, quick and steady, steady and I make myself stand and watch and watch and watch, watch him limp away quick with his torn ankle until he stops and he turns and he stands there, silent. He lifts his arm to me and holds it high for me. I do the same. And then he turns and that's it and my hand flies to my mouth and I find myself biting down on my thumb, tears unfolding themselves down my cheeks, down my neck, down and down and down, wetting my clothes. I watch him turn for the last time, watch him not look back again, not again, not again, not again, though I want him to, I need him to, though I stand there and stand there hoping that he does turn to look at me, to see that I'm still there, holding our ground, holding his place by my side, but he never does, he never does, only the brown of his T-shirt grays into a another man's summer suit and the escalator takes him away, like all of his responsibilities and duties and honor will take him away until I've lost him and he's gone and still I watch and watch and watch, I watch the hollow space where he's been, I watch the air, still warm from his body, his exhalations, and I push my head into my shoulder, pull the collar of my sweater into my nose, to catch his smell, to find his smell, the only smell, the only one, the only one, but it's gone, it's gone as he is and my eyes burn and I can no longer breathe. I can no longer bear my own weight and I wonder how I'll keep it together enough to get home.

I collapse in the muck of the public bathrooms. I lock myself into a stall and bury my head into the dirty stainless door and collapse, understanding nothing, knowing nothing but confusion. What will I do now but trace my steps back like a lost teenager who's frightened herself back home? I am spoiled, I am a horrible person, a cheater, a liar, a bad wife. But I don't care. I don't care. But it's beyond all that. I'm unrooted.

Under the door, women shuffle past with trolleys and bags and babies. So many babies, screaming and blubbering and wailing, laughing and loved, all so loved; I can feel the love like a kind of cool through the stale, windowless heat. All of this life blindly passing by, all of these women giving life, having given life—these girls and mothers and the elderly—they pass by like a long, poly-voiced undulation, and I feel soothed, the pettiness of my troubles suddenly swallowed up in, subsumed by the bigness of other lives, by the vigorous, belligerent profusion of life.

But I have nowhere to go. Something will change. Something with my husband. He'll know what's happened. I won't tell him but he'll know. The sadness so great, pushing itself out of the four walls of the bedroom, down the stairs, through the long hallway, echoing off the hardwood and plaster, filling our home. I'll hear his footsteps on the stairs and he'll find me in bed and I'll turn away. He'll find me with eyes latched on the blinds, on the sky, on the planes that trail past, and he'll sit with me and I'll tell him I don't know what it is, what's wrong, and I'll apologize. I'll say that it might be sickness, a summer flu, a little wave of depression—I'll tell him that something's wrong but that I'll be okay. That I'll get over it.

In the station bathroom, I want to crawl onto the piss-splattered floor and burrow down below it, past the tiles littered with stray tissues, deep past the train caverns and the grimy earth to the very bones of the city. But somehow it's okay. I'll get through this, the next step of my life, another beginning, somehow.

In the station waiting room I push my hands into my bag and find my rings and put them on. They flash in the manufactured light. The neighbors across speak Spanish and eat sandwiches. I can almost touch their legs, which are rounded into one another's. They look happy. Married. How long have they been married? Have they ever been divorced? Have they been together all along? Or have they just found one another? The woman tears her sandwich in two, passes the rest to her husband, who thanks her with his eyes. I want love like that.

I think about children. I want children, what my husband won't give me. What he never wanted to give me. I want you all to myself, he'd always said. I don't want to share you with anyone else. How at first I'd been flattered. But how wrong this is. How I'd found his journal, *I must fight the urge to possess her, mind body and soul,* and how it had frightened me, mind body and soul, but how I'd still married him, but how I'd still agreed to the abortion; how, in the heat wave, he'd gone to his cousin the fertility expert, how he'd said, Jennifer's pregnant, and how his cousin had smiled and answered, *Tanti auguri!*, and how he'd had to correct his cousin and say, No, we don't want it, we want to get rid of it, but not in Italy, somewhere safer, somewhere more sterile and cool, and I'd let him take me on the overnight train from Rome to Vienna, Vienna where I'd taken a pill for him and lain down on a bed and had taken a hard ginger cookie from one of the Austrian nurses and had cried and cried and said, Promise me we'll have children, promise me. Next year. I want a baby, as soon as we can. And he'd said, Next year, I promise, and I'd writhed in pain, my insides torn with regret and shame, and I'd believed him and I'd let him squeeze my hand as I'd stared at the emptiness of the walls, as I'd heard the German whispered in the corridors, cold and soothing, just like he'd wanted it, cold and soothing, and then I'd said to him, I think this was the last chance, our last chance.

In the station, the boy next to me has blocked his ears with white buds and stretches out his bare, tapey arms past the edges of his armrests to nowhere.

In the station, I neck my head up to the ceiling. I want to push up all the panels, all the cheap, dirty white panels. To find air. To find a way out.

When I get back home, the balloon is on the news. The children are on the news. I wonder if my husband is watching, if he knows. He's gone again, traveling, working. He's in one of his airports—Atlanta, Cincinnati, the nicotine triangle—up in his gravity of clouds, looking down like a false god as everyone twists in pain. I imagine looking down on the baseball diamonds, the backyard pools like blank eyes, the soccer pitches, the stands of pines with their abandoned picnic tables cut with my initials, with the hearts my lover knifed, his lewdnesses, his loves. I wonder if my husband forgot us, all of us, like the brown earth he lifted off from, like the mountains deflated by distance and space and time. Did he ask for the news from his neighbor? Did he unfold the paper, uncrease someone else's sorrow (dry, stale, yesterday's, but raw still)? Did he smell it as it came up off the page, as it grayed his fingers, his daily bit of peace?

The whoosh whoosh whoosh of air, the propane explosion. French dragon impaled in the clouds, two hundred foot drop, gondola on fire through green birches, black smoke through corn, soot through soy. The silence of the evening opened to the screams of men and women and little children. The pilot's body burning dead, blanketing a woman alive. The children's mother, she said in the paper, I don't know how my son will go to school tomorrow. I don't know, I don't know, I don't know.

I think about my lover's ideal world. How, a year ago, I tried to make it, tried to fit myself into it with fine, gloveless hands, tried to sew him in, sew myself in. Tried to enclose us both in wicker and hand us back to him, a faulty gift tied in blue string the color of heat, of his wife's eyes. I remember being in my bedroom alone, with him, in his bedroom alone, three hundred miles connected by phone line. It was the afternoon, another September so beautiful and crystalline as to be frightening, as if to suggest only the imminent reversal of perfection, of tragedy. I'd been in bed. I'd held my knees. I'd buried into the pillows like a boy and I'd say to him, *I want to be with you I want to leave I'm going to leave I can't stand it anymore this being apart, not one more day. I feel as if I'm dying slowly, as if I'm wounded, as if I'm walking and walking and walking this godforsaken earth and I'm not really me, I'm not alive anymore I'm dead.*

A balloon had appeared, the first one of the fall. The safe one, its sweepy lumberings across the horizon, its held breath one and two and three and the long primeval exhale of fire, the hushed roar slipping through sky, over chimneys, along rooftops. How I'd opened my mouth to the red nylon, taut and excessive and grazing the window glass, and how I'd gone close and closer still with the phone to my ear, his voice in my head, heady as it used to be (scratched and worn and Southern), and how I'd stolen his words and I'd pushed my fingers against the fly screen. How I'd wanted to claw out and get to him, to the pallor covering his heart. How I felt I was there, up in the sky like that, inflated with fire, touching my own roof like the beacon lights of a plane. How I'd said to him, close-eyed and glazed in hope, irrational, how I'd said, It's beautiful, It's beautiful, It's beautiful. I'd said to him, You should be here. You should be here to see this. You ought to see. And he'd said, Lie down. Lie down for me, sweet thing. Close your eyes and lie down for me. He should have been there. To see the thick of a woman's love, before it starts to run rabid like hate. Before it warms to the mild fever of loathing. Before it shifts and cools to the toxicity of indifference. You should have been there, I whispered. Before the news crews picked clean the carrion of one afternoon's tragedy. One tragedy to be replaced and forgotten, lost to others, and others, and others more, and others still.

John Blandly

THE WRITING GROUP ON WHEELS

I was up in Lake Placid, at the Lake Placid Film Festival, to see a few short films, ones that were accepted, unlike my own. I was not in a good mood.

I watched some films, and, yes, they were better than mine. I was by myself. The wife, a 1986 Miss Geronimo Sub (I like to brag), not feeling up to it, stayed at the motel.

I decided to hit a tavern on Main Street at the Mount Marcy Inn. I figured I owed it to myself.

I managed to get a seat at the bar, ordered a drink, and saw David Pleshe walk in. He had been a member of a writing group I was in.

We hadn't seen him for months.

"David," I called out. "Where've you been?"

He stopped and said, "Pancho, what are you doing here?"

So, it was blah, blah, blah.

Turned out, he was there to pick up someone.

"I'm, like, a designated driver. Official, well...maybe unofficial, Lake Placid designated driver. Come on. Meet my writing group."

"What writing group?"

"The Tupper Lake Writing Group. They're really wild, fantastic."

"Sure. Just let me finish my drink."

"No time for that. Bobby! Plastic cup!"

In a few seconds I was outside hiding a plastic cup filled with scotch on the rocks inside my coat.

Dave flipped open the double doors of a small school bus that was double-parked in the street with the motor running.

As I got on the bus, Dave said, "They're in the back. Hey kids, this is Pancho Mirage, the guy I told you about."

One woman, about 80 years old, turned around in her seat in the back of the bus. "You're Punchy Mirage?"

"Pancho."

"Whatever. Come on. Sit down."

I sat down in an unoccupied seat among four other writers closely huddled in the back of the bus as it shook and heaved making turns, hopping curbs, horns honking, brakes squealing, the whole nine yards.

"Like, the point of view shifts, like, to the shark...."

"Yes," another writer said. "Why is the shark thinking about that? He's got his fins in handcuffs, right?"

"Can I continue?" the first guy said.

"Oh, sorry. Right."

"Yeah, so, the point of view shifts to the shark."

"So?"

And it was like that all night, until the group broke up at a Holiday Inn parking lot, after Dave had picked up and dropped off three drinkers, one after another, at three local bars. They were mostly older folks who weren't that rambunctious.

The next time I saw Dave was in court. He'd been charged with running a livery service without a license. I'd been able to plea-bargain it down to disorderly conduct. We'd had a lot of time to talk waiting for his case to be called.

"So, are you still a spy?" I said to Dave.

"No way, but even if I was, I couldn't tell you."

"Oh, I get it."

Dave had mentioned to us that he'd been a spy in Hawaii.

"You know, it's not that glamorous. All spies don't look like 007."

"No?"

"No way. I'm, like, five-ten and I'm the tallest...I mean, I used to be the tallest spy around."

"What do you mean?"

"Spies. They're all, like, five-five, five-six maximum."

Then the case was called, and I haven't seen Dave since.

But the point I'd like to make is that Dave was a great guy. Until the local cabbies complained and put a stop to it, he drove that writing group around for free and picked up and dropped off drinkers without asking anyone to even pay for gas—had people throw up in his bus and all over him—just because he was a good person and thought he was doing the right thing and wanted to do something for society. There need to be more people like Dave.

Edward Hardy

THE DANGERS OF BLISS

I'm in the warm front seat of my friend Wendy's ancient white Volvo station wagon with its sticker-covered coffin box on the roof. Her son Finn and my twins, Luke and Ethan, are in the way-back, the fold-up seat that looks out the rear window, showing their bellies to the drivers on I-95. They're all six and have known each other since they could only crawl backwards. The actual back seat is stuffed with brown cartons of New Zealand yarn, as Wendy owns a knitting store. She frowns and pushes a mix that Finn likes into the CD player. The Ramones come up with "Rockaway Beach," which is fine by me.

We are fleeing overheated Providence for the hazy fields of East Greenwich, some twenty minutes away, to meet Gordon. I don't know Gordon but Wendy called at noon to see if the boys and I were free after school because Finn needed to not watch anything on a screen and Emily, her daughter, had a playdate. She said something about a farm and tomato plants, and because I was trapped in my third floor studio staring at screens while the gorgeous day trundled past, (once upon a time, in the very recent past, I produced a New England-wide news magazine show, now I'm editing wedding videos) I said OK. Only when Wendy picked us up she seemed preoccupied and a little pissed at me. She said she'd explain when we were up on the highway.

I'm afraid it has to do with what I said yesterday at pick-up. I was off all day, basically non-functional, because that morning I dreamed I was in a narrow green bar playing a set of big orange drums in a band with people I didn't know and Wendy was the bass player. I couldn't see her face but her bass was white and she had a Spider-Man Band-Aid on her thumb. Then, as I sat there behind the kit, Peanut, my favorite uncle who died a few years ago, kept hovering at my shoulder, shaking his cigarette and telling me that last month only 7.3 percent of Americans played a musical instrument. Seven point three. And if I could only pull it together and play again my problems would all "melt like the snows." Like the snows.

It's true that lately, ever since Cath and I switched roles, and it's been a complicated shift, I have been a guy without a gyroscope. Or more specifically, a guy without a gyroscope who drinks too much stout. Only this wasn't a normal dream; this was like dropping into a crisp diorama where you could look around the corners. Then after Luke came in to wake me up at 6:15, I was still in bed but I couldn't move, which caused a fair amount of panic. It would have freaked Cath out completely, but she had already left to start her commute to Boston. The not-moving thing wore off after a while but all yesterday the green bar kept tugging. And I never think in those terms—the burning bush, lost relatives proffering advice from the wings. I'm all for leaving that door open but, I don't know, maybe you reach a point and certain things begin to make sense? You're deep in the ditch and your favorite dead uncle shows up to suggest that now's the time to begin the quest for a particular bliss you've largely forgotten about? I can't pretend I didn't see it. So yesterday, on the hike to the cars after Wendy and I collected our kids, I asked if she played bass. Yeah, she said with a completely suspicious glance. Once upon a time. I told her some of the dream and asked if her bass was white. It is. That's why I think she's not talking.

"The Ramones are like the Beach Boys at our house," Wendy says, finally, our first bit of actual conversation since we left town.

"I like that," I say over the open-window roar. I'm pointing to her shoulder. There's a new tattoo, or at least one I've never seen. A pair of crossed knitting needles atop a wreath of ivy.

She rubs it and adjusts her orange tank top. The silence is starting to bug me. "OK, *now* can you tell me?"

"Gilbert." Her eyes narrow. "You just suck."

"What'd I do?"

"You asked about my fucking bass."

"Which is wrong because…."

"Because. Because." I've known Wendy for six years. We met when our kids were in daycare and I have never seen her flustered like this. "You got me thinking about it. You reintroduced the worm and last night I couldn't sleep, which is why I kept scowling yesterday as I walked away because I knew this would happen and you *knew* my bass was white."

"Drugs," I say. "You can take drugs for sleep."

"I did play and it ate up my life. More than once. It's supposed to be a *phase*. You're supposed to get over that and age out of it by now. Only last night I opened the case and played and my right hand felt like a claw, which sucked, so…."

"Ate it up how?"

"There's a history. There were ... a number of bands."

"There were?"

"The last one was all-girl, like Husker Dü and The Donnas. That one I truly loved. There was a swoopy one that would have been shoegazer but the word didn't exist back then. Before that I thought I was the suburban Cleveland white girl incarnation of Bootsy Collins. Parliament meets Talking Heads? I also wanted to be Tina. I can't believe you don't know any of this."

"Me either, but it's good to hear."

"I love playing but *being* in a band makes no sense. It takes all this energy, it keeps you up at night and nobody really cares. But it's some of the most fun I've ever had. I kept telling myself I wasn't missing it, and then you...."

"How long have you been without?"

"Since I was pregnant with Emily. Ten years? You really can't play bass by yourself, unless you're Jaco Pastorius. It's like the tuba. You need people. Last month I almost went the desperate Craigslist route. You know: Aging postpunk bassist slash goddess seeks similarly afflicted for practice while the kids are at school."

Finn shouts: "Can you play the Monday-Tuesday song on repeat?"

"Say thank you," Wendy calls.

"No, no, no," he says.

"You know," I say, "when I had my old job, people would sometimes listen to you. With kids, not so much."

Wendy smiles in a semi-skeptical way and skips the CD ahead until an English siren winds up to start "Police On My Back" by The Clash. "But you played," she says. "Right?"

"Yeah, fourth grade through college. Timpani, orchestra stuff, marching band geek. Plus a few near bands and then I stopped."

"It's a sin to leave an instrument unplayed. You know that. Did your bands play out?"

"One did, for maybe six months. It was mostly parties, drunk kids and pretend hippies circling in slow motion at a pond. Sometimes they fell in. That was the spacey Dead-Phish band. The other two broke up after the first gig. I appear to have that kind of karma."

"My last band broke up on stage in a fight over a stolen boyfriend." She taps her collarbone. "Not mine. There was an unplugging, a beer poured into a very nice amp. The other two girls stomped off so it's me and the drummer and I'm singing—and I *finished* the song, thank you. It makes a good story, now." She unfolds her black sunglasses with one hand. "You know how when you're playing and you hit the chorus the second time and it swells and there's that rush of sound and it's coming from you but it's not really of you and how it feels like you're in the absolute center of something so much bigger?"

"Yup."

The sunglasses slide on. "Tell me, who is this Peanut?"

"My uncle. My dead uncle. He was my mom's much older brother. He played piano and clarinet and scored horror movies. He had an orchestra in New York in the 1950s. They did all these wild arrangements with xylophones and glockenspiels and seven trombones. I found a clip once on YouTube."

"Tell me the dream," she says. "Could you hear songs?"

"No, and it's weird because the dream was all between the songs." I recount as much as I can: the green walls, the paneling, the orange drums sparkling weirdly in the powder blue lights, the accordion player with gold boots, the maroon Telecaster, the Spider-Man Band-Aid, the tall woman with the silver pony-tail, who's singing, Cath on a stool holding a copper-colored drink, the zigzag glow of Peanut's cigarette, which starts out unlit but glows at the end. And it feels OK, explaining this. So I go on and tell the other part, the one I didn't see until I dozed off an hour later on the couch as the boys watched TV, the one where I ended up back in the green bar and my dad was there, in a black tuxedo coat, sitting in the shadows next to Peanut. He only died last year.

Wendy leans forward, as if she's trying to see it all out beyond the windshield. "Those Spider-Man Band-Aids," she says. "We have a whole *box*."

I check on the boys. Their shirts are off. "Are you still strapped?"

"Yes," they chorus.

"If it's only a dream," I say, "why does it feel like something else? It's like the dream keeps remembering me."

"You mean the dream to become a rock star despite your normal, boring life? Or rather in the middle of your normal, boring life, which is actually a much, much bigger fantasy."

"This is a fantasy?"

"Lots of people live fantasy lives. Sportswriters. Firefighters. C.I.A. agents. Pilots. Politicians—they're still running for student council."

"But how could it…be? I mean, Cath's practically moving to Cambridge. Did I tell you? She's renting the third floor from a friend because commuting every day isn't working. She'll be up there three nights a week, which the kids will hate, and I don't think it's going to fly. I'm supposed to be editing Doug and Heidi's Nantucket wedding right now. I'm old and I don't know anybody."

"A person cannot do everything at once. That's why there's a list. Eat a cashew, go to Spain." Her fingers wiggle. "But you could be older and you do know me."

"Only it's not *my* dream to do this," I say. "It's the dream that happened, which is a different thing. Last night I had a dream about ordering a roast beef sub. It felt remedial." I rub a mosquito bite on my temple. "Peanut kept saying, 'Do this and your problems will melt like the snows.' How are you with ghosts?"

A sideways look. "My cousin's a medium."

"No shit."

"See, I don't not believe."

"That's sort of where I am."

"When did your Dad die?"

I'm surprised, but Wendy's conversations often take these blunt little turns. I have to count back. "Eleven months."

"What did he do again?"

"He was a college choral director. He played trumpet, some jazz. He had a dance band. He and Peanut were buddies."

A faint that-fits nod. "Grief's weird," she says, slowing down. "It shakes loose a lot of stuff and you never know when."

The green and purple Mardi Gras beads hanging from the mirror sway. A pick-up towing a trailer with half a dozen orange double kayaks passes us.

"You know, I used to be OK," I say. "Not that my happiness matters in the giant scheme of the universe, but…."

This brings a sharp laugh, as if how oblivious could I be? "Ya think you got enough going on? Job's gone, they took your chair off the grid, much domestic chaos….There are three ways to be happy: add good feelings, take away bad feelings, move on to a new subject."

"That's it? Three?"

We're veering toward the off ramp. "Maybe work isn't going to be the thing, for a while. Did you tell Cath about this?"

"The dream? No. I'm a little queasy about that. It didn't feel like I should. I don't know why. Maybe I do. She's stressed."

"Did you ever look up lucid dreams?"

"Yeah, I was doing that when you called. The not-being-able to move part happens when you jump from REM state, so your brain wakes up, only the regular sleep paralysis keeps going. Which of course rules out my first choice of a brain tumor."

"You're disappointed?"

"The thing is, REM dreams are supposed to leave you anxious and suspicious and...."

"This *didn't* leave you all wound up?"

She's correct of course. Wendy's pretty much always right. "Wait. Who is Gordon again?"

"Eamon knows him through birding, and Patti, his wife, is our pediatrician and she started coming to the store on Thursdays when we have those wine and dessert, stitch and bitch things. Gordon used to teach middle school social studies but he took a buy-out and now he's afraid he retired too early. Patti and I sometimes play tennis."

"You play tennis?"

"Gilbert. I *like* hitting things."

I'm suddenly both dumbfounded and a little amazed at the ways people migrate into your life. If we hadn't signed our kids up for the same daycare I would not be sitting in this car.

My hand goes out the window. We've been on this twisting two-lane road long enough that the houses have dwindled and there's an occasional full-sized field. At the next curve Wendy flashes her lights at an on-coming SUV. "Why'd you do that?"

"No reason. Only if they look like they need it. The big black ones, the occasional Escalade. I like to watch their brake lights in the mirror when they think there's a cop around the corner."

"And why are we going to see Gordon?"

"Because he plays guitar, silly. He has a drum kit in his barn. I called you right after he e-mailed. He said any time after three."

"Oh." That metallic tingle lands on my tongue. The Clash are back to sing, "What have I done?" I'm tapping my thighs. My right foot starts going. This is going to suck. I am going to suck. I haven't actually played in—it's too long to calculate. I'm not sure I actually can play.

Wendy turns up a gravel driveway and yells, "Shirts on." There's whooping in the way-back. We pass maple after maple until a tall yellow barn appears. She pulls around a gold Porsche that's at least thirty years old and parks behind a dented white Ford pick-up.

"Shoes?" I call. "Everybody got 'em?" I hop out, open the back and they do. I'm stunned.

Ethan points at the Porsche. "That's a *race* car," he says and they're off.

The house is an ancient colonial. It's a deeper yellow than the barn with black shutters, a fat center chimney and a screen porch on the back. The kids spiral past the vast oak and into the back yard. On a rise, out beyond the garden, Wendy points to a wood-framed greenhouse that looks homemade. The plastic sides are rolled up.

"Finn," Wendy calls, "when Patti's not here we stay outside. Got that?" Finn comes to rapt attention for two seconds and twirls away. "It's good here," she says. "They can run."

As I follow her across the lawn, the sharp tingle on my tongue returns. What if I really don't remember how to play? That can't be. But what if? I'm actually breathing a little hard when we get to the greenhouse. Gordon sits at the far end before a table made from an old door and two sawhorses. There's a white plastic bucket in front of him and a mound of black soil, only Gordon is leaning back in a lawn chair with his mouth open. Wendy sings his name, her voice dropping on the second syllable, and Gordon's head snaps forward. He rubs his thighs and stands. He's shortish, in work boots and soft tan pants. He's wearing a faded red and yellow plaid shirt cut off at the elbows and a green Red Sox hat. Sandy-red curls poke from the sides. He looks almost bear-like, but with a rounder face and a vague paunch.

Wendy glides on through the pale, diffuse greenhouse light. It smells like dirt and damp wood, layered with the bright lemony tang of tomato plants. We step over snaking turquoise hoses and pass tables littered with flats, then rows of white containers, most with three-foot-tall plants, their vines reaching for a run up to the wide, shoulder-high, horizontal metal racks.

Wendy's carrying a mix CD in an orange case. "How are you?"

Gordon brushes off his hands. "Still living the dream, dear."

"It's only a playlist," she says, "but there's some nice Allen Toussaint, Buddy and Julie Miller, Band of Joy, Decemberists."

"Thank you." Gordon's right hand rises to his heart.

Wendy makes the introduction and Gordon tells me I'm tall. I say "Thanks," as if I've been working on the height issue. And because I'm nervous, I flip into interview mode, the ancient default. "How old is this place?"

Gordon places the CD in a clearing on the table. "You mean the greenhouse?"

"No, the whole thing." I wave back toward the barn.

"Early 1800s. A distant relative of Patti's owned it, once upon a time."

Then as if these were the olden days and I happened to be scouting a segment about small scale intensive greenhouses, I keep on. We learn that Gordon built the greenhouse, that these are all cherry tomatoes and the idea is to grow heirloom varieties, or varieties that no one normally buys, and sell them at farmer's markets or to restaurants in Providence.

"The seedlings are all in," he says, "but these transplants came yesterday. I'm behind on getting them into the pots. They're 70 to 80 days from maturity."

He points down the aisle. "That's a section of Ruby Sweets and these are Red Figs, which look like little bowling pins. These are Coyotes, which will be the size of peas and taste like melon. I like the old varieties. It's time travel you can eat."

Wendy seems concerned. "Don't you need help?"

"If we could finish," Gordon says, "we could hose off and, you know...."

We nod. Gordon shows us how, and Wendy and I each transplant about a dozen plants into white buckets. Ten minutes later we're done and Gordon looks up. "Now what else was on the agenda? Oh yeah."

Wendy goes to retrieve her bass from the box on the Volvo's roof as I follow Gordon into the barn. I'm back to being jittery—first impressions, pretend auditions and all. I try again to count up the years since I've played, but the math won't resolve.

The barn smells sweet and cool, like oil and hay from decades past. Gordon waves at the muddy black Nissan pick-up with huge tires and chrome cut-outs of a naked woman on the mud flaps. "My daughter's," he says. "She's in California and worrying us." A dusty red lawn and garden tractor with a for sale sign sits in the first horse stall. There's a pop-up camper beside the stairs to the loft, but Gordon goes through an office door on the left. He snaps on the lights. Bare bulbs hang from long cords in the corners.

It is the perfect space. The walls are maybe twenty feet on a side and covered with dark, sideways paneling. Christmas lights run and twinkle around the edges. There's a pair of cracked yellow bar stools, a floor lamp that seems to have escaped from a living room in 1966, a black vinyl couch with a quilt on it and stacks of gear.

Gordon sighs, as if he hasn't been here in a while. "I should probably get rid of some of this." He sips from the bright blue squirt bottle he's been carrying. "Cherry juice. You want some? It's tart but good for the joints and everlasting health." He points to the harvest gold refrigerator in the near corner.

"Sure," I say. "In a bit." I wander in a little deeper and pause beside an Ampex bass rig that nearly reaches my chest. There are three variously-sized guitar amps lining one wall and a black road rack with six guitars. Another wall is filled with LPs and stacks of CDs. There's a p.a. in the center of the room, some mic stands, a tangle of pedals, multi-colored cables and power strips. The drums are in the back. It's an old Ludwig kit with a chrome snare and a very big bass drum, two floor toms and one 12-inch rack tom, all covered in that swirly, blue-gray pearl Beatles wrap like Ringo's kit. The cymbals are large, a 22-inch ride and an 18-inch crash. They're dull-looking, patina-heavy Zildjians.

"Smells like old dreams," Gordon says with a faint smile as he props open the line of half windows running across the front. "Old dreams of must."

Wendy appears with her bass case and a green plaid hat box. She frees the bass and shows it to me. It's white, of course, with a black pickguard and a dark wood neck with triangular inlays. "This it?" She seems to be getting a kick from my distress.

"That…is a thing of beauty," Gordon says. "What year?"

"1982. Rickenbacker, 4003."

I stare and nod. I can no longer touch bottom. I decide to go sit quietly behind the drums and change the subject. "Did you see the boys?"

"They're worm hunting," she says and clips a tuner to the headstock.

Gordon is slowly untangling cords and lining up pedals. Every time I think he looks familiar, I tell myself: No, he does not. But I keep gazing at the guitars in the road rack, hoping there isn't a maroon Telecaster sequestered among them. There isn't. Wendy's amp clicks on and I'm searching for drum sticks under the floor tom. I eventually find three that sort of match. The black throne creaks when I sit and everything's in the wrong spot. Playing drums is all about placement and reach and arm length, so when you're skyscraper tall like me you always end up adjusting other people's kits. I spin the throne up and hop the ride cymbal's stand back a few steps. I'm raising the snare when the jitters swoop back. What is the half life of motor memory?

Gordon lifts a black Gibson SG over his neck; the switch on his amp makes a heavy thwack, and when he bangs an A chord, it hangs and rumbles through the corners. He hits it again, takes off some reverb and retunes the low E. "What do you want to play?" he asks, letting his arms drop.

Wendy laughs. "Something melodic. I no longer thrash."

"Me neither." Gordon looks a tiny bit wistful.

I'm lowering the hi-hat and adjusting my way through the deepening suspicion that Wendy and Gordon are far better players than I ever was. I play a few soft and sloppy triplets, digit-ta-da, digit-ta-da, a lazy six-stroke roll and a lopsided fill down to the second floor tom. I hit the tom again and one of the lugs holding down the far side of the head springs into the air. I make the catch and thread it back in. This is going to suck. I am going to suck. And I can't leave because Wendy drove. That's the mantra I keep going while I somewhat desperately try to get my feet working. Hi-hat, kick drum, hi-hat, kick, kick, kick. Motor memory. They say it's the same as tying shoes or buckling your seat belt. Mislaid, but never lost. My neck starts to prickle. "I'm so rusty," I say.

"WD40?" Gordon strums something sad and waltz-like in E minor. "When did you last play?"

"Years." What must he be thinking? "Sorry."

He smiles and shakes his head. "Why'd you stop?"

"There's a list somewhere. Work. Too many moves. I gave away my kit, lost my friends who used to play." But sitting here beneath the Christmas lights, these sound like the weakest of excuses. "Because I'm an idiot?"

He raises an eyebrow as if to say: Could be.

Wendy slips into a small, snaky run and Gordon looks over approvingly. He's thinking: Where could I go with that? They're off and after a bit of hesitation I'm working in around the edges. A little high-hat, some clicks on the bell, a few more hi-hat triplets, add the kick, pull up a backbeat, double that and I'm in. But I miss a beat and think—uh-oh, so I stop, which is the worst thing you can do playing drums. Ever. Actually, I've done two of the worst things. You can't think and you can't stop. Wendy and Gordon keep going but look concerned so I stutter my way back in. I drop a couple of back beats but the kick drum keeps going. Then I really am in. The arms and feet are moving and I'm just there, behind it all, as if I'd always known how, as if this was what I was supposed to be doing all along. It's frightening.

I stay simple and in the groove for the longest time before gently trying to move around on the drums, a quick fill at the end of a phrase, then again. My hands mostly go where I want, only they land late and the fills don't quite fit the spaces. I'll hear something in my head but by the time I get there Wendy and Gordon have moved on, like I've just missed the bus. They're both solid and subtle and shockingly confident as if this were as easy as breath. Wendy seems amused when I miss, but I'm still in. I've crossed the membrane. I am under the bell of sound and things are beginning to levitate. This is bliss.

Every once in a while Gordon spills off in a new direction. Then all at once he turns the corner into "Feelin' Alright" and I only just recognize the song as he steps up to sing. He has a round baritone that seems to rise from the floor, which makes me think of my dad, but I can't do that. I can't think. After the last chorus the sound widens and builds, gaining height and space until Gordon nods and we all stop together and laugh.

I played.

A minute later I'm still amazed and relieved. Then I'm feeling ridiculous that it took so long to get me here and a little pathetic because this is making me deeply, genuinely happy. It feels illicit to be blissed out in a barn while Cath is up in Boston wrangling on the phone with the package designers. It is.

Wendy makes a boop-boopy sound high up the neck of the bass. She takes a small bow and I get it. This is a first date, for the three of us.

Gordon cackles. "Not bad for a power trio. That was—quite liquid. Gilbert, you have a nice, light touch."

"I do?"

"Know this one?" Gordon asks. "It's F and only F." He winds into a Chuck Berryish riff and leans in to sing: "Mr. Rabbit, Mr. Rabbit, your ears are kinda long." I've never heard this song but I'm in, just something simple with a backbeat and eighth notes on the hi-hat. "Ever little soul must shine, shine, shine," says the chorus. We run on after the third verse because Gordon can't remember the words. Eventually my right arm begins to cramp, so I skip the eighth notes and fall back to quarters. Wendy starts hopping on the downbeats until she lands on her cord and it pops out of her bass in a sharp ruffle of static. We tumble to a stop.

"Fuck," she says. "I *always* do that. I forget to loop my cord."

"What was that?" I ask. My ears ring and it feels good.

"Mr. Rabbit? I guess it's a kid's song now," Gordon says. "It's an old spiritual. Paul Westerberg covered it. I like it."

Wendy's checking her chunky blue watch. "Gilbert, it's that late. We gotta collect Emily." Her bass comes off. "Gordon," she says sounding a little out of breath. "We need a project. We should play regularly and see where it goes."

I'm thinking: We do? Yes, we do.

Gordon leans on a bar stool and laces his fingers across the black guitar. "Be careful what you wish for, dear."

"A play-out kind of project," she says. "As long as we're never famous. I can't be famous. It's one of those things."

He regards the propped-open windows. "I fear I am perhaps too old to play out."

"Since when are 50-year-olds not allowed to play out?" Wendy says.

"I'm 58."

"Oh, well, that's really different." She starts reeling in her bright green cord. "Whenever I turn on PBS, it's Stevie Wonder or Winwood or Eric Clapton. Or maybe that's all the same show."

"Or those Do Wop guys?" I say. "Every time they do a spin move, I think someone's going down with a heart attack."

Wendy says, "We can play dad rock. I don't care."

"You mean AARP rock?" Gordon unplugs his guitar. "Which is prog rock only much much slower." He coils the cord and leaves it atop his amp, tapping it with a knuckle. "This is a blissful thing, but then there's torpor and fatigue. I don't know…I can't even remember the last gig I went to. Besides, everybody's home now staring at their screens. Most of my friends, the ones down here, they never leave the house."

"Blues guys play into their eighties," Wendy says. "Sonic Youth, only they're not eighty. How about that sacred-obligation-to-your-talent?"

Gordon straightens. "But I fulfilled my obligation. You can't be going around putting flyers up on phone poles in late middle age."

"We'll get the kids to do it," Wendy says.

"I don't think my kids can reach," I say. "I don't trust them with a staple gun. Do people still do that? Flyers?"

Wendy stuffs the cord into the hat box. "No, you're right. It's another lost art. It is, however, a crime to know how to do something and refuse to do it. It's like keeping a secret."

"Some secrets are better kept," Gordon says.

And then, maybe it's the green bar talking, but I somehow say, "Wouldn't it be easier if we already were a band, once upon a time, and now we're simply getting back together?"

Wendy unclips her tuner. "This *did* feel a little preordained."

"If it works," Gordon says, sipping his cherry juice, "you'll forget how old you are and end up in inappropriate places after dark."

"What's wrong with that?" Wendy's phone pings and she frowns at a text. "Eamon's going to be late."

I'm still on the rug looking for my wallet, which fell from my pocket, but when I close my eyes I'm back behind the orange drums. "I saw it."

"Saw what?" Gordon asks.

Why did I say that? I can't tell Gordon about the green bar. I don't even know Gordon. "No, it's more…I get what you mean."

"Well," he says, sounding tired, "we'd all be wrecks in the end. I lost one marriage to a band."

"You told me that's because you two recorded together," Wendy says.

Gordon sits on the yellow stool. "In part. You get a little obsessed, a little haunted, it can eat your soul for lunch. The thing is, once you play those notes, they're gone forever. You can't get them back. Plus, you've got to consider the friendships. If it does go bad, they just chip away. Not all at once, but…."

The bass case clicks shut. "Doesn't have to happen."

"I had a lust for it. But I lost my lust. It has to do with age."

Wendy says, "They have drugs for that."

"I need it for longer than four hours."

"Any show that goes to eleven is worth its weight in ten thousand dollar bills." She laughs. "I can't believe I'm saying this."

Gordon points at the wall, as if we could see through to the greenhouse beyond. "I have far too much to take care of right now."

"Gordon darling, they're plants."

"But there certainly are a lot of them. Do you guys have songs?"

"Songs," I say. "I never thought of that."

Wendy consults her watch. "We gotta find the kids."

At first we can't, but they're inside playing Mario Kart on Gordon and Pattie's Wii. We herd them to the car and listen to All Things Considered on the ride back. Wendy calls Emily's friend's mom with an estimated time of arrival and I settle into the front seat, a little blurry but still stunned that I more or less remembered how to play. We're up on the highway and eventually it begins to seem strange that Wendy and I aren't talking about what just happened. Maybe I didn't play that well after all. Or well enough. We do talk about missing *Flight of the Conchords* and *Arrested Development* and whether first graders should watch *The Simpsons,* which we split on (I'm the no).

The kids want the CD from the way down so we're back with the Ramones and for most of the ride I just forget to talk. It's as if a wave has come in that cannot be sorted out. There's the residual strangeness of the dream and the green bar, and to be playing again after so long, to be under that bell of sound, to feel the alarming pull of bliss and know the dangers of reopening an old need, and that before yesterday morning, when I heard Peanut's sharp whisper, I never would have thought this could occur. It doesn't feel entirely possible to go back.

Then we're in Providence and crossing the Point Street Bridge as the boys sing an underground version of the Barney song: "I love you, you love me, let's get together and kill Barney. With a great big axe and blood on the floor, no more purple dinosaur."

"Guys," I call back, "that's gratuitous."

"What's gratuitous?" Finn yells.

"Never mind." Wendy's tongue crosses her lower lip. "I love to practice," she says. "There's some Zen, Montessori part of it that kills me. You're in the cocoon of the song, but still sort of free. You're in a bubble and moving through space."

"You mean like those plastic balls you can put your gerbil in so they can roll around the house?"

"Yeah, pretty much." Up on Wickenden Street, Wendy wants to know where I parked the van. I can't remember, so we circle until the kids spot it. What does it mean that I keep forgetting where I parked the van?

"Gordon seems dubious," I say as she pulls to the curb. "It really did sound like a no." Part of me hopes she agrees.

"He's worried about his tomatoes. No isn't always no with Gordon." Her hands drape over the top of the wheel and she watches with a deliberateness I'm not used to. "Gilbert," she says. "You need to gear up."

I can feel my head begin to shake. The tip of my tongue is on the roof of my mouth, pressing forward with the N of no. Instead I nod. It's only a nod and I only just then understand that it's true, we both really are suffering from the same debilitating affliction.

Anya Maria Johnson

Reconciliation

The room is under your name so you buzz in the men with the stretcher, back to me. Who would have thought we would be violent even in reconciliation? I think fast. Your hand is on the door as I ask you to name two chemicals that don't go together and you say everything goes together and I believe that you are some sort of chemist and it won't always be like this.

When you give the EMTs the address of the free clinic, they roll back on their heels and say, no, hospital. You say, no, *clinic.* Their radios say, 47-year-old woman with chronic nausea at something-or-other State Street.

I'm thinking no way, man, no way, I can't afford you. "Go get the lady with the tummy-ache," I say. I'm not going anywhere.

They roll away cursing while you make more calls. Over the mouthpiece your black eyes say *you* did this, *you,* and I nod encouragingly. Do you know how many times a day I want to touch you?

In another life I would have been borne away by those sterile white-coats, but in this one I swallow four Vicodin, tie tea towels around my feet, and hobble to a cab. Medicaid can cover the fare. When I ask the cabman for a receipt, he starts howling about the Better Business Bureau and having two or three *el niños* at home. I'm not sure I heard him right. He's beating time with his forehead on the steering wheel when I gimp out of the car and drag myself into the clinic, unnoticed.

As soon as the veil of ammonia hits me, I miss you. I miss your big blue veins and your indifference and how you make me do things, stupid things, without ever asking for them.

The clinic nurses shake their heads and make the pithy remarks their better sense requires them to. I rap my head as if to say, "It's pretty empty in here," because I don't imagine they'll find my death-wish romantic, and my feet are still raw and burning.

In case you're still angry, I spend the night with the girl next door. You track my scent and come knocking, but the neighbor's peroxide hair is heavy across my collarbone like a golden noose. As she maneuvers my hand across her moon-silvered chest I want to say, *Why are you doing this?* but I find I am mute and it is better in silence. Why weren't you ever this easy?

Back home you try to bathe my mangled feet in lukewarm water, but I scream and crawl under the bed. You lie prone with your cheek against the carpet and ask me why I did it. "I would walk through fire for you," I reply and realize that I constructed all of it to fulfill this cliché. Before your split lip can fold into a smile, you catch her smell on me, the flaxen line clinging to my neck.

I watch your smooth, brown legs walk away as I curl my crippled ones into myself. Chemist, I know you know that some elements can never co-exist.

John A. Lauricella

HUNTING OLD SAMMIE
[NOVEL EXCERPT; FIRST CHAPTER]

ONE / ARMAND

Featherbed silence of a summer night and still Armand Terranova cannot sleep. Anything can happen. One-and-a-half million tons of plate glass and steel girders have fallen from a cloudless sky. A windstorm of ash and dust has hurtled through the streets.

Liberty. Greenwich. Albany. Thames.

Armand pictures his house's doors, front, back, and side. He knows the deadbolts are locked because he has locked them, yet these seem flimsy enough to fail. Ditto the sash latches of the windows. And if they fail and someone enters, a ruffian or berserker, a murderer in a mask, only Armand will stand between it and his family.

Tree-broken moonlight throws cold shadows on the walls. He lifts the sheet and swings his legs clear, stands with the delicacy of a man about to attempt the high-wire. Leah craves sleep, loves it better than food or money. Armored in a tracksuit, she lies on her stomach with the sheet at her feet. No nighties anymore, no lacy scanties. It's like sleeping with a triathlete.

Men and women stumbled in the debris fog. Ashed-over, as gray as ghosts.

He slips around the bed and through the doorway, turns right into his home office, and from a small place only he knows retrieves the key. Smoothly it slips into the cylinder and in half a turn unlocks the BB-gun from its rack on the wall. Armand lifts the gun down. He pumps the mechanism, feels the resistance as compressed air fills the chamber. He heads across the landing and into his son's bedroom. From its big window Armand surveys the street and sidewalk, the sparse yard canopied by an ancient maple, the night-blue sky that seems to hang, billboard-like, between the great tree's branches and the limitless surround of interstellar space under which their home lies naked.

A woman in a business suit—blue? black? pearl gray?—stepped through a window. Her hair flew up as she started to fall, arms spread, legs extended in the empty air a quarter mile above the streets.

Washington. Cortlandt. Vesey. Church.

A cat pads up the driveway, right on cue. A big male, orange-and-white with fly-away fur, the oldest, largest, and ugliest of the next-door menagerie. Armand sees it often, knows it well, hates it just-because. It prowls across the moonlight, no doubt headed for Armand's patio, whose flagstones it and the others smugly foul. There are by Armand's count eleven cats in all, eleven, and Armand, despite having considered filing a complaint with Animal Control, has until now done nothing about it. The window being open, all he has to do is lift the screen. Which he does. The cat pauses; like a doomed president in an open car, it is exposed on the asphalt. Armand sights down the barrel, sees the yellow eyes in his crosshairs, and holds his breath. He can kill it; steady his hands, evenly squeeze, fire the BB into its brain. Kill it outright or wound it grievously so that his neighbor would have no choice but to have the animal euthanized.

Is Armand willing to start a war over catshit? That is the question he asks himself and the reason his finger lingers on the trigger. Is he? With two children in the house and his neighbor evidently a man with nothing to lose? A conglomeration of freebooting cats, three mangy dogs. Plenty of potential targets, yes, but what, all together, are they worth? Whereas Armand has everything.

The cat skulks off. Armand knows he has missed his chance; he isn't sharpshooter enough, the gun is not accurate enough, to hit a moving target in the near-dark. He squeezes the trigger just to enjoy the release, and the compressed-air pop propels the BB invisibly into the night. Armand hears it tick off the asphalt but can't tell just where. Anyway, the cat is gone.

Armand lowers the screen. He nudges the window down three inches, for the air has cooled. Alessandro is deeply asleep; Armand cannot even hear his breathing. He leaves the bedroom and returns the gun to its rack. It is set well above the children's heads, and Armand has to reach up to place it on the pegs. He secures the lock, returns the key to the secret small place, and silently descends the stairs.

His next-door neighbor is more or less Armand's age. Armand does not know the man's name so he calls him Jethro. Jethro lives with his mother, has a dark beard and ponytail streaked with gray, and wears a bandana on his head. If Armand had to guess, he would say Jethro tips the scales at 300 pounds. Simple as these facts are, Armand is not sure what they mean. Perhaps they are signs only of a misfit but even at that, how can Armand know how such a man might respond when another man, a neighbor recently arrived, married more-or-less happily with two children, suggests his cats be taken to the SPCA pending adoption?

People crawled under cars to shelter from pulverized concrete and plummeting steel. A firefighter, at least one, was killed by a falling man.

Armand crosses the kitchen, lecturing himself on the triviality of catshit. Through the back door's sectioned glass his eyes pick out the cat on the patio, now licking its paws, now leaping onto the cushions of the awninged swing and stretching out. He considers filling a saucepan with cold water and opening the door gently, calmly approaching with the surprise behind his back. That's legal—isn't it? Chasing off a cat with a bolt of cold water? It can't hurt the cat, however much it hates getting wet. And isn't that the point? For the cat to hate it and stay away?

He doesn't do it. Not that he wouldn't love it. But he isn't sure. The cat might attack him. God knows it has claws, and once the water is gone, what would Armand have? The saucepan? Could he fend off an angry cat with a saucepan? He is an ordinary guy, an ex-analyst, not an expert on self-defense. Also, someone might see him; you never know if some insomniac is peering out of a window. Anyway, he's weary, having worked all week on the house, not just in the yard but on the roof, specifically the porch roof, onto which he has crept with a six-inch steel blade fixed to a four-foot wooden shaft to scrape emerald-green moss off the asphalt shingles. That job took nearly an hour and hit Armand like a workout of sit-ups and back-bends. Leaning back so as not to topple off the roof, pushing forward to force the blade through the leather-tough moss. It will grow back, the moss, because the canopy of the Norway maple puts the roof in perpetual shadow.

The tree is at least a century old. It dwarfs the bungalow, which it would crush if its fall-line happened to go up-slope rather than down. Armand has contemplated the architectural puzzle of building a deer blind amid the maple's stout limbs, now fortified by two braided steel cables whose installation cost him three hundred dollars. Not to ambush the starveling deer that infest the surrounding hills and invade residential blocks to devour juniper and hosta and luscious mountain laurel (although now he has thought of it that's not a bad idea), but to fire a blue dart of low-velocity BB into the flesh of every trespassing cat that empties its bowels and bladder on Armand's grounds.

He should scamper upstairs right now and get the gun. It's a level shot at close range; all he has to do is open the door noiselessly and the cat will be as good as plugged. Maybe some blood on the cushions and a yowl to prickle the hair on his forearms, but at least he would be rid of it. Sure, there are others where the orange-and-white cat comes from. But he has to start somewhere.

Actually, for Armand it started with the house. Now it never ends. He expected that a six-month, basement-to-roof renovation, once done, would allow him and Leah and the kids to settle in. Feel at home, relax. But no. First the old driveway had to be ripped out and a new bed excavated and fresh gravel laid, all to the tune of $5500; then Leah wanted a patio in the back where the so-called grass was dying on the so-called lawn. The patio-building process was remarkably similar to the one that built the new driveway (excavation, gravel), and soon they had a flagstone expanse as large as a dance floor. Then the main sewer line had to be rooted out and the gutters cleaned of leaf-muck, and finally the rotting porch steps had to be demolished and new steps carpentered with twin railings, as per code.

And then Armand began to notice dark brown, almost black fecal pellets on the fresh treads of new wood, as well as along the base of his foundation. He heard raucous couplings or sudden fights under his bedroom window, which made sleep ever more elusive. Now the new grass he has been at pains to cultivate in the maple's perfect shade is burned brown by cat urine. Other spots are torn up, gouged and shredded. Injury added to insult: the cats do it on purpose, from the spite of their malicious hearts, as payback for the coyote urine Armand lays along a perimeter to ward them off. It doesn't work, not completely and never for long. Witness the cat on Armand's swing, stretched out for a nap.

Who knew cats liked to dig? The damage they inflict on the grass cannot really be called digging, in the dog sense of the word. It's more like tearing, ripping, rending, as if these punky felines are devouring an antelope in their dreams.

Armand stops watching and turns away. The cat on the swing would kill him if it could. Armand is sure all the cats hate him for hissing them off his porch, his grass, his driveway, the brick path and flagstone patio that together have cost more than 8Gs, not counting the wooden table and six chairs and matching bench seat and swing-with-awning Leah wanted, plus the umbrella and wrought-iron base they agreed they should have. Now cats lounge on the patio as if Armand has had the stones laid just for them, in particular that over-sized orange-and-white with its jaundiced eyes and fly-away fur, obviously male, who makes free with Armand's grounds in front of Armand's face, and whom Armand, returning from Ithaca Paint with new brushes and fresh rollers and additional gallons of Benjamin Moore exterior latex for his ongoing project of covering the craggy stucco, finds lying by the back door as if expecting Armand to let it in.

Not on his life. Not on its life. Not on your life, her life, their lives, all 99 of them. Armand hasn't prematurely retired and moved his family 200 miles north and west to steward the local fauna. He has come here—returned, actually, he and Leah—to escape the crowds and taxes and manic consumption of everything from gasoline to sushi that afflicts people who work too many hours and have too much money and live too close together while remaining half-recognized strangers on commuting trains. Fifteen years as a petroleum industry analyst were more than enough by five years, which he toughed out because the money was too good to give up. The steady paycheck and twice-a-year bonuses added up to much more than he makes investing on his own. But Leah, God love her, has a job that provides incoming cash and health insurance.

Armand climbs the stairs. Really, he has nothing to be upset about. He should not pay attention to his neighbor's pets. But it is annoying to be beset by catshit when he himself does not own a cat. It seems unnecessary: a simple problem whose solution should also be simple. Except he hasn't found it yet.

At the top of the stairs he stands on the landing and in the low glow of the nightlight looks at his face in the big mirror bolted to the wall. His life still amazes him: how it has changed, how he has changed it. When he was working, Armand felt rich—except that he had to keep working. He would never go back to the grinding hours, the prospectuses and annual reports, all of them hammered out in boilerplate and more than half, he suspected then and is convinced now, deft spin and bullshit. He is happy not to have to monitor the news, to be free to ignore, say, an oilfield in Saudi Arabia that has fallen below expected production levels two years running, or a pipeline in Iraq that has been sabotaged, again. It used to be Armand's bread and butter to know about such events the moment they happened. Now he concerns himself with home maintenance and daily chores, the native wildlife, other people's domesticated animals. Strange: A man once savvy about currency exchange and interest rates, global trade imbalances, economic "dark matter" and how these interacted to affect the petroleum industry, now cares where a cat takes a piss.

He knows how it happened. Looking into the dark mirror, Armand can travel backward without trying—back to the clement September morning when distant threats came home to roost.

He was at his desk in the midtown office at 8:46:40 and heard a faraway boom. A very big sound that lasted a long time. Computer screens flickered, telephone consoles lit up. First reports sounded incredible, as if someone were floating an outrageous, stupendously stupid joke. Then CNN switched live to downtown and minutes later everyone was watching what television could show, or would show, of human figures crowding windows of the North Tower, trapped on upper floors above the stricken segment, from which black smoke roiled; human figures walking into open sky and free-falling nine hundred, twelve hundred, thirteen hundred feet to the concrete plaza.

The smoke was dense, deeply black. Hell-smoke, as if the inferno's deepest pit had erupted. It poured from blown windows, billowed and spread and seemed each minute to grow more fierce, like a beast feeding on panic.

Moments later a high scream rent the sky and television showed a silver jet sharply banking. Its aluminum skin was strangely dark in the clear morning light. Everyone shouted a second before its wedge-like shape smashed into the South Tower and became an orange-red fireball amid a tremendous explosion of glass and steel.

People reached for cell phones but the system flooded and connections failed.

Land lines were tied up for hours, what felt like hours, and communications froze. Television showed the Towers from various angles; above, helicopters uselessly circled. For the first time in his life, he hopes for the last, Armand saw human beings wholly desperate, purely desperate, desperate unto death. Men and women trapped 100 stories above the street waved white towels in an appeal no one could answer because no rescue was possible.

People Armand knew did not get out: other analysts, colleagues with whom he might check a fact or piece of news in careful conversations, lest some scrap of proprietary intelligence be revealed. On September 11 they became the news, part of its awful proximity, and everything changed.

A lot of people started looking for a way out. Armand held on six months, dug in and defied them. *I shit down the throats of terrorists,* he told himself each morning, staring into the bathroom mirror, lit much more brightly than the one on his landing, in his rebuilt home, almost three years later. And he meant the boast, wished he, 40-plus-year-old Armand Terranova, could strap on a Kevlar vest and parachute into Afghanistan and with his rifle and his bare hands bring red, white, and blue, star-spangled payback to the Islamic heroes hiding in caves. And when that job was finished, hunt down the rest in their training camps and mosques, their shared apartments in Hamburg, their safe houses in Karachi, Istanbul, Yemen—and Los Angeles, he soon learned, and San Diego, and Paterson, New Jersey. Never mind that it was beyond his strength, never mind that he had no training. Armand dreamed of catching bin Laden cornered in a cave and killing him like a rat, then bringing his head back to Manhattan on a pike.

In his last six working months, Armand played the good soldier. With everyone else, he endured super-sensitized metal detectors and empty-pockets, pat-down searches every day. Queasy with doubt, he tried to ride out the markets' downturn. Then they made the break and moved to Ithaca, where the grasping greed isn't close to what it is throughout the New York megalopolis, despite the local college kids roaring up and down the hills in silver BMWs and gold SUVs the size of bedrooms. Most of them, Armand knows, come from families that live in places just like the one he and his family have fled.

He blinks and the mirror's images disappear. He turns and, passing though the doorway next to Alessandro's, ghosts into Julietta's bedroom. The floor creaks but his daughter sleeps in the same well of deep unconsciousness into which Leah and Alessandro also fall. Julietta lies on her side, head tilted slightly back and up, as if she has dropped off while staring at the sconce fixed to the lavender wall beside her bed. Armand painted her bedroom himself, as well as Alessandro's (light blue walls, night-blue ceiling; luminous plastic stars ticky-tacked to the inner sky so that Alex could imagine himself in space), as well as his and Leah's. Also the bathrooms and his home office and Leah's office off the new kitchen and the kitchen itself, also the dining and living rooms—in short, every wall and ceiling and inch of trim, and all the doors, too. He and Leah went all the way, replaced everything that wasn't the thing they wanted, to the point that Armand cannot look at any wall or ceiling, not even the refinished floors, without thinking of all it took to get it to look as it does, be what it is. The tear-down of ruined plaster ceilings, the installation of sheetrock, the screws that hold the sheetrock in place countersunk and spackled; the taping of seams, the spackling of tape and surface flaws, the patient sanding-smooth and the fine white dust such sanding creates; the sizing and priming; the first coat of paint, the second.

Corkscrew willow. Light cocoa. Mocha cream.

Pulling nails from window trim and filling the holes; extracting screws from the same trim and filling those; the sanding, always the sanding, to level excess wood fill, to remove alligatored paint, to clean a vertical surface neglected for 30, 40 years. Then the priming. Then the painting. One coat for base, a second for coverage, a third for luster. Leah picked the colors.

Skysail blue. Arizona tan. Autumn wheat. Travertine.

Armand stands at the casement, cranked open a hand's-breadth. Again he hears it from the rundown house next door, an old-lady cackle that explodes in a cough. It is the same smoker's hack he hears through his bathroom window, which also faces the Cape Cod. Armand has never seen the mother's face; he does not know the son's name. He is taller than Armand, maybe six feet, but the weight shortens him. He never looks at Armand, never nods, waves, or says hello, as if one of them is invisible.

Tube light strobes behind the curtains of a ground-floor window. The curtains are drawn and Armand cannot see who stares at television in the heart of night. The old lady, he guesses, up at all hours, while Jethro retreats to his room with a tube of his own and video relief. He lowers the sound or squelches it. Mother mustn't know. What does he think Mother thinks? A man of 35, 40, it is tough to tell his age, living at home: not a man's life.

Armand checks the upstairs windows. All seem dark; he can't tell if the liquid sheen is soft interior light bleeding through thin shades or a reflection of the milky moon. It troubles him that an unmarried recluse lives next door, in a bedraggled house whose rear windows face his daughter's bedroom, because whoever Jethro is, a sad shy guy whom women turn wordless, or something sinister, a man's desire must express itself. Armand has heard repeatedly that the suicide teams were young unmarried men. At a CU symposium on the first anniversary of 9/11, the talking heads made the point again. And Armand thought of his neighbor.

The man seems to be jobless and seldom leaves his house. He does not even bother to walk the dogs, just goads them into the small park across the street or into Armand's front yard. If he seemed in any way normal, Armand would knock on his door and invite him outside for a man-to-man about the difference between a neighbor's lawn and a vacant lot, between curbing your dog and allowing it to shit on your neighbor's new porch steps, about the possibility of litter boxes in one's cellar to service the excretory needs of one's wandering cats, and *What say we have those felines fixed, 'ay Jethro?* At this point, Armand does not trust himself to remain civil. Besides, Jethro might come to the door with a shotgun in his fist.

Y'all talkin' 'bout mah cats? What y'all got to say? Huh? Huh?

Let it go. Maybe Jethro is nutso and odds are he's armed. It's only catshit and dogshit, dumb animals pissing new grass to death and not, Armand thinks, looking at his daughter, his baby who is almost 7, a cause for war. Especially not when your daughter's eyelids are electric with dreams, and her dreams are secrets you can never share, and the meaning of her life will unfold so far in the future you cannot live long enough to learn it. Julietta's dark hair is glossy and straight and smells like apples. Armand kneels beside her and holds his head close to hers. Her eyelashes are long and delicately curved in the way people a hundred years ago would have described as buggy whips, a phrase no one uses anymore because no one understands. In this way knowledge is lost. Armand does not use the phrase despite thinking it always when he sees his daughter. Nor does he describe Julietta's tender skin as custard, or her round, dark eyes as pools. He knows everyone has heard it, that no one would listen or care, that they are indifferent to his beloveds and would ridicule the language he uses to cherish them.

He stands, stares from his daughter's window down at the shabby house. The world is deadly. Terrorists conspire in a Michigan mosque, in Dearborn, if Armand is to believe what TV news tells him, plotting to detonate a dirty bomb on Fifth Avenue at lunch hour, and all he has to protect Julietta and Alessandro and Leah and himself are a shovel and a hammer, a pick-axe bought at a barn sale, and a garden spade from the hardware store downtown, chiefly used to remove sundry excrement from the vicinity of his windows. There is the BB-gun, yes, which might serve to chase off shit-happy cats but is sure to be useless when killers appear.

It galls him, *gall* being another word he does not find much in print and precisely the word Armand believes best describes his mixed feeling of resentment and fear. It is one thing to lie low and hope the enemy misses you in pursuit of larger targets. But when a man gets shit on and shit on and shit on, he cannot help turning angry. Standing beside his daughter as she sleeps in the peace of an ordinary night, Armand understands that he cannot attack his neighbor. He doubts a word with him is possible, assumes that broaching the subject will end in an argument or worse. Most galling of all, Armand cannot even superficially wound even one of the cats, which the law protects as well as humans and in some circumstances treats better.

On September 11, human beings fell from tremendous heights. One, two... eight, ten, sixty, two hundred—how many jumped? They jumped singly or together, men and women holding hands, holding tightly, all accelerating in awful descent, aware of what was happening to them and about to happen.

Like small bombs, their bodies hit the plaza.

In a quiet way that provokes no response because it is hidden, Armand will fight. He is determined to live the life he has imagined in the house he has bought with the money he has earned, the house he and his family have made their home. A life that does not include shoveling shit.

Stephen Marion

Gold

Zoomer was seated in a big black recliner in the fully laid back position. He had a board across his lap and the board was filled with prescription bottles and he was shifting them around like chess pieces. The woman went straight to the kitchen and began to make coffee. Things will smell a lot better with coffee, she said.

Well, Zoomer said without looking up. Houdini has been located.

It aint nobody but Marcus, said Parker. He turned on the television and stared at it.

Oh no, said Zoomer. He opened one vial and sniffed. That there is Jailhouse Houdini. They are calling him that on the news. Wait and see if they aint. The sheriff said he is turning this place upside down looking for him.

That aint true, said Marcus. Because I seen him tonight.

Zoomer laughed. I bet you did, he said.

What are you doing at my granddaddy's house? Marcus asked.

Zoomer looked surprised. Doing a check, he said. When somebody dies, they usually call me in to do a check. He unreclined himself suddenly and some of the pill bottles fell and rolled on the floor.

That is my granddaddy's medicine, said Marcus.

He aint going to be needing it, said Zoomer. Marcus noticed that he was barefoot. He already had one particular vial in his shirt pocket.

He checks the obituaries, said Parker. That's how he does it, Marcus.

But you just let him.

Parker didn't say anything. He had taken off his glasses, which were darkened toward the top of the lenses.

I really need to get to know you better, Marcus, Parker said. And all that stuff. Really. Coffee will help.

Parker leaned toward him and uncoiled his right arm and settled his chin into the open palm and let the fingers play with his lower lip. I'm proud of you, buddy, he said.

For what?

For being the Jailhouse Houdini everyone knows and loves, said Zoomer.

Shut up, Zoomer, said Parker. I wasn't talking to you.

Or all that stuff, said Zoomer.

I mean, said Parker, where are you going?

Right now?

Whenever.

Right now we need to get back over there to the funeral home soon as we can. I just come over here with you for some coffee.

Parker laughed. Do you all want a Co-Cola? he asked.

Not me. It makes the pills fizz, said Zoomer.

I do, said Marcus.

I'm making coffee! said the woman.

See, we have got all this delicious food, Parker said, going to the refrigerator. People has brought it from all over. Up the country, what have you. You eat, Marcus.

I done eat at Starla's.

Parker handed him a can of beer. His hand was trembling. It had a big ring on the pinkie. The ring had a horseshoe formed of diamonds or something that looked like diamonds. Parker drew a kitchen chair over to Marcus. Okay, he said.

This is a beer, said Marcus.

We call them Co-Colas, said Parker. He gave a big laugh and motioned for Marcus to speak. Around here we do. Marcus didn't know what to say. He drank from his beer. They could hear Zoomer vigorously chewing up a pill.

Awful, he said.

You know that your sister Starla aint been over in four years, Parker said. Four years.

That is a long time not to see your father, said the woman.

She told me, said Marcus

I'm surprised she told you that. She didn't say why, did she?

Not really, Marcus said. He looked down.

I figured she did. She might not of told you the truth, Marcus. Parker rolled his eyes and made a motion again as if he wanted Marcus to start something.

What? said Marcus

Just anything. Parker made a flourish with one arm. We all need to know you better. Start with that. He flicked one finger at Marcus's hands.

Marcus looked at them. They are a lot better, he said, since Starla put some orange stuff on them.

Good for Starla, said Parker. How did it happen?

They got froze off, said Marcus.

He was running from the law, Zoomer said.

That wasn't what done it. They put me in the back of a truck and took me back to jail. That's what done it.

Parker motioned for the hands and Marcus gave them to him. He examined and touched them for a long time, shaking his head softly. It was like having your hands in a woman's hands, except Parker's hands were rough and knotted around the knuckles. Marcus looked at his father's knuckles and wished that he still had his own. We done heard all about it, Parker said. But what about your dreams?

My dreams.

Your dreams.

I got me a girlfriend, said Marcus, trying to change the subject.

Parker threw back his head and started to clap with only his palms and without cupping his hands. His arms were muscular with big veins that ran all around them. Tell us everything about her, Marcus, he said.

Well, it was a real cold day when we met, Marcus said. I was out in the snow and she was too.

Very romantic, said Parker, working his mouth as if he were chewing up the information and savoring it.

Sometimes I think I know everything about her, said Marcus. But sometimes it don't feel like I know nothing. She is funny that way.

He had a pair of her panties, said Zoomer.

Shut up, Zoomer.

Panties? Parker asked. What kind of panties?

It was quiet. Zoomer had lost a pill in the recliner and was searching. Tell him, Marcus, he said, but Marcus didn't want to discuss the subject of the panties with his father. That was weird.

It don't matter, Parker said. He seemed hurt. Marcus saw that Parker had all kinds of ways of pulling things out of you.

White, Marcus said, shrugging.

White panties, said Parker. You having a pair of her panties and all that stuff. Does that mean the two of you are intimate?

Intimate, said Marcus.

Did you fuck her, Zoomer said.

Fucking is not necessarily intimacy, said Parker with a scolding tone. Is it, Melanie?

The coffee is ready, she sang out from the kitchen.

The answer is no, said Zoomer. Can't you tell? He don't know the first thing about fucking, Parker.

I was in jail, said Marcus. That was how come her to give me the panties.

I have never been in jail, said Parker. That is one place I have never ever been.

You just aint never been in the right place at the right time then, said Zoomer. Aint that right, Marcus?

Marcus wished Zoomer would hush. For some reason, he wanted to talk some more with Parker. He had some questions he wanted to ask, but Parker had gotten up and gone to the eating table and was starting to clear it off. As if cued, Zoomer had gotten up too and gone to sit down at the table.

Come on and set down, said Parker to Marcus.

I'm Melanie, the woman said to him when he went to the table. She was finding saucers for the cups. We use mixed up saucers and cups, she said. That is a signature of the household. She put her hand lightly on Marcus's shoulder and said, Your father is so proud of you.

Melanie had a leathery ugly face but at least she was lean.

This has come to me, said Parker, making a vague gesture that could have taken in the house or brushed crumbs from the table. I took care of my dad.

He took care of his dad, said Melanie. Parker come and took care of him to the end and this is his now. I am so proud of how he done for his dad.

Parker waved her away and Melanie jumped back as if she had been hit hard.

I done a lot of things in my life, said Parker, but this I did do.

Marcus remembered Starla saying he probably came in at the last second. He thought they were about to eat but Parker placed a paper grocery bag in front of Zoomer and a smaller paper bag in front of him. He unrolled a large white plastic trash bag for himself and neatly arranged it at his own place. He got down under the table and brought up a box and set the box on the table and took out cans of spray paint.

Compliments of me, said Zoomer. He immediately popped his top and threw open his paper bag and sprayed it full.

Quit it, said Parker. He hit Zoomer hard in the shoulder with his fist and Zoomer stopped. Parker sat down and said, Let's bow.

Zoomer and Parker bowed their heads, so Marcus did too.

Heavenly Father, said Parker, forgive us for what we are about to do. But you took my daddy away, Lord. Surely you see how it is down here. Look down here at the three of us, Lord. Look at poor old Marcus. He didn't have no daddy to speak of and who is that thanks to? Thanks to yours truly, of course. And I am so ashamed of that.

Marcus opened his eyes because he thought Parker was about to cry, but he just seemed serious. Zoomer had one eye closed very tightly and his fist around the paint can. Marcus looked at Melanie, too. She was standing a little ways from the table and her head was bowed.

Lord, said Parker, you made us this here beautiful earth and what do we do? Even the wintertime, aint it beautiful? Aint it good that Marcus aint in jail this very evening and that he is right here with us, even though they aint nothing I can never do to make it up to him? In Jesus' name, Amen.

Zoomer cheered. You sure do pray good, said Marcus.

He's a preacher, Zoomer said, spraying inside his bag.

Used to be, said Parker. Big used to be. I aint no preacher no more.

Honey, said Melanie, didn't you have something to discuss with Marcus?

Stop spraying, Parker told Zoomer, and he quit.

I think he has a little fatherly advice for you, said Melanie. She twisted up her face, as if fatherly advice were good medicine but tasted very bad.

Parker scooted over to Marcus and leaned up in his face as if the others couldn't overhear. He had his dark glasses back on and Marcus saw little glitters of gold in his mustache and in the pores of his face. Parker had a big jawbone.

Buddy, he said, I know it don't seem like it right now, but it is going to pay you to go on back to that jailhouse. Shoot, you don't even have to go, but you need to be at that hearing.

What hearing?

About your legal matter.

My legal matter.

The one where you are suing that son of a bitch.

I aint suing no son of a bitch.

Yes you are, son. It was in the paper.

You mean that.

Yes yes that.

That won't amount to nothing. Marcus said it hopefully.

It is very hard to predict, Marcus, said Melanie.

Parker turned cautiously around, keeping his neck stiff the whole time. Shut the fuck up! he shouted at Melanie. Shut the goddamn fuck up right now!

Melanie looked down.

Ten million dollars is a shitload of money, son, said Parker.

I aint going back to jail.

You don't even have to go back to jail. He had taken up pleading again. Marcus saw that his daddy was excellent at pleading. But if you was to need help to get to the hearing, we would be more than glad to help you. I can't drive but Melanie here is driving me everywhere I need to go and we have got gas money a plenty so it is just a matter of you asking. Do you know that?

You drove over here, said Marcus.

Shit, Parker said. I did, didn't I? How come you let me do that, Melanie?

Most of the time he don't, said Melanie.

Now do you? Do you know?

Know what? said Marcus.

That we are here to help you.

Okay.

Well all right then. Because if you was to miss that hearing, your suit will be dismissed. Aint that right, Melanie?

I used to work for a attorney, said Melanie.

Parker sprayed a whole can of paint in his bag, which he had popped open like a housewife about to insert a pillow into her clean pillowcase, and began a second. Zoomer had already huffed his bag and he had a gold rim around his face.

My brain is gold, he said.

Your brain is shit, said Parker.

Zoomer shot him a look, but it was almost dreamy. You'll be sorry you ever said that, he said.

The room smelled like a workshop. Parker quickly removed his glasses and gathered the mouth of his bag to his own mouth and just stayed that way with his eyes looking at Marcus. In a minute he gave a big suck and his eyes went like the dogs' eyes at the shelter when you put them down. Marcus didn't want to look so he sprayed his own bag and put his face in it and breathed in and it went right up to the roof of his head and coated it. Immediately the angel hole opened up and the angels came pouring down it as they never had before. He felt as if he had just been in a bad car wreck. Zoomer stuck out his tongue and it was gold. He wiggled it.

Lookie, he said.

Ew, said Parker.

It tastes bad too, said Zoomer.

Boys, boys, said Melanie. She was sipping her coffee.

The television played. After Parker had done his bag a few minutes and his face was gold, he lay down in the floor and began to twitch. Muscles that you couldn't twitch but could only twitch themselves were the ones twitching. Zoomer began to pace around the room looking at everything. Marcus went back to his own chair and sat down and tried to see the room. It was his grandfather's room. He wanted to see it. But he couldn't. He guessed Starla could tell him about it. He would have to ask her. Marcus saw that Zoomer was bent over Parker on the floor and he was making a kind of eh, ah, sound. The son of a bitch better not have been taking advantage of Parker because he was passed out. Marcus hollered that out. At least he felt he did. Eh, said Zoomer. Eh. Marcus didn't want to go over there and look because he was afraid Zoomer's dick would be out. He was bad to get his dick out when he was high.

Sure enough, when Melanie came out of the bathroom she started screaming. It was screaming of the highest pitch Marcus had ever heard, and she would scream one scream and then load up for another. Marcus jumped up to push Zoomer off of Parker, but when he got there he saw that Zoomer had cut Parker's throat. He was just finishing it up very carefully, like a child with his first drawing, and Melanie had sunk down to her knees and had her hand cupped to her mouth but the only thing coming out was the screams. Blood was moving across the linoleum floor quicker than water from a leak. Marcus felt his arms and their hands, such as they were, at the ends of them flailing, and Zoomer was off him, but he landed in the blood and rolled onto his back and dropped the knife, which was a pocketknife.

Mmmm, said Zoomer, as if it was a really good food.

Call somebody! screamed Melanie.

Marcus got Parker by the arm and tried to drag him toward the door. His face had come loose at the neck. Help me, he hollered to Melanie, but she recoiled as if she had been cursed.

We got to get him to the hospital, Marcus hollered.

It aint no use, said Zoomer. He was looking up at the ceiling.

Marcus and Melanie dragged Parker by the arms through the room to the door. Melanie was stronger than Marcus. Outside it had gotten warmer, and the tree limbs and the bushes moved and whirred. Marcus knew Parker was still breathing because it bubbled and he made groaning sounds every time he breathed. When they reached the car, Melanie started screaming again and she wouldn't stop and Marcus ran around the car several times like a dog and she never would stop so he finally hit her across the face and it messed up his hand. Marcus thought Melanie had bitten him or something. She leaned down and was spitting out blood but she was still crying. Her head was more fragile than he had expected. Marcus realized he was crying too.

The keys were in Parker's pocket, but the pocket had filled up with blood, which was a lot warmer than Marcus had expected. He got the trunk open and it was completely empty. Marcus tried to hoist Parker up to the trunk himself, but he kept slipping in the blood. Melanie wouldn't help.

Help me, goddamn it, Marcus hollered, and Melanie kind of helped but kept on sobbing and screaming. Marcus didn't close the trunk because he was afraid Parker would suffocate and then they would blame him for it. He tried to start the car and it caught on the first turn. He got out and tried to make Melanie drive.

I don't know where I'm at! Marcus called out, but Melanie kept screaming. She would sob several times and then scream real loud. Finally Marcus pushed her inside as hard as he could and jumped in and started off down the road. He had gone around two curves before he realized he didn't have his lights on.

• • •

The fuel gauge on Parker's car read empty but it never would run out. He had driven all kinds of miles in the night and he wondered how many. If he had looked at the odometer when all this started he could have known, but why would he ever have looked at the odometer then? Marcus examined the other gauges, the speedometer one where the needle jittered up and down and some others with which he was not familiar. At about 10 a.m., exactly as the little death folder in his pocket said, Marcus saw the funeral procession leaving the funeral home and waited a while and fell in behind it.

The dawn had been enormous and red. Marcus wondered if the others had seen it. He had tried to pick up Starla at her house but nobody was home. The house was exactly as they had left it. Under the dawn, which was silent at Starla's house, the walls were moist and square. Marcus stood in front of it in his baggy black pants, which had Parker's blood all over them. He guessed that they had called Starla to the hospital because of Parker. Marcus would have gone himself, but he couldn't. There was no use, he knew. Parker was dead. He guessed that the sheriff had already come for Zoomer and taken him to jail. Zoomer was going to find out about more than a hundred and eighty days, day for day, this time.

Marcus felt he had done all he could. When they had found the ambulance, Melanie had still been screaming. She had screamed every time she drew a breath ever since they had been in the car, and Marcus absolutely could not shut her up. He had not realized a woman's lungs could do this. She would draw breath and scream and draw breath and scream and pretty soon even the drawing of breath was a moan, and she clawed at the inside of the car like the cats did in the cages at the shelter. The ambulance was parked at a little restaurant and Marcus, gesturing wildly with Melanie screaming, slid up to a stop beside it. The emergency medical technicians were inside sucking on toothpicks. A sign in the parking lot said, Pray for Stan. When the paramedics saw it was Marcus, they tried to start the ambulance and leave, but by then he was out of the car with blood all over him and they had to get out.

Shit, said one of them, a skinny one, when Marcus got the trunk open.

They wouldn't let Marcus come. They loaded Parker, whose golden face was turned a funny way with one eye half open and the other fully open. Melanie jumped in the back of the ambulance, but they closed the doors on Marcus and took off. Marcus stood in the gravel parking lot, which smelled of cooking, in the warm wind. A county patrol car flew by with its siren and lights going. Marcus went back to Parker's car, which had clear plastic over the seats, and sat behind the wheel for a long time. His ears could still hear Melanie screaming.

Marcus turned his lights on like the others' cars. The funeral procession cut off the main highway after a while and took one back road and then a second and a third. Cars pulled over and stopped when they saw the procession and even stayed pulled over when Marcus came along, just in case he was part of the procession too. Even one man on a tractor stopped and removed his cap. When the procession pulled off at a little church, Marcus drove on up the road until he found an open field and stopped. It was warm. Some frogs were singing about one field over. It was a lower field that must have had water in it. Marcus started across the field in the direction of the church. He got one foot wet crossing the low place and the frogs stopped when they sensed him. But the ground began to rise and by the time he reached the church, which had a graveyard spread out behind it, he was on a broad hill and was able to stand next to a cedar and watch everything.

They took the coffin first by its brass rails with three men per side, their empty arms risen out with hands dangling at the ends exactly as they did for any other weight. Its carriers ducked their heads, and the coffin disappeared under the tent. People had come out of the cars and linked their arms together to walk into the cemetery, which they entered through a little gate that the funeral man held open. Another funeral man carried the casket spray, holding it high and sweeping it around like the robe of a king, and a space developed between all the people and the preacher, but he could still be identified by his Bible.

Marcus went ahead and reached down inside himself and felt around. This aint hard, his cousin Anna had said last night. The cemetery in the morning is the hardest. Marcus had been certain the hardness, that which the funeral men stepped so carefully around as if it were newly painted, would have formed by now, but he couldn't find it. He felt the trunk of the cedar tree, which had green rust on it, and looked for Starla, but he couldn't find her either. Marcus went over and went over each female, but they were all either so young their legs were still light or too old to be Starla. It made him question whether he knew Starla at all because she had to be there. Marcus had gone over them all several times when he first noticed the one about ten steps behind. At first he thought it was a woman because of the big blue scarf, but it was Parker. He could tell by the walk. Parker walked as if he had been set down in a very rocky place against his will, even though the grass was smooth. His hands were way out as if he expected to fall at any moment, and from a distance it seemed as if he were herding them all through the gate.

I be God damn, said Marcus.

Parker, who was wearing big black sunglasses, went straight under the tent. Some of the others did too. Still others bent under and then emerged again and took their arms and directed others beneath the tent, and sometimes the others didn't seem to want to go, but eventually they did, with the rest of them arrayed around the back of the tent, and they grew still, so still it was possible to feel the loosening of the ground beneath the warm wind. Way up the hill behind Marcus was a black walnut tree all by itself, the way hills tend to have them, and in the top of it two crows hollered out, but the sound of their hollering was softened with distance.

Marcus wanted to tell Starla that Parker was alive. He could have been the first to tell her and they would have had that together. From this day on they might have had an attitude, the same one, toward their father, and have started it from the same place together. But Marcus kept thinking of the gap in Parker's neck last night and the golden face of his father, like a mummy's death mask, and how his head twisted back as if he were trying to let something out of his neck, some energy or spirit that had needed let out for a long time. The thought of it made Marcus hurt in the fingers that were gone. It made it harder in the warm wind to find air to breathe. He guessed that whatever it was, whatever had come out of Parker, was in the air now, or that he himself had breathed it in and that even Melanie had breathed it and shot it back out again with each scream.

He never did find Starla. Marcus examined his picture of Starla in his mind, but he found it wasn't even a very good picture. Instead it was partly the smell of her house, her bacon and eggs, the way she held the dogs, the way she walked as if she were in a city, and several of the things she had said. Marcus still watched as the bunch of them loosened up around the tent, and the preacher went around shaking all the hands. Parker went away to the cars immediately, but all kinds of others stayed. It was a long time before Marcus noticed the men, the gravediggers, standing over at the corner of the graveyard and the pasture. They were smoking and facing the other way, as if they were embarrassed, but Marcus felt them waiting. There were three. They seemed to be having a service of their own, and Marcus looked at the gravediggers and looked at his cousins and he knew the gravediggers' service best. Like them, he didn't mind to work.

When the last car went away they moved slowly over to the grave and Marcus went down the hill. Before he could reach the fence the funeral men, pointing and gesturing at the gravediggers, had struck their funeral tent and were carrying it toward a gray van, which finally left with the hearse.

Hey, Marcus said to the gravediggers, and one of them said, Hey, back, but quietly, and the others just kept working. One clod struck the coffin box and made a loud bong, but pretty soon they softened up. Marcus watched them as if he were overseeing their work. They had the sod coiled up in rolls.

That is real neat, said Marcus, how you got the grass rolled up.

It's the only way to go, said the one who had said hey. He was the only one who had a beard. The other two were Mexicans.

I bet it is, said Marcus. He was looking around. You aint got another shovel, do you?

No, the bearded gravedigger said. We are plumb out. Plus, it would be bad luck. It'd be bad luck for you to just come up and help. You would of had to of been here from the start. Aint that right, boys?

They nodded and kept digging. One of them was down in the grave, smoothing out the dirt.

I don't care to work, said Marcus.

I bet, said another voice behind him. Marcus turned around to see. The boy had on tan coveralls, and in a minute Marcus could tell by the way he stood that he was a girl. The girl had thin blond hair that was stuck down her collar. Marcus kept looking at her and thinking how a girl's body was inside the coveralls. It was like a story book where the animal had swallowed the child. She had just about finished a bouquet from the flowers in the arrangements.

I don't see you working neither, Marcus said finally. He looked her over good several times, and she saw that in the way that females always feel when they are being looked at, even when their backs are turned.

What is wrong with you? she said. You aren't sad because your granddaddy died, are you?

No, said Marcus. I never did know him.

Marcus couldn't help but think about how everything juggled around in his life, such that he never had crossed paths with his sister until lately or his father until last night or his grandfather until after he was already dead.

We work, she was saying. Don't we, boys?

They laughed.

We do a little bit of everything.

You have to, said Marcus.

Her daddy is a master of the backhoe, the bearded one said. He is a backhoe master.

How could you work with them hands like that? she asked. When she asked it her tongue peeked out of her lips and stayed there as if this were how she thought. Marcus saw its silver underfin. He started to pick up his hands and look at them but he refused. Find ways I guess, he said. I don't really need them no more.

The gravediggers laughed. Be careful, you, said one of the two Mexicans. She put you to work.

If you all need help, Marcus said.

Nobody responded.

The girl's tongue was still out. She took out one long-stemmed flower and put it in another spot of her bouquet. It had one of those green tubes of water on the end. That is a shame about Starla, she said.

Marcus had started to pick up a rock that was in their cover dirt, but he stopped. What are you talking about? he said.

About her killing herself and all, said the girl, looking straight in his eyes.

I seen her last night, said Marcus. There aint no truth to that.

It was last night it all happened. This morning, I guess.

The shovels cut into the dirt pile. That aint true, he said quietly.

How's that? the girl asked, holding up the bouquet. Marcus started to say something but the bearded gravedigger spoke up before he could. It's real pretty, Pam, he said. Marcus felt stupid because she hadn't been talking to him.

I think it is, Pam said. She turned around and started back toward the parking lot.

I thought you said you all needed help, Marcus said, but she kept going, so he called it out louder, and then a third time. The second time she turned around and came back a little ways.

Ride with them, she said. Did you think you were riding with me?

The gravediggers laughed. Marcus didn't say anything. Her car, an old brown Camaro, went flying up the road. They were beginning to unroll the roll of sod, and Marcus wondered if he should help now or if it was still bad luck.

Christian Zwahlen

The Truth Is They're Dying

When I was a kid my uncle told me that the Eastman Kodak Company made clouds. I believed him because when I looked south out of the fourteenth-floor windows of the John F. Kennedy Memorial Towers where I lived, the long black stacks of Kodak Park stretched like fingers up into the sky and pumped out these white clouds of chemicals. And the clouds weren't black or sooty like the clouds from the coal plant out to the west on the lake. They were cotton white and touched with light grays and blues like the sky. You could smell the chemicals, especially in the mornings and at night. It reminded me of the smell of earwax. It smelled like nausea. It smelled like a fever.

My grandmother used to tell a couple of stories about how my father worked at Kodak. In one of the stories, my father was making photo paper with pulp and water in a giant sink. A sink the size of a house. He got drunk and fell asleep and the building he was working in got flooded and he got fired and moved away. In another version of the story, my father got drunk and fell into the sink and drowned. I have no idea if the story is true or not. Either version of it. I do know that my grandmother did not like my father very much and that nobody knows what happened to my father. My mother joined a religious cult in Georgia and I haven't heard from her in about ten years. I tried to call her once but she wouldn't talk to me. I tried to get a job at Kodak once too, but they wouldn't hire me. Which is how I got started delivering newspapers.

I have one hundred and eleven customers in the Towers. My papers get dropped off in the lobby in the middle of the night by my manager. His name is Bill and he says I should have every paper delivered by six o'clock in the morning because that's when the local morning news comes on the television, and after that no one's going to want to read the paper. I have all my papers delivered by 5:30. I use the elevator. Then I wander around the halls and put my ear to people's doors and listen. I once listened to this man named Francis sing a song in Italian behind his door. He lives here all alone, too. He thinks my name is Ned, because that's what I told him it is. But that's not my real name. It's one of my made-up names. I make up names for myself. I name myself after British royalty.

I also have a key. I got it from one of the maintenance guys. I use it to go into people's rooms at night or during the day when no one's around. The other night I went into Emery Vogel's room and listened to him snore. Emery is a very old man. He was a friend of my grandmother's. After a little while, about ten minutes, I left Emery alone and took the elevator down and walked outside and down the street to Lake Ontario. In the winter I go down to the lake at night and wish it were summer so that I could go skinny dipping. In the summer I go down to the lake and wish it were winter so I could run wild and pale like smoke in and out of the snow drifts and along the frozen waves.

But tonight it's fall. The air is cold and when I breathe it in it calms me in a place underneath. Right down to my bottom. And something lifts. I don't worry about my grandmother. She wouldn't like it about the key. She wouldn't like it that I go into people's rooms.

Since I can't see it in the dark, the lake feels even bigger than usual. At first I can only hear it. In a little while though, my eyes adjust and I can sort of make out the water. It looks like something gray and wide and gone. To the west there are the waterfront houses. That's where the businessmen and lawyers and judges live. There are some lights on in their windows. There are some fake candles burning in their widow walks. I start to think about my grandmother, but I stop myself.

On my way back from the lake I walk through the empty playground behind the bathhouse. There is a blue floodlight there and I can see yellow locust leaves in the sand under the swings. I walk down past the bars and listen to the music on Lake Avenue. From across the street, I see a man and a woman kissing out in front of the Penny Arcade, which is a biker bar and a nightclub. The man smokes a cigarette and he holds it between his thumb and ring finger behind his back when he kisses the woman. I watch them for a really long time. The woman has beautiful shoes. They are tall and red. At one point she lifts one of her feet in the air behind her as she kisses the man and tilts her head way back. Seeing that surprises me, but I like it. It also makes me sad. I want to kiss someone that way. I want to lift my foot in the air when someone kisses me. I want to lean my head way back like a snake with a trick jaw and swallow someone up whole. When I was a boy I used to eat cigarette butts I found on the street. But I stopped that shit. My grandmother helped me with that.

The truth is, there might be something wrong with me. Something in my head. Sometimes I'm there and then sometimes I'm not. This is a problem. Also, I am not very good looking. When I was small people told me I was cute, but now my eyes are too big and my nose is too small. My forehead is so tall that it looks like I'm wearing a wig sometimes.

When I get back from the lake, my papers are out in front of the tower waiting for me. It's four o'clock in the morning. I carry my stacks of newspapers into the lobby in three trips. The heat is on too high in the lobby and everything feels wrong and heavy and yellow. My papers smell good, though. They smell like paper and ink and the cigarettes my manager Bill smokes. I set down my third stack of papers in the lobby by the elevators and press the up button. I load the papers into the elevator. They are strapped together in bundles with yellow plastic straps, and the straps bite into my hand when I carry too many bundles at once. I get all the papers into one corner of the elevator and then I go up and start on the top floor. I take an armful of papers and leave each one neatly in front of my customers' doors. When I come back to the elevator, I call it from whatever floor it's on, and my papers are still there in the corner. They ride around the tower without me. I like that. I like to think of them traveling around from floor to floor without me. It makes me smile when I think about it.

I finish my paper route by 5:15. I take that key out of my back pocket and listen in front of this woman Edna's door. Edna is a very beautiful woman who I think has a crush on me. I think maybe she will kiss me if I let her. I stand on her welcome mat. It is green and has a white and yellow flower made of plastic in the corner. I can't hear anything inside. I listen for a long time and then I key in.

I have been in Edna's apartment before. It's dark and blue, even in the daytime. But now at 5:20 in the morning it's especially dark and blue. I walk down the hallway to where her bedroom is. I feel as if I have become unstitched. Like maybe I'll get frayed and then I'll slip away, piece by piece. Little pieces will get left around. In one apartment and then another. In the elevator and down Lake Avenue. Out in front of the Penny Arcade. With the locust leaves in the sand under the swing set, and all along the beach.

"Edna," I whisper.

But she's asleep. She looks so small in her bed. There is a crucifix above her head. There is a bathrobe on the floor and a pair of pink slippers. I lie down on the floor, crawl under her bed and lie down directly beneath her.

It smells like old socks under there and it makes me want to say a prayer for her. She is probably ten years older than me. She is probably like 42 years old. I pray that she will live a really long time. If she wants to.

"Edna," I whisper, and she stirs. I stay under there for a while. At least five minutes.

"Edna," I say. "Don't you know who I am?"

I wait around some more and then I get bored, so I crawl out and go into her kitchen and steal a vase from the cupboard.

Back up on my floor, I see a man I haven't seen in a long time. He is tall and his hair looks fake. His eyes are wiped out, like a woman who wears mascara and cries. But he doesn't have any mascara on. His eyes just look wiped out that same way. His name is Jerome. He doesn't live on my floor. He lives on another floor. I used to deliver him the paper, but he never paid for it so I cut his ass out.

"Hello, Jason," he says to me. I have no idea why he calls me Jason. I never would have told him my name was Jason. That's not a Christian name or a royal one either and I would never have told him that it was my name. He stops for a minute and looks around, like maybe he's confused. Like how did I get on this floor or something.

"My name's not Jason," I say. "It's George."

"Where are you going with that vase?" he says.

"Don't worry about it," I say, which is kind of like saying mind your own business, but not quite as mean.

Back in my grandmother's apartment, I fill the vase with red wine and then I set my grandmother's picture down next to me and drink while the two of us watch *Good Morning America.* I get up for a minute and see the sun come up out over the lake. That was the whole reason my grandmother got us this place. Because she loved the sunrise. And she loved the lake. She used to swim every day in the lake during the summer. I used to time her. She'd swim out over to the mouth of the river and back. I can't swim. I can't even really get in the water. It makes me confused. It makes me sick to my stomach. Once, I was in the river as a child and my ear got something dirty in it and the next day it blew up like a cauliflower and exploded.

I finish my wine and fall asleep. I sleep for a long time. Right before I wake up I have a dream about the salmon that run up out of Lake Ontario and into the Genesee River to spawn in the fall. Sometimes you see them swimming in the shallows, downtown up near the falls. They look strong, like a person's words. Like a person's deepest thoughts. They look like how I want my words to come out. Like how I wish the sounds would come out of my mouth. But the truth is that, the fish, they're dying.

I wake up later and look out the window to see rain coming in over the lake. It probably came all the way from across the lake in Canada. It probably fell in Toronto. And now it falls here. It falls all down the side of the John F. Kennedy Memorial Towers, which is where I live. All down the north side of the towers, all down the windows on the fourteenth floor, which is where my apartment is. It will rain like this for a lot of October and some of November, and then it will turn to snow.

I have binoculars and sometimes I think I can see Canada across the lake, but it's not true. You can't see that far. But sometimes you can see big container ships with Russian and Swedish names on them headed for the Saint Lawrence Seaway. And sometimes I see cement boats come up the river. Once I thought I saw a submarine. It was in the middle of a storm. It appeared and then it disappeared. It was probably headed for Buffalo.

I used to live in my apartment with my grandmother, but she died and left me the place all to myself. I have a picture of her above the television set. It's an older picture from the 1970s. But she looks good in it. Her hair is done and she has these long earrings on. Sometimes I talk to her.

I go back down to Edna's apartment and knock on her door.

"Hi, Edna," I say when she opens the door. She looks good. She's wearing a dress and high heels.

"Hi, Henry," she says. She calls me Henry because that's what I told her my name is.

"Hi, Edna," I say again and I look right at her. I hold up her vase.

"Oh," she says.

"I found this upstairs in my grandmother's room. For some reason I thought maybe it belonged to you."

"Oh, yes. I think it is. It does. I think it does."

"Maybe she borrowed it from you or something."

"Oh, yes, maybe," she says. "Wow."

"Yeah," I say.

"Would you like to come in?"

"Yeah," I say. "I would."

We sit down in her living room. She's on the twelfth floor. She has a beautiful view of the lake. It makes me want to jump out the window and fly away.

"Can I get you something to drink, Henry?"

"Wine, Edna," I say. "I'd like a glass of wine."

We sit on the couch and drink wine and stare at each other for a long time. She turns on the TV with the remote and I stand up and walk over to it and turn it off.

"Don't watch TV," I say.

I wait for her to get up and run over to me and kiss me, but she never does.

"Henry, are you okay?" she says.

"I think I'm just drunk," I say. "I miss my grandmother."

Edna doesn't say anything.

"I'd better go," I say.

"Okay," she says, but she doesn't get up or anything. I see myself out.

I go back upstairs to my apartment and finish off my bottle of wine and watch the dusk come on the city. It comes on like water, rising slowly in the low places and seeping into all the corners. I watch the red lights of the Kodak building fade on and glow. I watch the falcons that live on top of the tower start to swoop. They're hunting pigeons. They remind me of the salmon in the river. They remind me of a lot of things. My father worked at Kodak. I already told you about that.

The phone wakes me up a little while later. It's dark in the apartment and outside the lake is just black. I can see the Bull's Head lighthouse shining at the end of the pier. I can hear music.

"Hello?" I say.

"Hello, Henry?"

"Hello?" I say.

"Hello, Henry? It's Edna."

Downstairs in Edna's apartment, I let her put her hands all over my chest and my shoulders. I let her kiss my ears and my face. She takes my shoes off and has me sit down on the floor. She lies down in my arms. She feels pleasantly heavy. When she puts her tongue in my mouth I become aware of all these strange smells. Her hair, for example. It smells like a forest. And then I am unstitched again. I am scattered like seed. There are pieces of me all around. Once I saw a plastic bag float way up in the air. Past the fourteenth floor and away out over the lake. That's what I feel like. A plastic bag going up and away. Not having any place to go, really. Just getting blown away.

"Henry," Edna says.

"Yes, Edna," I say.

"I want you to love me. I want you to love me right now."

"What do you mean?" I say.

"You know," she says. "You know what I mean."

I clear my throat. I don't think that's really what she wants me to do. She looks away from me. She has a large, light-brown mole under her jaw. It looks like a moth caught in a bowl of milk.

"Oh, yes," I say. "I know what you mean."

Edna kisses my face some more and then stops and waits for me to do something important.

"Edna," I say, "don't you realize that I'm not very good looking?"

"That's not true," she says. "I think you're beautiful."

"Edna," I say, "I have to go. I have to go up to my apartment. I'll be right back."

Before I leave I go into the kitchen and steal the vase again.

Instead of going to my apartment, I go to Jerome's apartment. I knock on the door but there's no answer and so I key myself in. I've never been in Jerome's apartment before. The walls are all white. Even the carpeting is white. In the living room there is a giant American flag hanging on the wall and a polar bear skin lying on the floor. The bear's mouth is open a little and it's snarling. I really like polar bears. I like the American flag, too. But I don't like the way they look in Jerome's living room. The way they look in there makes me sick. I leave the vase in the middle of the living room floor and steal a bottle of whiskey from the kitchen.

I take the bottle of whiskey down to the beach. It's dark down there and loud. I hear waves and wind and nothing else, which is a great relief. I try to remember that nice feeling I had when I used to sit down there in the summer and time my grandmother as she swam. She had a long, steady stroke, and white hair, like the flash of the moon. She smiled when she swam. It made me happy to sit in the sand and watch her. But I cannot get that feeling back. I can't remember it even. Not really. Not the way I can remember other things. Things I can touch or see. But I can't really remember any feelings. Not the way I want to anyway. Nothing so close as that. I drink too much of the whiskey and walk down the sandy boardwalk. Usually there are seagulls out here, floating like kites above the driftwood. But not at night. I don't know where they go at night. I walk down to the antique merry-go-round, which is all boarded up for the season. In the summer, they let you ride all day for a dollar. I like to ride on the wooden ostrich.

I finish the whiskey and throw up a little and a seagull eats some of it and then I walk back up Lake Avenue toward the Towers. I pass the Nelson Funeral Home and Most Precious Blood Catholic Church. The side doors of the church are always unlocked and so I go inside. It's huge and empty and dark inside. It's dark all the way down to my feet. And cool. There's the flicker of a candle up on the altar next to the tabernacle. It's there to keep the Blessed Sacrament company. So Jesus doesn't get lonely. There's a crucifix lit up with a soft, white glow. Above the crucifix are the Latin words, "Agnus Dei Qui Tolis Peccata Mundi Miserere Nobis," which my grandmother told me means "Lamb of God You Take Away the Sins of the World Have Mercy on Us."

I think about getting kissed by Edna. I wonder if I'll ever see her again. I think she wants me to have sex with her, which I don't want. But I might do it anyway. I mean, I don't want to key my way into other people's apartments and spy on them while they're asleep either, but I do that anyway. And I don't want to live alone, but I do that anyway, too. My grandmother didn't want to die, but she did anyway. Sometimes it's just like you don't have a choice.

When my grandmother died she was lying in her bed and I was holding her hand. She tried to tell me something, but she couldn't get the words out. She was worried. She was not ready to go away into it. That much I knew. But her hands got cold and she stopped trying to tell me whatever it was she wanted to tell me. And then she faded away. It wasn't sudden, and it wasn't slow either. It was just like breathing, only the opposite. She breathed, and then she didn't. I was very, very angry. I crawled under her bed and wouldn't come out. My uncle was there. He told me I had to come out.

First he told me I had five minutes to come out. Then he told me I had to come out by the time Nels Nelson, the funeral director, got there. But when Nels crouched down and asked me to come out, I just flipped him the bird. Finally, my uncle got mean and dragged me out by the foot and made me look at her as they wheeled her out of the apartment and into the hallway. He said if I didn't watch I'd never come to terms with her death. But that's a crock of shit. Of course I'll never come to terms with it. Whatever the hell that's supposed to mean. I did run out into the hallway, though, and yell at Nels Nelson. He was looking at his watch and waiting for the elevator. I told him not to take her away. I touched her hand, but it was so cold. And she didn't look like my grandmother anymore. She didn't look like anyone I knew.

Brianne Wood

WHEN THERE'S NO TOMORROW

He idly watched the last of the soap bubbles slip down the drain as he rinsed off. He turned the cold water on full blast and made himself stand under the stream for the count of fifteen, as much to clear his head as to make sure he was fully awake. The cotton towel made quick work of the moisture on his body. Dressing in the clothes he had laid out the night before, he stepped out into the early Southern California sun filtering through the haze. It was a typical subdivision for the area, Spanish tile roof, neutral-colored single story home, avocado or palm tree in the front yard, house number freshly painted on the curbstone and the ever-present sound of lawn sprinklers sending arcs of water across the lush green grass. He walked the four blocks to the bus stop.

The bus was crowded, but he found a seat near the back. From his vantage point, he had a clear view of most of his fellow passengers. Most were dressed as if working in an office downtown. Every one of them had earbuds in place and were busy texting. No one spoke or even noticed the other passengers. He thought it odd that people demanded to know the latest news from around the world, but no one knew their neighbors anymore. He pulled the rope signaling a stop and got off the bus.

The lobby of Mercy General Hospital was cool, bright, and as active as a beehive. He had inquired at the front desk as to where he was going. He made his way to the bank of elevators and waited patiently with an assortment of visitors, nurses, doctors, and delivery people. When the elevator arrived, he stepped in and pushed the button for his floor. The car rose slowly and silently, stopping at every floor. On the seventh floor, he stepped out of the elevator and made his way to room 7205.

The room was awash in sunlight. A small figure lay in the bed, barely creating a ripple under the blanket. "Good morning, Mr. Petrillo," said a smiling uniform standing beside the bed. "Morning," he replied. The unifrom hung a chart on the foot of the bed, lightly touched his arm and before heading out the door, said, "The doctor will be in with you shortly." He took up the uniform's position at the side of the bed, bent, and kissed his mother on the cheek. Noticing a thin line of perspiration on her upper lip, he removed a blanket and ran a washcloth under cool water.

As he cooled her face, thoughts of his childhood came rushing back to him. Mom, running tirelessly behind him as he learned to ride a two-wheeler. Mom, drying his tears and holding him close as she bandaged wounded knees. Mom, attending every game and practice and being his loudest cheerleader. Mom, in her garden, tending her plants. He also remembered the teenage years, when he hated his mother and told her so daily, called her every name in the book and wished she would drop dead at least twice a day. He regretted those times and had never really told his mother so.

He finished wiping her face and wondered if she was thinking of the same memories. He knew the answer to that. The doctor had said brain dead: no activity. There were no memories left for her. No time left to tell her how much he loved her and how sorry he was. Her only choices now were to stay on the machine and be a vegetable, or her son could donate her organs. The donations would mean his mother died, but her organs would keep other people alive. Her lungs could run behind another child as he learned to ride a two-wheeler. Her kidneys could take another person to the ballfield to cheer on a rising star. Her liver could help someone tend their garden for years more to come. Her heart could heal many minor boo-boos, break at the harsh words of a teenager, and, yet, love them all the more.

At that moment, the doctor walked in. "Glad you could make it, Mr. Petrillo. I'm sorry, but I really need a decision as soon as possible."

"That's okay," said Mr. Petrillo, with tears filling his eyes. "I've reached my decision."

Elizabeth Wyckoff

UNDERWATER

Vince, the shark, noticed me first. He approached through the waiting area, threading his way through over-stuffed couches and coffee tables stacked with *Today's Senior* magazines. The cardboard fin waggled where it had been scotch-taped to his headband. He circled me once before stopping to shake my hand. "I'm Vince," he said. "You here for the dance?"

"I'm a chaperone," I said. Vince smiled. I was only fourteen. I unfolded the scrap of paper, a business card, in my hand. My mother had scrawled *Ronnie Bennett* on the blank side as I stepped out of her car a few minutes earlier. She'd been in a rush. Her two cursive "t"s trailed off toward the edge of the card like swelling waves.

"Do you know the nurses?" I asked. "I need to find Ronnie Bennett."

"Ronster the Monster." Vince grinned. "She's in the ballroom, decorating." He didn't look like the men in the South Woods brochure: clean-shaven gentlemen in turtlenecks with snowy helmets of hair. Vince sported a grisly patchwork of stubble on his chin, and one eye wandered alarmingly behind his plastic frames. He wore black sweatpants that cinched at the ankle. "You don't want to get roped into decorating," he said. "Trust me on that."

Ronster the Monster was new to me and I wondered what nickname Vince had for my mother. She'd been working at South Woods Summit since it had opened six months ago. Tonight, she claimed to be supporting one of her friends at an AA meeting downtown and had convinced me to chaperone the dance as her replacement. She'd been trying to get me to volunteer at the home since we'd attended the opening ceremony over the summer. That was the longest amount of time I'd spent at South Woods: an entire afternoon under a tent with a hundred muggy, senior citizens. We had watched in silence while a hunch-backed old woman tottered across the sidewalk in puckery shoes and sliced through the Opening Day ribbon with a big pair of gardening shears. Everyone clapped. Then one of my mother's nurse friends removed the shears from the woman's hands before she could drop them, blade-first, toward her toes.

"Old people are lonely," my mother told me. "They'd love to spend time with someone young, like you. You'll inspire youthful memories." From our row of metal folding chairs, grayish fluff covered every head in front of us.

"Besides," she said, "you could make a new friend. Have someone to talk to." I sensed her making the transition into one of those conversations. The kind that gave my throat a hot-teakettle ache. Though she never said it aloud, I knew my mother worried. I was not like her—friendly, beautiful, normal. I was an odd child, with the potential to be trapped inside my head forever. I'd begun to recognize the particular look that would settle on her face when those concerns rose to the surface, like I was no longer a person she recognized at all.

"I think you should come with me," Vince said, tilting his fin toward the hallway. "Be my chaperone. To hell with decorations." The paper corners of the business card stabbed into my fingers. I almost never disobeyed my mother, but she'd left me here. And an old person wanted to spend time with me, just like she'd predicted.

Vince had magazine pin-ups from the forties taped to the wall beside his bed. Doris Day above the alarm clock, reclining in a beach chair. Betty Grable behind the lampshade, curls piled up on her head like a pineapple. I sat on his mattress. My backpack, placed carefully on the floor, held a pair of goggles and a snorkel—my costume for the dance's underwater theme.

When Vince shut the door, closing us in, he seemed to forget about me completely. He sat down at his desk and started pulling things out of a drawer: matchbook, olive jar, cardboard cigar box. We'd met ten minutes ago and already I could feel myself becoming invisible.

Years before South Woods Summit existed, the massive building had been St. Bernadette's Boarding School for the Deaf and the Blind. On a handful of occasions when she'd had a few glasses of wine and was feeling reminiscent, my mother had recounted stories about the old school and the children that had lived there when she was young. I'd heard that my mother and her friends had gone streaking across the grounds of St. Bernadette's as teenagers. Mom wasn't pleased that Donna, one of her nurse friends, had blabbed it. Apparently, they ran the full length of the arboretum, up through the tennis courts, then back into the woods, completely naked and in the middle of the day. They'd figured they wouldn't get caught because the deaf kids would never hear them coming, and the blind ones wouldn't be able to see them anyway.

It wasn't hard for me to imagine my mother having that much fun. Thumping through the forest, barefoot, over damp undergrowth. Hair lifting in the wind. In photographs of her as a young woman, she looked nothing like me. She wore sweaters that hung gracefully from her shoulders, and translucent, fluttery scarves. She reminded me of some rare species of bird—the kind people carry binoculars around just to glimpse. In most of the photos, she was part of a group—shaggy, tangled people draping their arms around one another. But I could always pick her out of the crowd. Even the deaf and blind students must have sensed her presence.

I didn't know any specific details about the St. Bernadette's children or where they had gone when their school closed, but when I was younger, I thought about them. I knew they wouldn't be kids anymore, and I liked to picture them as deaf and blind adults, well-adjusted to the realities of their lives as I hoped I would be in adulthood. In my imagination, they were my mother's age. They lived far away, in distant cities, and sat cross-legged in front of fireplaces. They sipped cider on soft rugs with their families. They had created bright lives for themselves in places that were dark and silent as the bottom of the sea.

Vince looked up from his desk and squinted, as if trying to distinguish me from the bedspread. He seemed to be wondering if I were really human. I had often wondered this myself.

"So, you've done this before?" Two gray patches of hair fluffed out from behind his ears like milkweed pods.

"Sure," I said.

He raised one eyebrow and I was immediately relieved. A pot-smoking teenager was something I could never pull off. Vince went back to work at his desk, shaking his head. I tried to remember what I knew about marijuana. Mr. Henderson had mentioned it one day in Biology—while talking about adrenaline and neurotransmitters and the sympathetic nervous system—but I'd learned more by eavesdropping on my mother and her friends. All summer, they had dropped by our house, sometimes unannounced, and stayed late into the evenings, discussing life over drinks in the backyard.

The nurses talked about all of the troubled people in their lives: out-of-work husbands, sons in after-school detention, thirty-year-old children from previous marriages who struggled through dead-end day jobs in order to live as artists or musicians. Sometimes, they talked about their own parents, who lived upstate or downstate in nursing homes or alone in the emptied carcasses of their old houses. My mother and her friends all regretted not knowing their parents better, murmuring in assent whenever anyone made a comment about the difficulties of parenting. They hadn't made it easy for their parents, they agreed. But now, taking long sips from their tumblers, their voices rising into the night, they realized parenting was a nearly impossible task.

A few curls of Vince's back hair seemed to peek out at me over the edge of his t-shirt. "I'll bet you didn't see your night with the old folks panning out like this." He turned to me and pushed up on the glasses that covered half of his face with lens. They were the shape of something I was learning in geometry: a trapezoid. Or maybe a rhombus. "Nurses let us get away with it now and then. Medicinal purposes, of course."

I nodded, then sat still, trying to blend back into the bedspread.

"Quite the chatterbox," he said without looking up.

His closet was full of earth-toned sweaters. I tried my best not to look at Vince, the drugs, or the half-naked pin-ups. It was overwhelming, the number of things in the world that weren't what you expected them to be. In my imagination, things seemed rosier decades ago: families were large, men were attentive, women wore bathing caps and full-body wet suits into the ocean. In reality, though, young girls had been posing on beach towels exposing their cleavage for all of time. Knowing it gave my throat that hot feeling. Up above Betty Grable's hair, a spider hovered on the wall. A piece of punctuation, waiting for me to speak.

"I like your sweaters," I finally said.

"Well, now we're talking," said Vince. "I've got quite a collection. Some of those date back to the Truman administration."

I searched for something else to say. I barely knew who Truman was. The ceiling fan hung over my spot on the bed and I realized that everything around me was in motion. The edges of Vince's un-tucked sheets lapped at my calves.

"Sometimes I wonder what's going to happen to them," he said, "all those old sweaters." A narrow canyon formed briefly between his eyes.

I walked over to the closet and took a brown sleeve between my fingers. "I could take them to a thrift shop," I suggested. "A nice trendy one."

"A trendy one?"

"Sure."

"Who would buy them?"

"I don't know," I said. "A girl who shops at thrift stores." I imagined the girl fingering through the racks. She would be lonely and shy, and this sweater with embroidered geese would appear before her, as if from a dream. A warm, migratory dream. Eyes would wander to her when she wore this sweater in photographs.

"It's a men's large," said Vince.

"Well, it'd be roomy. But in a good way." Maybe, I thought, roomy was about to make a comeback. Maybe the lonely girl in Vince's geese sweater would spearhead the movement.

"I like your thinking," Vince said. He turned back to his desk, but I thought more about the lucky girl in his sweater. Maybe the sweater would be the key to an amazing new life for her. Maybe in two years time, she would be on television. She'd be the star of a hit series about a group of attractive high school students who become unlikely friends. The girl would only get the part because of the sweater, which she would wear to her audition. The casting director would be mesmerized by the intricacies of the geese. I ran my fingers over the dense threads of their beaks, and the dark fabric used to show where wings overlapped.

"Perfecto." Vince kissed the finished joint and dropped it into his breast pocket. He looked in the mirror and readjusted his shark fin. Then he came over and sat next to me on the bed. A few strands of his hair were picked up by the wind and waved at the back of his head like broken cobwebs.

"You should get ready to go under water," he said.

I pulled the snorkel out of my backpack and situated the diving goggles on my forehead like sunglasses.

Vince smiled and placed his hand on my knee. My heart pumped so hard, I wondered if Vince could feel its pulse way down in my limbs. I tried to remember the last time anyone had touched me for that long and couldn't think of anyone besides my mother.

It had been months ago, my mother recently back from a night out with her friends. From my window, I watched her car pull into the driveway. Then I curled back under the sheets to listen to her move around below me. As she came upstairs, I closed my eyes, pretending to be asleep. Her feet shushed down the hall and toward my room like a drum beat. Most nights, she stood in the doorway for several seconds, making sure my lungs were working under the covers. But on this night, she came closer. I heard her at the door, then the foot of the bed, then next to my headboard. She made so many movements on the carpet that she must have been sitting down. My heart beat like crazy, but I knew that if I did not open my eyes—if not one eyelash fluttered—I might learn something about my mother, right at that moment. I smelled her hot, familiar breath. I tried to picture her in some telling position: leaning back with her head against the wall, or cross-legged with her chin in her hands, or on her knees before me as if in prayer. I was under her gaze, that much I knew. And then I felt her hand on my shoulder. She rested her palm there, lightly, not on the blanket, or the sheet, but on my skin. She held it there while she breathed and I breathed and I must have fallen asleep just like that, because the room had filled with sun by the time I woke up, and in front of my bed, the carpet was bare.

Now Vince's palm felt hot on my skin and his fingers curved out like spider's legs over my knee. When I turned, I met his eyes.

"Come on, Bess," he said. "It's time."

The door to the outside world was propped open with a coffee can full of cigarette butts. Vince and I were the first ones to sneak out, but soon, other old men began to gather in the darkness. They emerged slowly, one by one, out of the white light of the back hallway, allowing the triangular beam on the pavement to widen. When they let go of the door, the light disappeared and they pulled chairs out of the shadows, scraping them over the cement. Our eyes adjusted to the dark and I felt us all, the whole group, settling into our nocturnal selves.

Before I knew it, Vince was holding the joint to his mouth. We had formed a rough circle with our chairs and the men watched him silently. Their glasses reflected a swarm of flies in the lamplight by the building's edge. Vince inhaled in silence.

When he removed the paper from his mouth, he stretched his arm over without meeting my eyes. I could see nothing but the red pearl of its tip.

"It's all yours," he said.

I tried to imagine what my mother would say if I was high when she picked me up. If she did notice, her reaction wouldn't be dramatic, but she'd heave one of those sighs that seemed to contain all of her life's exhaustions in one breath: the old, dying people and her odd, quiet child. A sigh to say: *I could see this coming with my eyes closed.* I didn't want to be the cause of one of those sighs. I was supposed to be sighing with my mother, or her with me, because we were all each other had. But, then again, maybe she wouldn't notice at all. And that would be even worse.

I took the joint and breathed in.

The circle erupted as soon as I removed it from my mouth. Vince released a cloud of smoke from his throat with a howl. The others hooted and broke into wide, whiskery grins.

Vince put his hand on the back of my neck. He leaned toward me and his hair touched my head, downy against the curve of my ear. I coughed and our heads separated, then knocked back together.

I waited for something to happen. For something to become clear, or for a secret to reveal itself in small details that only I could see. There was a broken branch on the ground that looked like a severed chicken's foot. A caterpillar dangled, dark and noodly, off the brim of an old man's newsboy cap. I considered the fact that I should not have made this decision and, on my neck, Vince's hand was now cold.

"Atta girl," he whispered into my ear.

By the time Vince and I showed up, arm in arm, the Underwater Ball was in full swing. The overhead lights had been wrapped in blue cellophane, casting the room in a ghoulish sapphire hue. We weren't just underwater, we were so far below sea level that the residents had evolved into glowing creatures as a matter of survival. An overweight man bounced by us, swept up in the twirling current of the dance floor, with a headlamp dangling from a wire over his forehead. A deep sea anglerfish.

Vince was smiling and nodding his head. Slicing the darkness with his shimmering shark fin.

"Looking good, Gertrude!" he bellowed at a jellyfish over by the refreshments. She held a pink umbrella above her head, and beneath it, she was a vision of dangling tentacles: iridescent saran wrap, dental floss, and gift-wrapping ribbons.

Gertrude smiled back at Vince, then let her tongue loll out of her mouth to show us that parts of her body were becoming tentacle-like as well. I was impressed. She was morphing into a jellyfish from the inside out. To hell with costumes, Gertrude had probably said to herself. She had channeled the spirits of ancient squid-kingdoms and allowed their pulsing forms to take possession of her soul.

The nurses were staked out around the edges of the room with blank looks on their faces. They sat in metal chairs, arms crossed under sagging breasts and matching nametags. I recognized Ronnie among them. I knew, from eavesdropping, that she'd recently separated from her husband, who carved bears and moose out of tree trunks with a chainsaw. He had been living with another woman in town for the past few weeks, even though his chainsaws were still lying in a heap in Ronnie's garage. She'd explained the whole thing to my mother over gin and tonics while I'd done homework in the other room. It made no sense: I knew that Ronster the Monster had angrily tipped over the wooden bears on her own front lawn, but I could eavesdrop all day for my mother to reveal something about herself and she never would. She kept all of her stories coiled tight, like stethoscopes stuffed deep into her pockets.

Taking my hand in one of his, Vince led me out into the thick of the crowd. I hadn't been expecting it, but there were others as wild as Gertrude. Others who had not just acquiesced to the nurses' consensus on an underwater theme, but had surrendered to the powers of Triton himself. As I trailed behind Vince, I watched them all as if they were behind aquarium glass. A tall starfish inched toward us in a bowlegged mosey, arms and legs splayed out from her body like a pinwheel. There was a blowfish at the edge of the DJ booth with his thinning gray hair fashioned into spikes. Behind the blowfish, I saw what must have been a sea monster—someone scale-covered and shadowy—lurking around the tinsel curtain by the restroom doors. I barely caught a glimpse of him and the dark algae dripping from his beard before he disappeared from my view altogether. The most stunning creature was a woman dressed as sunken treasure. She twirled in the center of the dance floor with hundreds of foil-wrapped chocolate coins pasted to her turtleneck. A small map with a red X was pinned to her breast.

In science with Mr. Henderson, we had learned that no one knew for sure whether time or space was real. The realists believed it all, believed in everything. But, the idealists weren't easily convinced. They didn't think it was possible for time or space to exist outside of the human mind. In Henderson's class, I could see it from both sides. But now I knew it was all in my head. I felt my power over them both: time slowing into a series of photographic freeze-frames, and space, first shrinking into the X on the woman's breast, then expanding into the tiny world of her imaginary map.

The DJ announced a slow song and someone in the corner started blowing bubbles through a giant plastic wand.

"Are you okay?" Vince asked me. I really wasn't sure. He pressed my hands onto his shoulders and placed his own, gently, on my hips.

"I'm not going to hurt you," he said. A ray of light from the disco ball glimmered off the edge of his tooth.

I was going to have to navigate this on my own. I breathed and tried to concentrate on tactile senses: my hand on the soft lumps of his shoulders; my feet, slow and clumsy on the carpet; and the strap of my goggles cutting into my ear. Focusing on these sensations was all I could do to keep from spinning off into space.

"Bess?" Vince said.

I swallowed. Bubbles came drifting down around our heads.

"Remember that girl? The girl you said might buy my sweaters?"

We were getting closer turn by turn and I felt like we were circling toward the bottom of a drain.

"Do you think she'd ever wonder who owned the sweater before her?"

Vince looked at me then, his eyebrows slanting up in the centers like mating caterpillars. I didn't want to hurt his feelings, but I knew that the imaginary girl would never wonder such a thing. After all, she was a teenager. She would be thinking about ways to avoid eating alone in the cafeteria. She would wonder about the condoms she found in her mother's drawer in the bathroom, and the way her mother's hair smelled when she came home certain nights. Her teenage head would be too full of questions about her father and whether he was an odd, quiet man, and whether that was a question she would ever be brave enough to ask. She wouldn't have room for Vince, too.

"I think she would," I said. And Vince pulled me closer, desperately, like I was the only buoy for miles.

It felt like I had turned with him for an eternity, making slow orbits around the room. I found myself looking down and thinking about the carpet. About the dirt down there like buried treasure at the bottom of the sea. All of us were responsible, even me. Over the past six months, hundreds of shoes had taken part: loafers secretly making their deposits, old slippers dropping their loam like jewels. Perhaps several bare soles, even, had touched those fibers and left behind bits of themselves. I realized there were pieces of my mother there, too. Things that she had carried in and left with these strangers. Food particles, human matter, dust, earth. I couldn't see them, but I knew they existed: molecules somewhere beneath the surface, sinking along slow, separate paths to the bottom.

Vince had been staring up at the ceiling, but now his eyes shifted back to mine. He narrowed them into the darkness, and I closed my eyes.

"Can you see me?" I asked. I waited for Vince's voice to rise above the thrum of the room. Instead I felt a hand on my shoulder. And without looking, I knew it was Ronnie.

"Bess?" I turned and appraised her through my goggles. She squinted into my face, searching. "I can't believe you're here. Your mom just called. I said I hadn't seen you all night." Her eyes flitted between me and Vince in shock, spindly eyelashes flapping like the wings of little moths. "Could you take off the goggles, please?"

"My fault," Vince cut in. He stepped forward. "This was all my idea."

"Well, you can tell it to Mary when she gets here." Ronnie's grip on my shoulder tightened. "Like you don't give her enough headaches already. You have to go and kidnap her daughter."

Vince's fin rotated slowly on the top of his head as he turned to me, registering. I imagined what he saw: my dark hair, skin pale as a fingernail, eyes sunk deep into my face like two stones dropped into a pond. All the same as my mother.

In the moment when Vince turned to face Ronnie, that small wrinkle in time, I made my move. I didn't want to hear any more about people growing up and getting older. I didn't want to know anything about my mother that she didn't tell me herself. I slunk backward in a kind of moonwalk before I turned and started to sprint. The sea swept by in a blue flurry of bubbles and seaweed streamers. I ducked around the slow-dancing aquatic species. When I found the gray metal door, I threw my shoulder against it and stumbled out into the cold, gulping for air. I couldn't stop. My arms swung out into the night. My feet flew across the gravel and into cool wet grass. The night expanded before me, ballooning and stretching as I rushed into it.

I'd almost reached the tree line by the time I heard the voices of Ronnie and Vince. Those hulking, leafy shapes before me were even darker than the sky—a forest of black holes. "Bess!" I pulled the goggles from my forehead and flung them into space. "Bess!" But I kept moving forward. I focused on every sensation, committing it all to memory. The first secret I would keep from my mother: cool air spilling over my face like a wave, incredible darkness in the spaces between the trees, and the quiet hum of the night that contained her, in a car, moving back toward me.

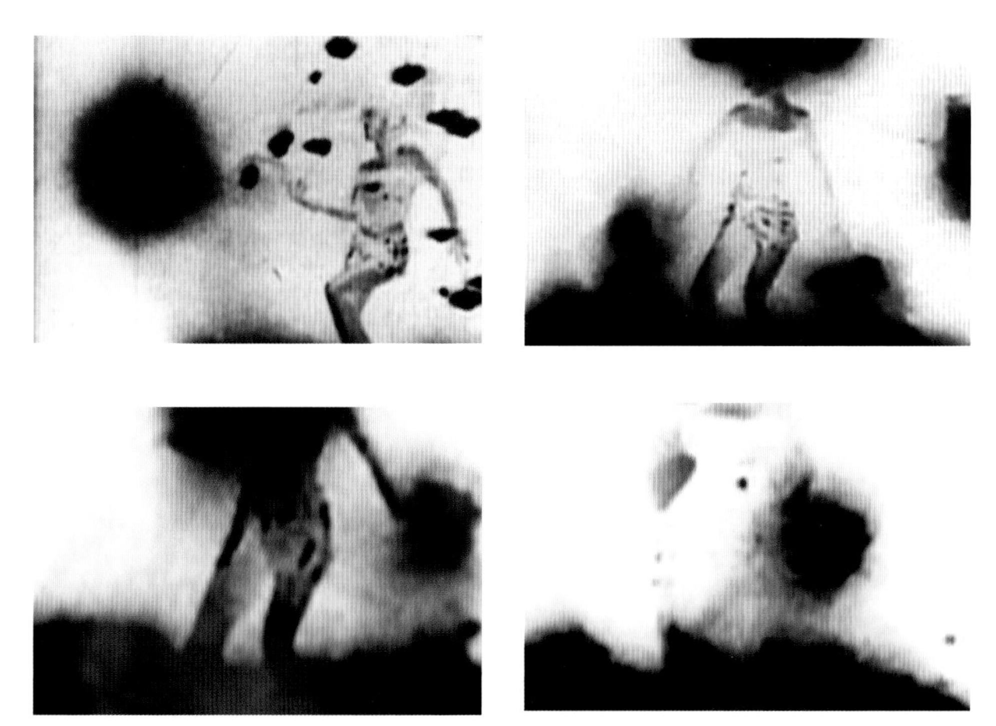

STEPHANIE LOVELESS, *Torch Song,* video stills, 2008

Torch Song is a video, sound, and performance piece, exploring unresolved desire. Using Super 8 stock, I filmed a female fire dancer and hand-processed the footage. I then digitally solarized, looped, and disintegrated the image. Palpable tension between attraction/discomfort and power/immobility emerged for me as I worked obsessively with her image. To accompany the footage, I produced an a cappella version of Oscar D'León Llorarás, a Venezuelan pop song that tells a story of love and revenge. The exuberant pleasure-in-pain of the song inspired me to insert my own body in the work. Standing beside the video projection, I vocalized a focused, strained repetition of the syllable "ah" for the duration of the piece.

Stephanie Loveless

Lori Nix, *Botanic Garden,* paper, plexiglass, resin, wire, foam core, wood, acrylic paint, polymer clay, beads, plaster, natural materials (dimensions vary), 2008

I do not know what will be our undoing: unbridled progress, climate change, nuclear annihilation, a nasty virus, an object hurtling through space, or something not yet imagined. Nix's series, "The City," imagines a future post-mankind. What will become of the cities and our symbols of culture, capitalism, and humanity? Upon our exodus, ceilings cave in, water mains break, buildings and bridges collapse under the weight of rust and mold. At first glance, these post-apocalyptic dioramas may strike a delicate nerve, but one might take notice of a new kind of urban renewal. A city devoid of its inhabitants is not divorced of life. Local flora and fauna now flourish in the same institutions of science and art, once dedicated to man's triumphs over Mother Nature. We view these scenes from a safe distance, able to indulge in our morbid fascination with what is wrong in the world.

Mitra Abbapour, curator of photography, Museum of Modern Art, NYC

Lori Nix, *Laundromat at Night,* foam, plastic, polymer clay, wire, plexiglass, wood, cardboard, paper, plaster, natural materials (dimensions vary), 2008

LORI NIX, *Beauty Shop,* foam, plaster, beads, wood, paper, polymer clay, cardboard (dimensions vary), 2010

Lori Nix, *Vacuum Showroom,* plaster, foam board, thread, polymer clay, horsehair cloth, latex paint, found materials, natural materials (dimensions vary), 2006

BARBARA STOUT, *Wellspring,* Ink wash on paper, 24" by 24", 2008

Studies of Spirit is a work consisting of over 25 individual portrait components. These larger-than-life portraits collectively contain a global span of ethnicities and range of ages. *Studies of Spirit* examines where differences and ordinariness are overpowered by each unique countenance which is accentuated by the uniform format. As I work on each piece, I am drawn in by the nuances of each face, engrossed by a certain chin indentation, the hollow of an ear canal, how an almost imperceptible shift of an eyelid or shadow on a lip can transform the expression. Applying the ink in layered washes gives the pieces an especially soft finish, like skin itself, and transports me to the original inspiration for this work.

Barbara Stout

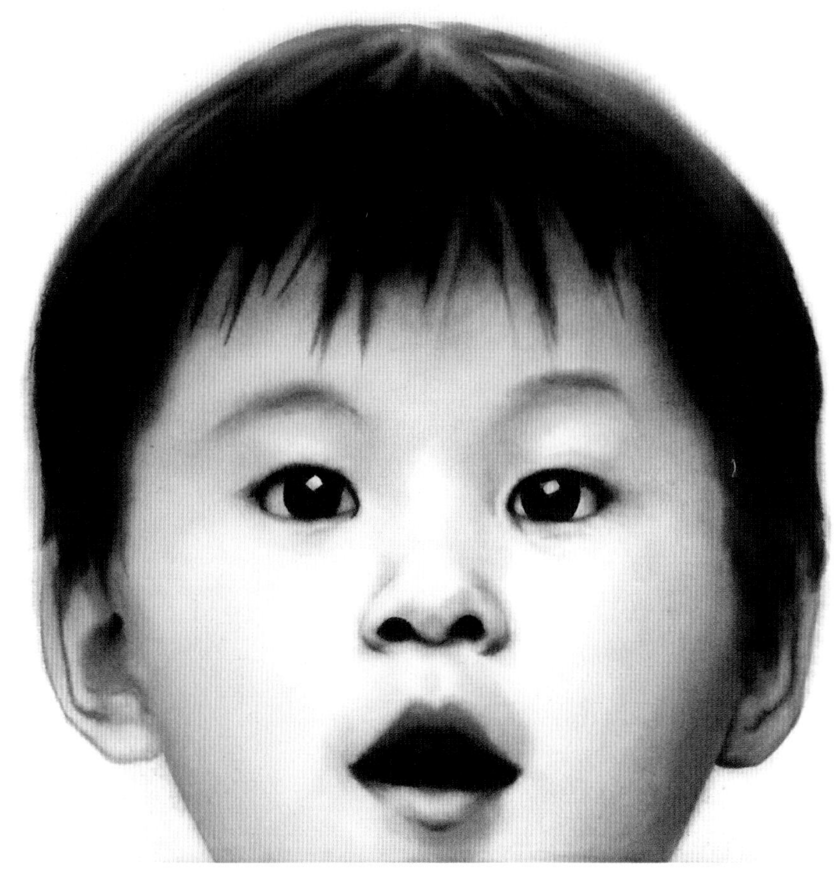

BARBARA STOUT, *New World,* Ink wash on paper, 24" by 24", 2009

CHRISTOPHER MCEVOY, *All We Have Is Now,* oil on panel, 14"x22", 2011

In my recent work, the act of painting documents the struggle between our interior and exterior world, the visceral and personal, as it relates to the physicality of our existence. My paintings dwell in the space between abstraction and representation. Within the canvas I strive to reconcile disparate states by morphing imagery to create a hybrid pictorial reality that serves as a dialogue between the intangible and corporeal, entropy and unity, devastation and rejuvenation. I have created these paintings out of a desire to explore phenomena of contemporary reality experienced as an intersection of place and cumulative experience. I'm interested in the contrast of physical presence with the fluid nature of memory and perception.

Christopher McEvoy

CHRISTOPHER MCEVOY, *Some Kind of Nature,* oil on panel, 14"x22", 2011

ANN REICHLIN, *Counterpoint,* welded wire fabric, reinforcement rod, steel lath, wire, 17'x59'x43', 2010

Dealing with issues of transience, fragility and memory, my work sits at the confluence between sculpture, architecture, and drawing. My site-specific piece *Counterpoint* was on view at the Munson-Williams-Proctor Arts Institute Museum of Art as part of my 2010 solo exhibition, *Ann Reichlin: Counterpoint.* Constructed of steel grid, lath, reinforcement rod and wire, *Counterpoint* was built in response to the Philip Johnson designed sculpture court. An exploration of the idea of arrested and precarious motion, *Counterpoint* used the Museum's logical and rational proportions as a foil. Initially inspired by the idea of an inverted, fragmented dome, *Counterpoint* evolved into a room-sized steel gesture drawing in which the parts were in a state of becoming and unraveling.

Ann Reichlin

ANN REICHLIN, *Counterpoint* (detail), welded wire fabric, reinforcement rod, steel lath, wire, 17'x59'x43', 2010

KAREN M. BRUMMUND, *Storm Road,* public installation, photograph, paper, barn (dimensions vary), 2008

My public installations transform the surfaces of our environment. The installation begins with a picture (or drawing) of the building. It is enlarged to the same scale as the facade and printed on office paper. Each sheet systematically covers the building and hangs in direct relationship with the subject. Over time, the sheets of paper weather and fall off. The uncertain process performs like an ephemeral drawing, creating new marks and lines. The real and the represented interlace, composing a new image that is outside these two starting points. As time-based drawings, the translation is in flux and the representation becomes a conversation.

Karen M. Brummund

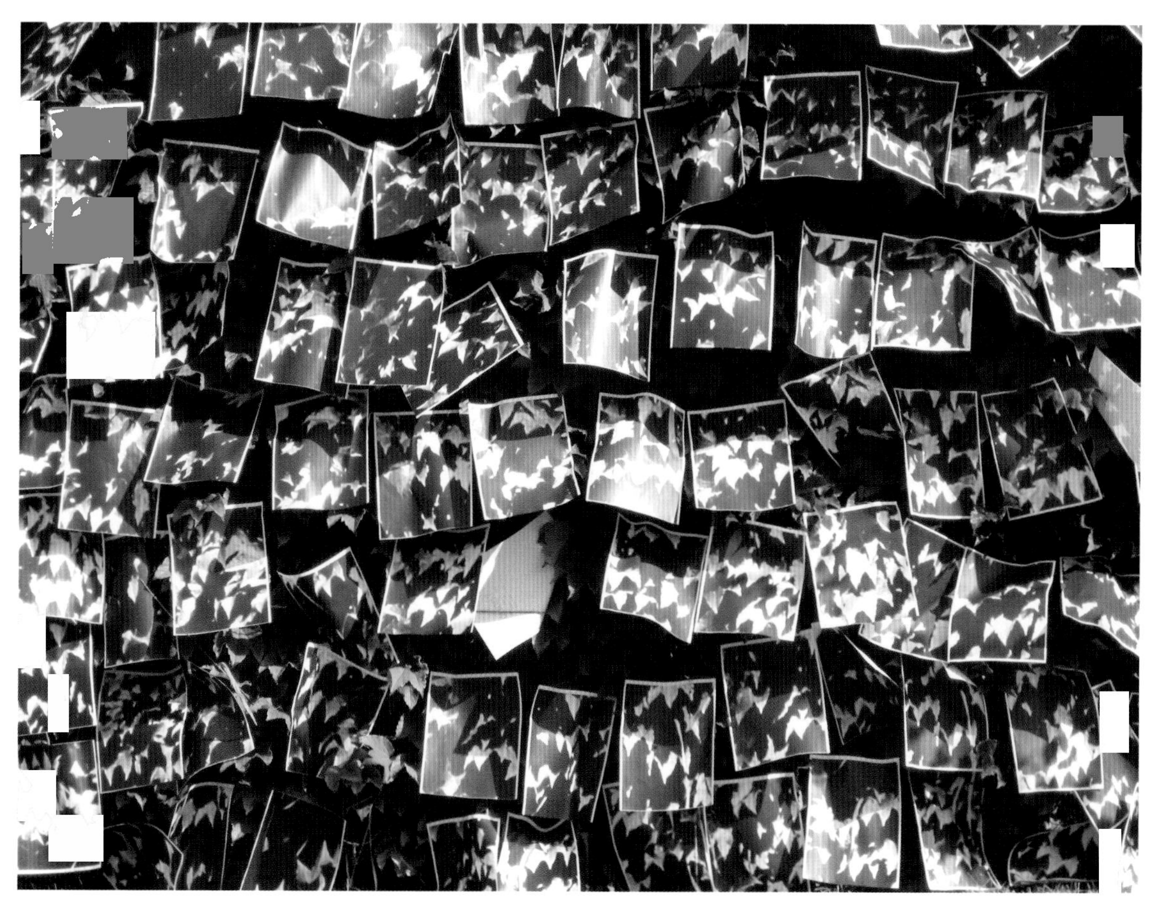

KAREN M. BRUMMUND, *316 Waverly Place,* installation, photograph, photocopies, ivy (dimensions vary), 2009

MARNA BELL, *Hudson XXIV,* archival pigment print (dimensions vary), 2010

My many trips back home to New York City on the train have helped me to remember lost pieces of time where life seemed simpler and less veiled. By revisiting the same landscapes in different seasons and under different weather conditions I was able to capture the past before it disappeared. As a painter and now as a photographer I have been drawn to the meditative quality of the Hudson River and the sacred aspects of the natural environment. This series is reminiscent of a more romantic era, when God and Nature were viewed as one.

Marna Bell

MARNA BELL, *Hudson XVII,* archival pigment print (dimensions vary), 2010

JUDE LEWIS, *Fait Accompli,* wood, aniline dye, color transparency images inside each "pod"; 13' across x variable dimensions.

This is an interactive piece where viewers must swivel each pod to see the image inside. Images are of the diversity of outcomes possible within members of the same "family." Anthropomorphism is often characterized as a narrow, subjective practice. For me, it is anything but. I believe that when we "ascribe human qualities to nonhuman entities" we will at some point inevitably turn the tables, and learn more about ourselves and others. A dog's defense of territory and need for routine help me to understand human jealousy and insecurity. Plants that need specific conditions to flourish help me to understand human failings. A fluted column supporting the weight of a building helps me to accept my obligations with a bit more grace. I find inspiration and reassurance in these simple connections. By incorporating traces of human qualities into the objects that I make, I wish to share these associations and possibilities with others.

Jude Lewis

JUDE LEWIS, *(I did, I will, I can't) Take a Chance,* wood, oil paint, aniline dye, color transparency images, 60"x18"x24", 2005

ALEXANDRIA SMITH, *untitled histories,* Conté/charcoal on Kraft paper, 48"x70", 2011

Working through two concurrent bodies of work in the disciplines of drawing and painting, I have created works that explore the theme of cultural and sexual identity through the lens of childhood and adolescence. The loosely autobiographical character of "Marjorie" is the focus of my large-scale charcoal and small pen and ink drawings. Through an intuitive, narrative approach, Marjorie is thrust into a world somewhere between the mythical and the real. She navigates a banal, minimalist world as a "coming of age" metaphor in an attempt to discover home, womanhood, and racial understanding. This explicit and implied narrative speaks to a larger story of the struggle towards understanding identity, cultural history, sexuality, and surviving psychic trauma.

Alexandria Smith

ALEXANDRIA SMITH, *swing lo, swing hi,* Conté/charcoal on Kraft paper, 48"x68", 2011

JUAN CRUZ, *El Reino (the Kingdom),* oil on canvas, 60 1/3"x60 1/3", 2011

In my work, I am constantly discovering new images and seeing new visions. These images reveal themselves to me, and speak to my inner self. I try to give these images life and meaning. Through the years, I have found a sacred connection with my work. This connection has been my guiding light toward the path to freedom. In addition, my work often shows the daily struggle of the people of the third world, surviving in an uncompromising modern world.

Juan Cruz

JUAN CRUZ, *La Santa*, oil on canvas, 36"x72", 1987

STEVE PEARLMAN, *Blue Flip Flops,* color photograph (dimensions vary), 2010

Diane Arbus said, "I really believe that there are things no one would see if I didn't see them." I'd like to think that this statement is true for the images that I capture with my camera. Through photography, I attempt to find uncommon elements in the common, and to make the familiar seem unusual. My hope is that the images that I make isolate small fragments from our cluttered visual landscape, in a way that we can all embrace. It's such a simple thing to press the shutter release on a camera. Isn't it wonderful that such a simple act can bring such joy?

Steve Pearlman

STEVE PEARLMAN, *Whale watching,* color photograph (dimensions vary), 2008

Marc-Anthony Polizzi, *Big Red and Shiny,* found materials, paint (dimensions vary for installation), 2010

My work uses a process of reconstruction and unification to examine the domesticated chaos of the postconsumer world. This area where the relatively ordered and relatively disordered coexist and interact might seem like a contradiction, considering the more austere and violent sense of chaos. However, it is in this gray area that I construct my work. These installations draw on the history and narrative properties of found objects to bring out the human connection often lost in the glimmer and glitz of an ever-growing material culture.

Marc-Anthony Polizzi

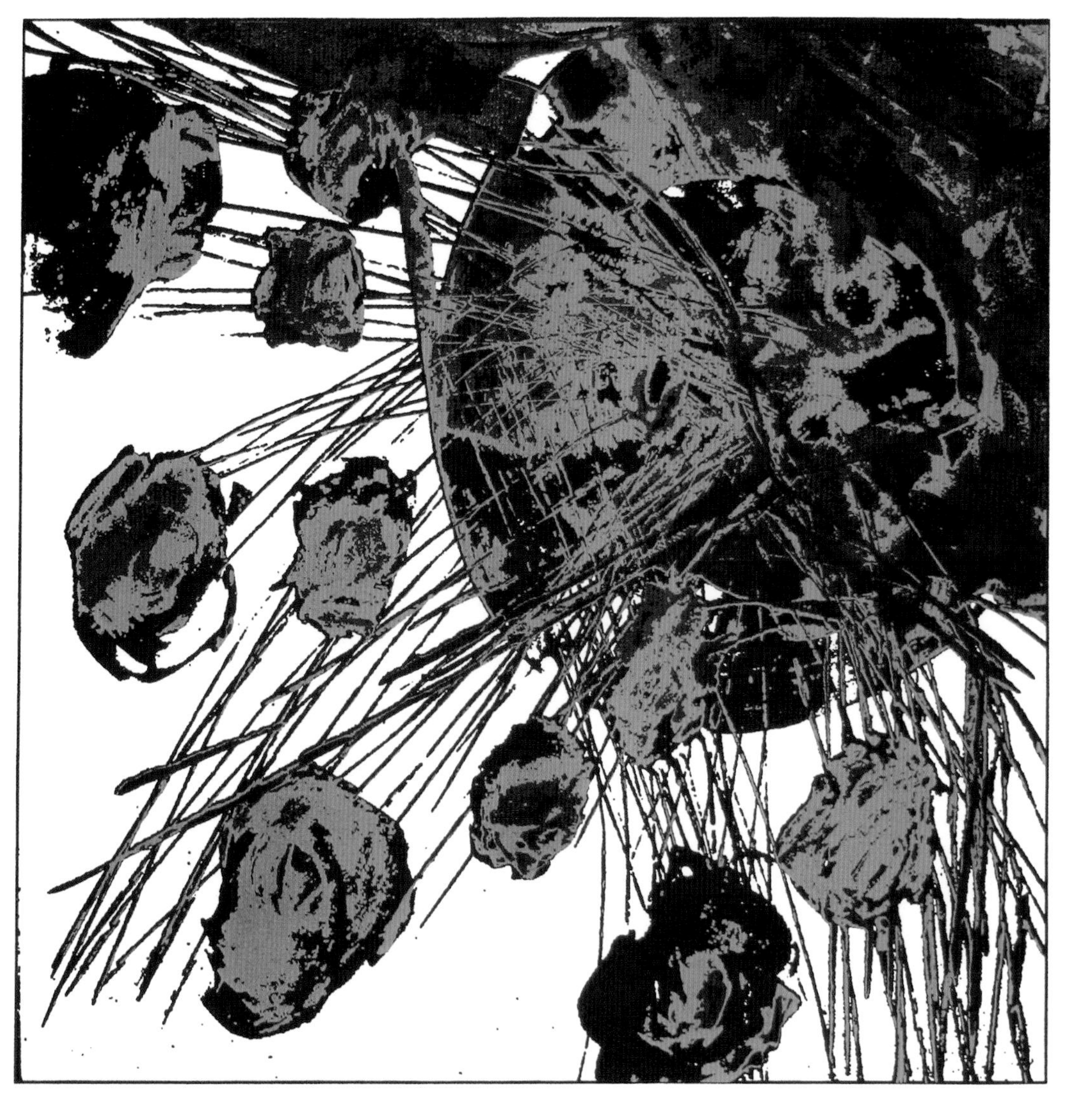

RUTH SPROUL, *Space—Projects for the Living,* screen print on paper, 24"x24", 2011

First I made small ink drawings by pushing ink around on plexiglass, not knowing where I was headed until I was there. Then I blew up some of the drawings and further altered them, and made large screen prints from them. Although they are drawings, they almost have a photographic quality. Photographs magically made without a camera, straight from my brain. Part of the collective unconscious.

Ruth Sproul

ALEX BIEGLER, *house. O tree spreading like the tree of Genesis,* oil on birch, 8'x8', 2011

My work acts as an active participant in alternative cultural mythologies for the purpose of exhibiting, through representation, how our current cultural projection affects and dictates our inheritance of knowledge. This inheritance, disseminated through story, embodies the evolutionary direction of both our culture and our species. By engaging with these stories, we gain perspective on what we know and how we know.

Alex Biegler

PETER T. BENNETT, *Core LB #2,* aluminum, 6"x7"x2", 2011

At the dawn of 20th century modernism, aluminum was considered to be one of the primary building blocks in the development of a structural utopia. The modernists believed that new design, new building and new materials were the appropriate expressions of our cultural optimism. Aluminum not only supported this new design esthetic and made new ideas possible, it became an active protagonist in the modernist dialogue. The material became a vehicle for sensory communication and possessed properties that seemed limitless and near magical. Aluminum was quite possibly the 20th century's first truly modern material.

Peter T. Bennett

Bartow + Metzgar

STRATIMENTATION: INVESTIGATIONS OF A METAMORPHIC LANDSCAPE

This project, undertaken by the collaborative team of Bartow + Metzgar from 2009 to 2011, involves the investigation of the "natural history" of the DeCordova Sculpture Park + Museum in Lincoln, Massachusetts, and an articulation of the complex intersections among the various geographical, geological and historical features of the site.

Collection 20-322

Date **06.08.10**

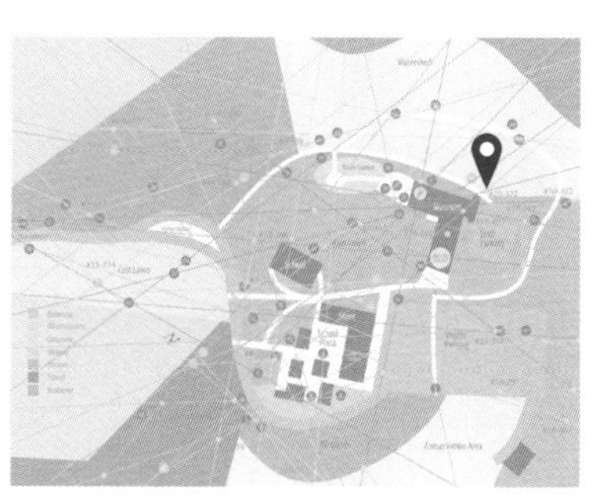

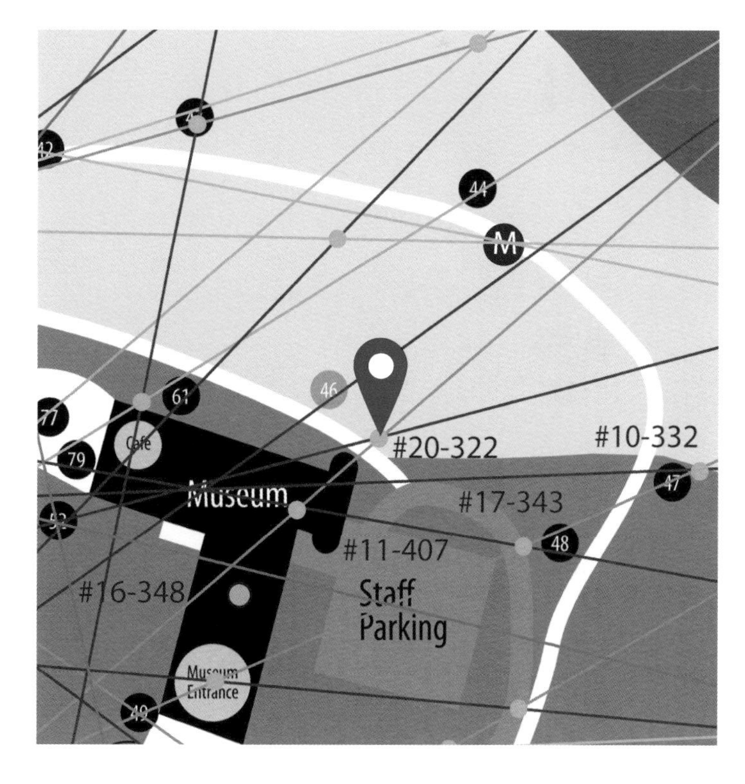

Collection
20-322

ORGANIC

23 Samples / 1-16

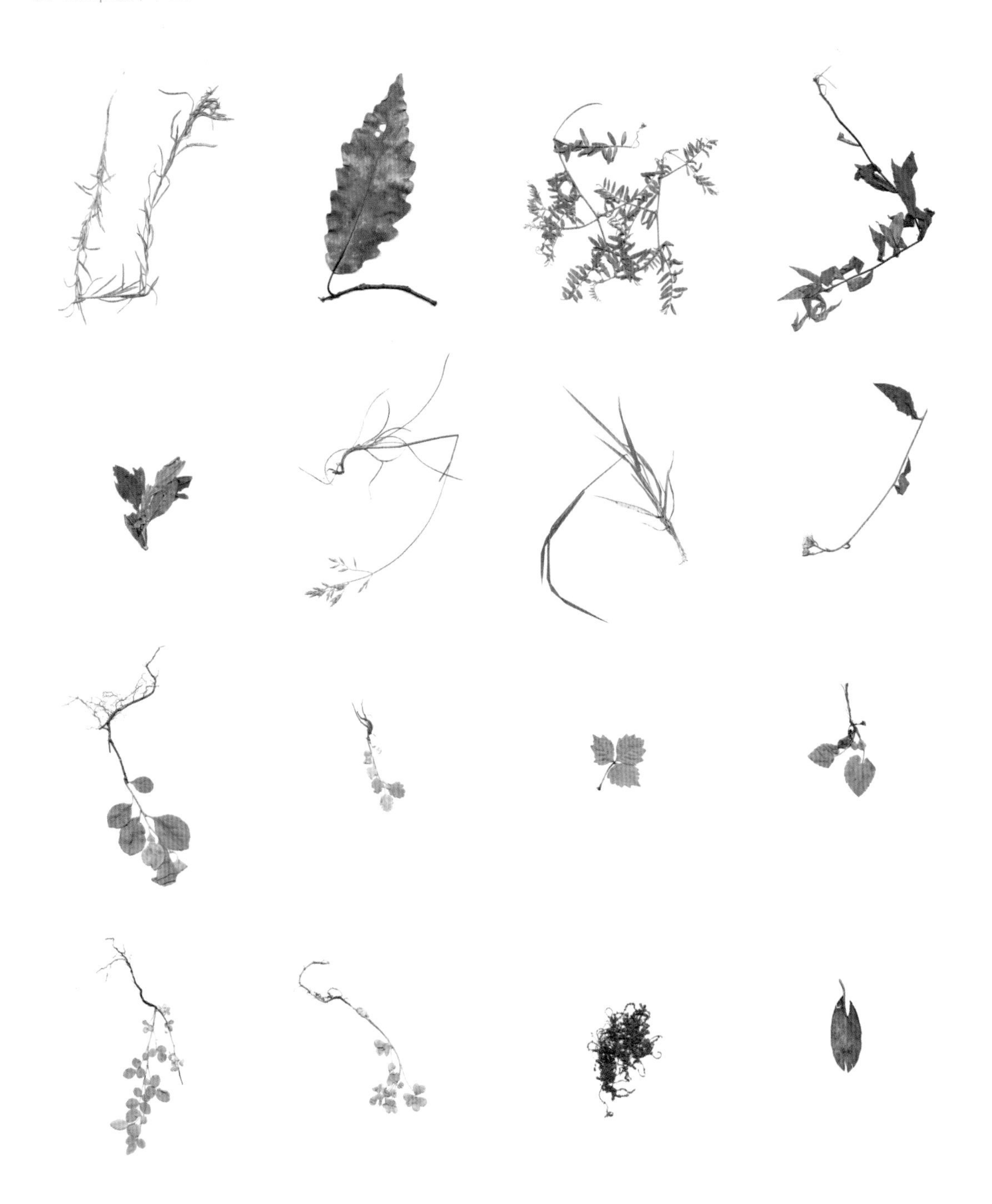

Collection includes organic and inorganic samples, soil samples, a geologic sample, and a lithic bacteria culture.

Collection 20-322

ORGANIC AND INORGANIC

17-23

GEOLOGIC

1 Sample

BACTERIAL

1 Sample

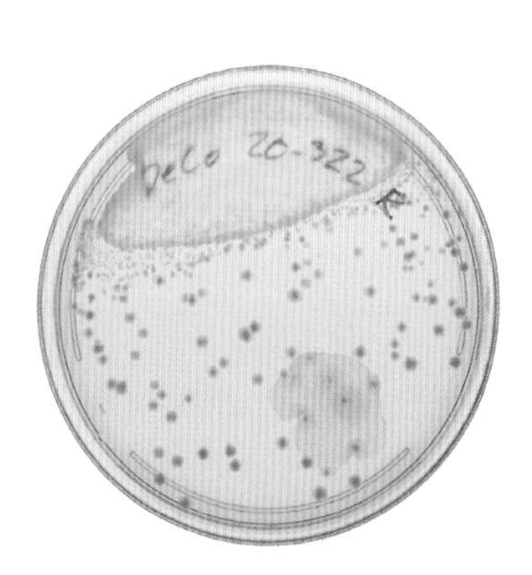

Two-person: From 2009-2011 the artist collaborative Bartow + Metzgar investigated the geography, geology, and biology of the DeCordova Sculpture Park + Museum in Lincoln, Massachusetts. Their project *Stratimentation: an investigation of a metamorphic landscape* focused on the dynamic quality of biological systems involving the human and nonhuman across time from both a local and global perspective.

Terrain: The geography of Lincoln, Massachusetts, like many other portions of New England, was shaped in large part by glacial activity as recent as 10,000 years ago. Little has changed in a relatively short period of time (geologically speaking) from the last glacial episode, known as Wisconsin glaciation, to the present. The first peoples of North America had inhabited the area we know as Massachusetts for well over 15,000 years and would have experienced this glacial event. Their agricultural and hunting practices involved episodes of deforestation and afforestation which also had an impact on the terrain of New England; this shaping of geography produced habitat for the human and nonhuman environment. Humans and the "natural" world have long been entangled yet we imagine that a distinct separation exist between the two, but this thought is misleading and oversimplifies the complex interactions that humans have with the nonhuman. Even at the scale of the human body - the terrain of the individual - we are a host of human and nonhuman interactions of more than 1000 different species of bacteria, fungi, mites, and viruses. Henry David Thoreau, a resident of Concord, the next town west of Lincoln, understood this inseparable condition well over 150 years ago. In a journal entry dated March 8, 1842 he writes, 'properly speaking, there can be no history but natural history'[1], a fully modern sentiment but difficult to grasp for those who imagine a nature/culture divide.

Time: Best understood as event, where forces act upon the physical world at different speeds and intensities at various scales of material and biological interaction. Why not then consider place as an expression of time? *Stratimentation: an investigation of a metamorphic landscape* is an experiment with time as an expression of physical and biological engagement.

Temporality: Geography and climate continually shift from one biophysical condition (system) to another. Their effects on the environment involve many scales of life, differing speeds of development, and a wide range of intensities. DeCordova's temporal condition can be experienced in a multitude of ways but prominent among them are its atmospheric qualities; ever-present and readily experienced from season to season, day to day, morning to night, minute to minute. B+M captured this temporal condition with environmental audio and video across the space of 1-1/2 years at twenty-two different collection points on the DeCordova site. Environmental samples (soil, rock, flora, cultural detritus, fungi, and insects) were also collected and registered into a project archive. The rock samples were cultured for bacteria, as were selected pieces from the Museum's Permanent Collection. Collectively, these temporal records reveal a dynamic range of localized environments that have a qualitative impact on the flora, fungi, bacteria, and animal life.

Tools: B+M's investigation of the DeCordova site involved several tools (listed below) designed to engage place from the position of the nonhuman with a specific interest in capturing nonhuman forces from a nonrepresentational perspective. These tools were developed to express linkages between the human and nonhuman; they produce material, biological, and durative hybrids.

1 **A field station** - for conducting research on site. The structure *(Morphology Field Station for Sensing Place)* was designed from the topography of the DeCordova site and clad with cedar shingles, a common architectural treatment for the

region. The field station was designed as a three-dimensional map of the DeCordova site. Its physical presence was a sculptural anomaly, a hybrid of art and habitable space which acted as a place holder for B+M's investigative program.

2 **Tree drawing apparatus** – a drawing mechanism that captures the movement of a branch in the wind over time. The drawings produced from this exercise are literal translations which describe localized atmospheres; they develop out of a specific alignment of human and nonhuman things, e.g., wind, tree, atmosphere (sun, shade, moisture, temperature), pen, paper, elevation -- nonhuman event makers.

3 **Microbial drawing apparatus** – a sheet of vellum is placed between two Plexi-glass sheets and buried below the surface of the ground for a period of time. Bacteria is pulled between the Plexi sheets onto the vellum surface where an interaction of soil, water, minerals, temperature, and bacteria produce a biological drawing that is removed from representational constraints. The microbial drawing is a literal transcription of time as material-biological process.

4 **Maps/systems** – the terrain of DeCordova's campus is interspersed with many sculptural objects made from a variety of materials, e.g., wood, bronze, glass, steel, rubber, paper, stone. Visitors of DeCordova's Sculpture Park are given a map that notes the location of each sculpture. B+M used the Park map to produce a system for extracting twenty-two random collection points on the DeCordova site. The system was based on material differences between all of the sculptures. It was also used to sample DeCordova's Permanent Collection by selecting works for bacterial cultures (a nonhuman entanglement with cultural phenomena).

Test: Ideas work best when they test the world. Ideas must materialize as actions or physical-material hybrids if their robustness and resilience are to be fully explored. The failure of an idea is often due to its lack of articulation, but a failure is revelatory if it is used to rethink one's proposition – in essence, to begin again. B+M's investigations at DeCordova focused on questions about time and place. How do we experience place beyond representational concerns? How do we comprehend biological interactions that are visually accessible but difficult to imagine as biological systems, e.g., fungi-trees-bacteria? What tools are needed to sense place more deeply, experientially? How are we world-makers? These questions lead to practices that test the world from a localized geography but strongly relate on a global scale.

'We are not in the world we are of the world'.[2]

1. Henry D. Thoreau, Journal, Volume 1, 1837-1844, Princeton, NJ, 1981, p. 370
2. Iain Kerr of spurse, an art and architecture collective based in NY that B+M have collaborated with on previous projects

---

Bartow + Metzgar began their collaborative practice in 1999. Their research varies from project to project with a strong interest in the urban environment and systems involving the human and nonhuman. They often collaborate with practitioners from other disciplines: geology, mycology, microbiology, geography, film, and architecture. Recent projects have been exhibited at the DeCordova Sculpture Park + Museum, Lincoln, MA; Locust Projects, Miami, FL; Action Art Actuel, Saint-Jean-sur-Richelieu, Quebec, CAN; and the Urban Institute for Contemporary Art, Grand Rapids, MI. More on Stratimentation can be found at B+M's blog ***stratimentation.wordpress.com*** and more on their collaborative work can be found at ***bartowmetzgar.wordpress.com***.

JIMMY ELLERBE, *Still Life with African Mask,* charcoal on paper, 18"x24", 2011

My hope is to become a professional artist and entrepreneur after finishing art school. My interest is in drawing, painting, and three-dimensional arts. During the summer of 2011, I completed Learning Lots, the Near West Side summer art program here in Syracuse. I learned to draw, paint, design three dimensionally, and weld. I made a mural, worked on a sculpture, and helped with group projects. I also had a chance to work on my art portfolio, doing self-portrait, still life, and nature drawings. I would like to thank Ms. Yvonne Buchanan and Ms. Dorene Quinn for their encouragement and guidance.

Jimmy Ellerbe

WILKA ROIG, *Invisible 2,* silver gelatin print (dimensions vary), 2011

My work occurs in the realm of personal and social space, questioning how individuals develop feelings of selfhood, connection, and belonging. I explore conscious and subconscious identification and individual symbols of power and culture. I attempt to reveal the self through sameness/difference, the relationship of self/other, relationships to time/place. The production of my work is often an interactive and dialog-based performance; I create situations and set up actions that result in photographs, texts, and installations. This process displaces the self and decenters the viewer, disrupting the usual artist/audience relationship. I expose the process of performance, challenging the powers of creation, identity, and community.

Wilka Roig

Wilka Roig, *Invisible 8,* silver gelatin print (dimensions vary), 2011

WILKA ROIG, *Invisible 10,* silver gelatin print (dimensions vary), 2011

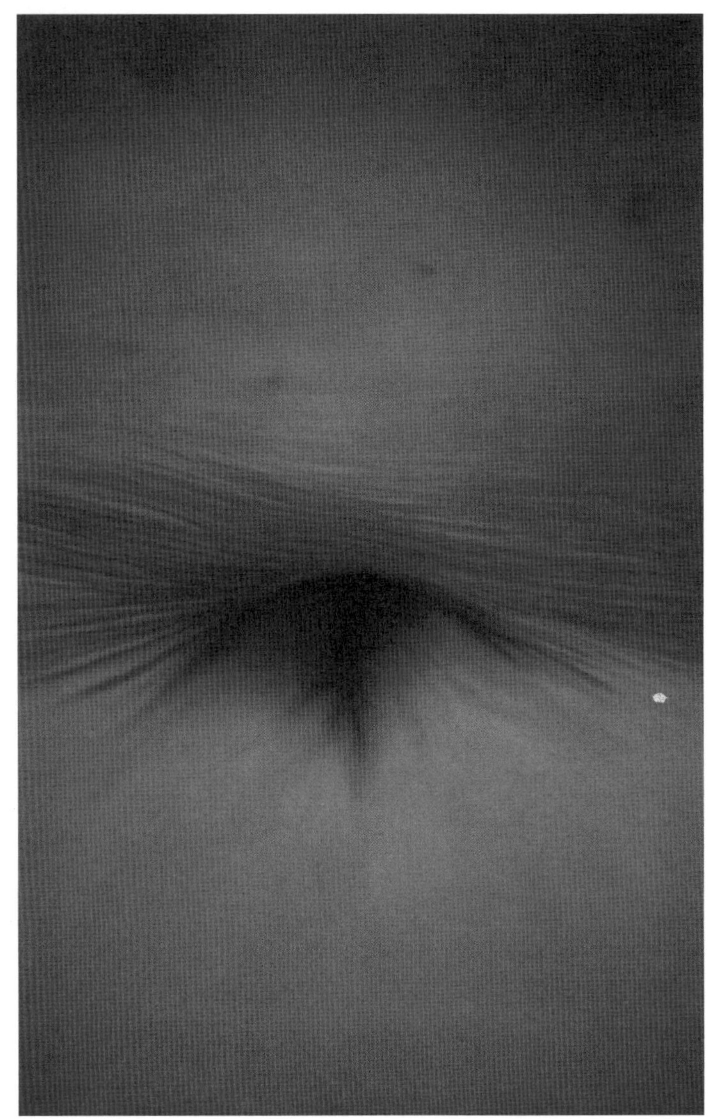

SUSAN D'AMATO, *Dad,* Charcoal/Pastel, 60"x42", 2000

My work explores visual and conceptual correspondences between the human body and universal forms. This series of large-scale charcoal drawings depicts specific intimate features of the body as metaphor to contemplate our identity, vulnerability and mortality. The drawings of my parents' aging bodies accentuate the aspects of time, gravity, and physical transformation, emphasizing the body as the vessel of accumulated experience and continuous change. Wrinkles, heavy flesh and spots mark their individual identities, while simultaneously transforming them into landscape. In "Mom," subtle variations of tone describe the weighted, once stretched flesh and age spots of the skin. Two scars of birth and passage are present; mirrored with the navel scar is the Cesarean scar, referencing lineage (*my passage to air*) and the cycle of life as it moves through body to body.

Susan D'Amato

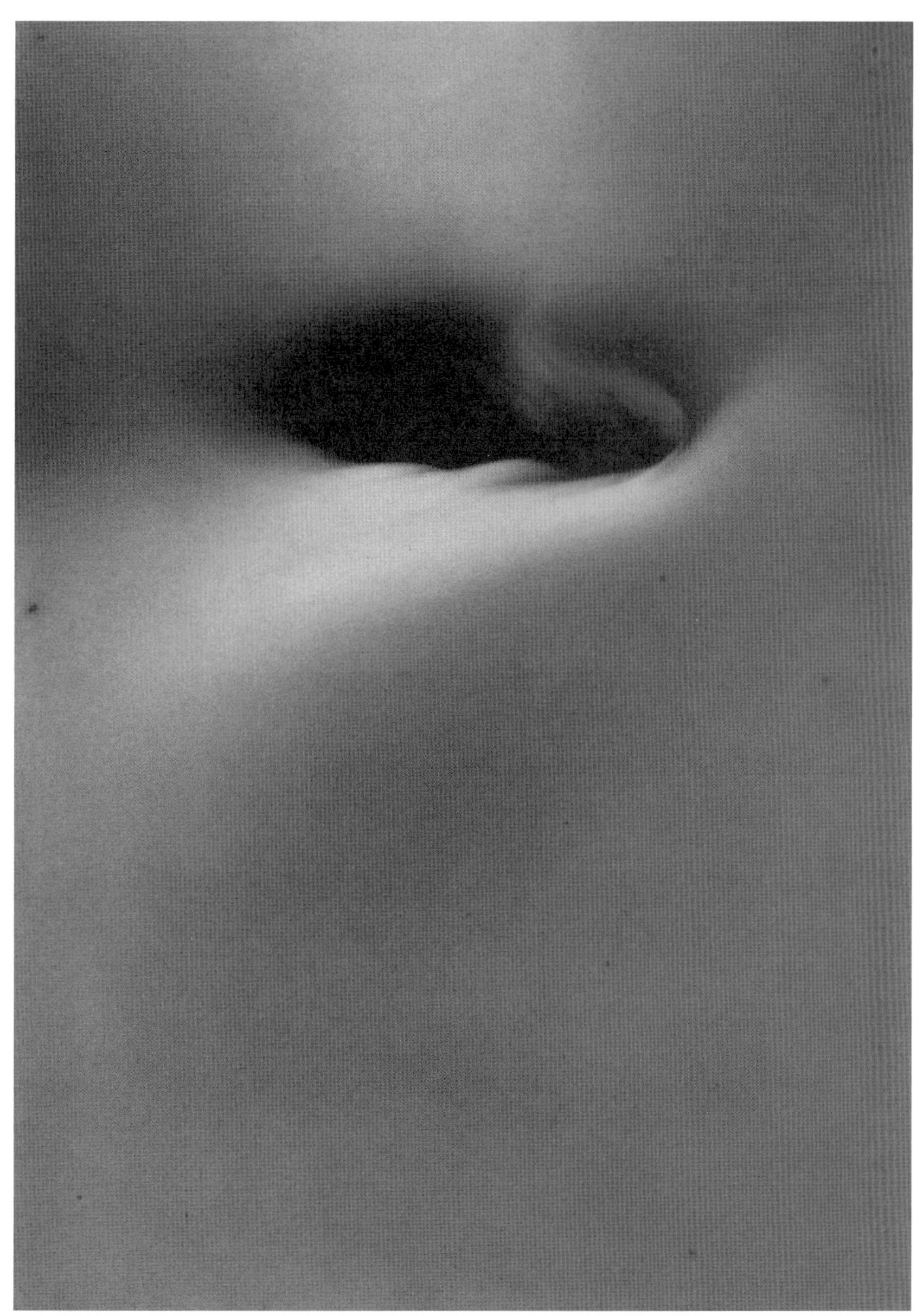

SUSAN D'AMATO, *Hierophony,* Charcoal/Pastel, 60"x42", 2000

Kazim Ali

FROM *THE BOOK OF MIRIAM THE PROPHETESS*

1. THE PRAYER AT THE RIVER BANK

this hand made hard by work & slavery has never
yet turned against its own blood.   this hand though
chattel has never murdered.   here at the edge
of the river   ankles choked with water-reeds &
eyes burning   thirteen I am
dripping with my first blood &   now
my first murder.

                                        in the name of my blood
dropping to the riverbank & in the name of blood

let this small basket of my brother sink like a stone
and the deep rush him to death quickly

let Miriam the slave-daughter of Hebrews walk
from this cold sacrifice into freedom.

let even the waves part to make way for us.

and oh dear Nameless One let never again in the history of the world
a slave woman be at odds with the tide.

oh One of rushing water
let never again in the history of slave-women
                                the ocean swallow up our babies.

2. The Plagues

bat toothed & locust winged the pyramids remember
Joseph's dream.   seven years abundance.   seven
years famine.

seven times seven of wandering under the empty sky.

something's always falling out of the sky:

cockroaches hitting the stones like coconuts.
frogs slapping down with quiet burps.   manna & quail for heaven's sake.

well,

I wait for the time our savior might rise up out of the good ground.
when the bush won't burn.   when the river won't bleed.

3. The River Turns Red

I had hoped to terrify
by our fierce & dreadful
miracles.

but my brother turned the river red &
the Queen's face flowered.

she leaned over & hissed
in the *Firaun's* ear:

there.
now your quarrel with the Hebrew God is over.

let these people go.
even the Goddess of the Nile is giving you her Sacred sign.

Bruce Bennett

The Horsemeat Restaurant

We were eating our lunch at
the horsemeat restaurant while
they were killing a horse in the
kitchen.

We could witness it through the
open space in the wall separating
the dining area from the chefs and
the hissing stovetops.

The horse had been positioned
with his neck over a basin, and the
throat had been cut. Blood was
sloshing into the container.

The waiters were immaculate
in white, and the presentation was
impeccable. There were hamburgers
and sausages, but also tender strips
of steak and exquisitely thin carpaccio.

The horse was standing splay-
legged, and would certainly have
fallen, were it not for the apparatus
rigged from the ceiling.

Occasionally, diners would glance
up, but would quickly return to their
conversation. There was that, and the
clink clink of silverware against china,
and the constant clicking of glasses.

If the horse made any sound,
no one could hear it.

Molly Burdick

Winter

The days are getting shorter;
The nights are getting longer.
The sun is rising less and setting more;
We head deeper into the night.
Winter's fingers curl around us;
Grip our hearts,
Filled with fear and awe.
Tears freeze upon forming;
So child, don't cry.
Just keep walking into the night.

Elinor Cramer

Chetwynd's Guide

When you dream of catching a train
that plunges through the night
toward some destination
you never reach, how would you know
after these many years—
until reading Chetwynd's dream book—
it's your longing for the dead?
He warns against trains,
their trajectory of grief.
If only you had dreamed of a small house,
he says, with a red door
between mullioned windows—
your mother's face.
You wouldn't have fussed half the day,
kitchen to bath to the bookshelf,
chasing after the silver coach
shunted from its wheels,
and lowered into the ground.

Jessica Cuello

Chamber

My shoebox rattled with shells
found at a garage sale:
Honey Cowrie, Perspective Sundial,
Chambered Nautilus—sliced
perfectly across, a hole punctured
in each chamber where the dead had lived.

Far from salt-thick water, I listened
to the low echo, breath from bone.
I put my mouth against the pink lip
of the conch, its curl of teeth.

Once I crawled into my brother's room
without breathing; I meant to show I
moved invisibly; I wanted his eye
to stray from his comic.

Num Cung

FALLING

simple life
taken away by conflicts
war has become true
such time was never before—
people dying between bullets, on bloody ground
taken home from the heart
destroying any future life
everyone cries
all voices in the air, falling rain
bullets taking many souls to unfair deaths
safety vanishes naturally
when lies become truth,
truth becomes lies
people pay for the future sorely
life depletes by fate
war lives to die

Angela DeSantis Dailey

How the Ear is Half a Heart

the snug curl of flesh
over flexible frame

leans away from the brain
toward other-than

what she is: a cupped palm
a sponge of cartilage: stoic

soft-bellied clam
vulnerable funnel

poised to swallow only
waves: echoes: digits of air

so that: what is
without her

enters her
fisted curve

sliding over bone
and open membrane

into the resonant chamber
of mnemonic fluttering

Francis DiClemente

The Bridesmaid

The most adorable pregnant bridesmaid ever
Waddles down the church's center aisle,
Unable to hide her protruding belly.
And with her feet swollen,
Her lower back sore and forehead warm,
She endures the ceremony standing
On the altar beside the joyous couple.
But she nearly passes out while
Posing for pictures in the lakefront park.

Inside the reception hall,
She almost vomits at the sight
Of shrimp cocktail and Chicken Florentine.
She orders hot tea and lemon from the top-shelf bar,
And dines on rolls and garden salad.
This single-mom-to-be, though not merry,
Offers a smile when others turn to stare,
And bobs her head to the music
As the guests hit the dance floor.

She nibbles on a sliver of white-frosted wedding cake,
And asks for guidance from her parish priest, wise old Father Meyer.
Then the bride overthrows the eager females huddled
Near the dance floor and the bouquet lands
Softly in the expectant mother's lap.
Her face turns red as everyone looks at her.
So she just grabs the bouquet and throws it back.

George Drew

Doing a Blurb for Jared

Imagine Lorca in his final moments,
on his knees outside some dusty hovel,
his assassins spitting on him and mocking
his manhood with their homo-hating barbs.

Imagine this Andalusian lover of beauty
stripped of anything remotely metaphoric,
images crash-diving in the dirt like planes
shot from the blue sky over Granada;

then imagine the assassins' rifle barrels
leveled straight at his head; imagine those
last few seconds, the crotch-hugging horror.
Imagine infinity, its middle finger raised.

Imagine Lorca, there in the Fuente Grande,
on his knees, death's jackals tearing at him;
then, just for a moment before the moment
of his dying, imagine him suffused with joy,

joy rebuffing horror, horror neutered, poems
leaping to his tongue, tongue spinning words.
Imagine Lorca smiling as the rifles stammer.
Imagine him and you know how I imagine you.

Myron Ernst

At the End of Summer

It isn't so much the colors
or the drying up
or the crispness
in the air,
it's about the twisting.

It isn't so much the colors
or the drying up
or the crispness
in the air—
more than the brittleness,
it's about the twisting,
the bending of leaves and light;
it's more the way the whole
muscle of the body bends.

Old in a Heat Wave in July

The man in the wicker chair
finishes his cigarillo
and tosses the still burning end of it
over the railing; it lands on the parched lawn below.
What weak, morning breeze there was, has stopped;
it is a dead calm and very hot.
The woman, who cannot bear the heat,
is inside, stretched on her back,
on bare sheets. She has been listening
to slow piano waltzes all afternoon long.
A red car, burning oil, labors up the steep road.
Their son left that morning, but he will be back
in a week or so to advise them again on how
to continue their lives until the end. It is very hot,
and the man in the wicker chair is resting
from having cleared the last of the clumps of wild grass
pushing up for life from the dust of the gravel driveway.
The task is done. This is what it is then;
the tossed cigarillo, the heat in July,
the woman within, breathing heavily on moist sheets,
and an earlier movement of air that has stopped.
It is cooler now, and the tinkling of the waltzes
fades with the sun. The ticking of the hall clock
has slowed, and it forgot to chime the hour.
The man goes in to wind it. It will run for a week,
and then he will wind it again.

Lisa Feinstein

Irene's House

I went through your house last night,
opened the unlocked door,
torn screen flapping
like laundry-line delicates,
climbed down cellar stairs
so much like my own, a mirror image
of wooden steps cascading

to the old, cinderblock basement,
your rich Carpathian voice,
grey curled hair
and your solitude so late in life.

I stood quiet in the kitchen,
my neighbor,
my friend, half smoked cigarettes,
a Hungarian newspaper
still on the table, four years
after they carried you
through the front door, past the summer
sleeping porch.

I crept through hallways, stumbling
over floorboards in the dark,
spinning slowly
in rooms where your children grew,
yellowed curtains, no claw-foot here,
reaching for my glasses to see
scratchy records, Zorba the Greek,
chicken wing bones.
An old telephone
sitting on a box,

no cord, no outlet, barely a wall
between us—the things
your family left for the mice, the vestiges
nobody came for, never packed in boxes or bothered
to cart off when you died,
leaving your home shallow,
vacant, empty-eyed, hollow, but remarkably clean

despite broken windows,
attic pigeons,
peeling paint, crumbling plaster,
and the city closing in,

growing about your abandoned home,
like vines on a fairytale castle.

Eric Geissinger

The Calm

It is a curious thing, the calm of distance.
In battle few men dare to sight
the enemy's head and squeeze the trigger,
Preferring, rather, the torso.
But miles above, no man waits
when told the city sleeps below,
and downward drop munitions.

A failure of imagination? Of course.

It is a curious thing, the calm of distance.
For in the room, within your gaze,
your tears invoke complete devotion,
I am forever yours…
yet when I turn my traitorous back
and fail to write, or call: it's funny.
I cannot hear your sobs.

Would that that were true,
Poetry can save the world
If only they experienced that
Subtle soul-expansion which
We poets *(yes, WE)*
So value.

An inculcation to massacres.
Yes, inculcation, many lives my verse
Could save, force feed the kids, youth, teens.

Poetry *can* save the world, you see!
It can it really can.
By night I sometimes believe,
Always, by light of day, never.

Mary Gilliland

Stirrings

She spends nights on her feet
tipping pills into throats of the aged,
swabbing their bedsores, chucking wet linen,
the rotator cuff hurling pain's metal
the length of her arm.
At midshift, at three, at the gooseneck lamp
lighting her station, she writes up the charts.

In the mornings, sleepheavy,
she wheedles her daughter's pressed thumbs
from the abdomen under the nightie,
guides them to the pitcher's handle,
slides the cereal under the milk
and with luck holds her tongue at bodily
nonsense, the girl nine years old.

She takes off her nurse's uniform
and slides into bed, the man turning his back,
hands balled in the clamp of his knees.

Christine Hamm

The Stars are Yellow, Surrounded by Black

At 6 am, I splay my tender feet
on cold pink tile, pretending

I can't remember your name. House
in the palm of my hand. Stink beetle

nestling in my ear, whispering, *this*
is the way we wash our hands. Skin

color was always SALMON PINK, like
this sky. My families were never

big enough, floated off to one side.
You have to use the whole page,

the teacher said as she gave me a fresh
box of wax. The blues didn't taste

as good as they smelled. When she
asked me to make a face, I drew

your mouth in black, a place
like a locked door, and me
on the wrong side, or under it.

Cliff Henderson

In the Charity of Commerce

What is it in these dusty, blighted places, halfway to nowhere, kids with grimy faces, playing in the gutters, in the summer rain, not grown, yet blossoming in cheap fashion, finding fields to fall in, or later rusty cars, promise rationed, or not ever there. What is it, trains rush through not stopping, entire blocks for shopping, show windows empty but for signs to offer them for sale, where rivers fouled that in spring flooding spill chemicals they're told they must ingest again someday to go on living, if living is the name we choose to call it. Why do they keep on giving, nothing left to give, to those who keep on taking, now they have it all.

Akua Lezli Hope

Seneca

The first time your visiting nephew
rode Captain Bill's narrative boat
he was afraid. Though the dark
polished wood interior, solid,
brown, comforting with flowered
seat cushions, was bright as a Sunday parlor,
sunshine on boat's wake made waves
teeth and knives. You know how
to swim, yellow orange candy-colored
lifesavers overhead. Nothing bad
will happen to you, but it already had.
Skinny adolescent narrator pauses, captain details
where those before walked. Assiniki, stony place
of people whose path is that faint narrow rock ledge
descending, disappearing into gray shattering shore wall
Salt mines across this deepest Finger Lake
another mysterious steaming of stuff from below.
All this strangeness and feeling yourself
a small, small thing on a big indifference.

Mike Jurkovic

Broken Bones

They test this
And they test that
And still I feel
Like shit.

Maybe it's memory
Accustomed to the pain
Of hand and idleness,
Prone to the ink of the grifter.

The salacious and sacred
Knit an odd rigor mortis,
Each demanding
A specialized hunt
For cause and effect,
X-ray, tincture.

Pink eye. Blue Cross.
A knot of fibrous swelling.

The little volcanoes
We douse with aspirin,
The cure we all
Mistake as joy.

If only we
Could tell each other,
How much we love
Their broken bones

Poetry
On a prescription pad
Discarded
In empty waiting rooms

Chrissy Kolaya

First Memory, 1954

First there are the sirens,
flashing lights,
a commotion of adults.
He remembers cradling his sister,
a baby then, watching
through the screen door,
his father, other men,
policemen, and
his mother shushing.

A glimpse of his aunt on the sofa,
face bruised, eye blackened,

and the door slams.

The men
with their smell of whiskey
and engines
snarling outside.

The sound of gravel under tires
means both departure and arrival.

At fifty he sits to tell a story
and can remember only pieces:
a door closing,
cigarettes,
the weight and heft of the baby in his arms,
men with their quick
angry movements,

and the women
who lay their hands
on the arms of their men,

hands that say:
slow
and *think*.

***

It's possible he killed someone,
the son thinks
years later.

Evidence:

the way everything stopped abruptly.
One minute
they were out for blood—

    his aunt
    seventeen
    bleeding into the couch cushions beneath her,

    men
    pacing on the porch

    it went on for days,

    the hunt
    for the
    boys
    responsible

—and the next
it was
over.

What had happened?

He couldn't say.

Just that he believes his father to be the kind of man who

hands around a throat

might keep squeezing.

Ilyse Kusnetz

The Eagle's Nest

On the first day, Easy Company liberates
10,000 bottles of Goering's vintage wine.

One soldier clutches a toilet to his chest,
as if it were a toddler. *I'm gonna shit*

in the same toilet Hitler did!
he shouts over and over again.

In a small cellar, my uncle Louis finds
broken plates and children's books,

spread facedown like sleeping butterflies.
He tells me this in his own cellar,

one Saturday after *shul.* It is 1972,
and I am six, scrunched between

musty columns of *Time* and *Life*,
shelves strewn with dusty bottles,

spare parts for obsolete machines.
My thin voice presses the air, as if

testing the spidery key
of an ancient typewriter: *But Uncle,*

who did those books belong to? His walrusy
mustache waggling as he laughs—

the laugh of a man who once-upon-a-time
uncorked his hate and drank it.

Tatianna Lebron

Catch a Dream

As I walk slowly away up away from the graffiti marked sidewalks.
Thinking to myself how does the grass become dead as the flowers along this bed.
The sun becomes blinding and the clouds are my protector.
Below there seem to be wrappers upon wrappers.
I say to myself where would I go?

The sounds are increasing as the cars buzz by.
When the words won't come out and only cussing seeps through the airways
they speak.
Kids start to laugh and all I want to be is a part of what used to be me.
Cops rush by, as the siren follows right along with it.
I look at myself what could I be?

Feelings are mutual just like they say.
The little girl I used to be was always happy and giddy.
No second thoughts could come across my heart.
As I drift away, feeling sleepy and groundless.
I ask myself how can I be what I want to be?

I sit soundless on the curb to my house.
The grass itches the back of my thigh as if it's questioning why am I here?
The sidewalks graze across my feet cold and dark.
I want to scream and nothing comes out.
Flowers I pluck feel like silk and smooth away my thoughts.
I stand up I am exactly everything I can be and will be?

Charlene Langfur

Analysis of the Best Possible Day

No material theory involved, only light. Everything's all right.
Amino acids, lipoproteins start off the day like any other.

Early on, a few pied warblers warble, the dog croons.
I'm dressed in a cotton shirt, cleaned, ironed,
a shirt the color of the sea at noon.
I give a class in school on advancing a single thought.
How to hold an essay together
in any weather or difficulty.
The mind likes maps.

In the newspaper, articles about gene pools, buried artifacts,
war in Asia.
Four soldiers died today in Afghanistan.
I think they were lost in the mountains and I picture the steel gray
rocks where they were found.
The war is like air.
It is always there in America now.
We do not talk of it as if it has a beginning or an end anymore.
I think of the soldiers
when I pass the giant sunflowers in front of my house.

All in all, today is like other days and what's new sticks to it
early on. The clock on the wall keeps its steady little beat.
Its eternal numbers. The rhythm of the stars and heavens.
At eleven I'm ready for a hot meal
garlic and pasta, organic olive oil from Spain.
I have game.
I have what counts. Even at the end with no one to smile at me
on my way but a black dog, tail wagging
I am not lagging.
In the east, light turns crepuscular, catches at the shadows.
The long float of loss, recession, unemployment,
the color
of your leaving,
ideas for solutions on a pad of paper to hold a small
world together as it passes. Flower doodlings. A draft of a poem
about a good day, the poem holding the day together,
a place in it for the soldiers, the dog's path, the lack of love, in the west—
the lilac colored sky

Naton Leslie

The Lost Episodes

If film steals the past,
then the child grubbing
in dirt out the side
door of our house trailer,
lot triked to hardpack,
is surely me, and the sister

who pulls me straight
for the 8mm, pokes me,
is an evil Shirley Temple
directing me in her movie.

Photograph/gravure/engraved.

I'm captured with a fistful
of birthday cake at two,
wanting a carnival ride
at four, but film recalls

me yanking a safety fence
and here comes Shirley
to pull that fence too,
as that is being filmed,
letting no part escape,

trying out for toddler
at five. When the camera
lights are gone, she twists
my face in her hands.

A picture of George Kish,
who inherited a scrapyard,
shows the lucky, violent
man throwing an arm around
my shoulders as he promised

not to punch me. I drove
blocks in Masury to find
a woman I knew was lost
to an image of a wallet-
sized future, who thought
a wild youth led to content

age and albums. These are
tracks, persisting in
the hard dirt, in memory,
vision in chemical light.

Lyn Lifshin

The Woman Who Talked to Hitchcock's Birds

she said she could
talk to them, they knew
she could understand.
She said they'd been
patient but they had
issues, they'd waited,
they just wanted
freedom. But they had
had enough, they
wanted revenge, they
wanted justice. She
was birdlike in her own
way, a beak of a nose,
panicky motions like
a scared bird. They
related to her, not to
those who stole their
feathers for hats,
shot them down. One
said her mate had been
shot down, cooked
and eaten. Some were
plucked for pillows
and coats, the trim on
designer dresses.
Enough was enough.

And what of the birds
in cages, cooed over
but never allowed
a free life? They'd
been given warning: a
rush of feathers
down a chimney, a
sea gull swooping down
for a peck. It wasn't
enough. It was hardly
noticed. People flock
to the country, slash down
trees we nest in. Do
they care about a trail of
eggshells, the smog and
wires our radar can't work
in? And they call a few
smashed windows, a few
shattered cups terror and chaos?

Jay Leeming

At the Falls

The river loud and roaring today,
the waterfall a thunderstorm
that never moves. Clouds of spray

rinse fallen sycamore leaves for hours.
Years ago an abandoned millhouse
was swept away by this river in flood,

swallowed whole, carried downstream
and thrown over the falls' high edge.
Miraculous how that building

was once a blueprint spread out
on a desk, was once lines on paper
and pine trees rooted in earth;

trees felled and then cut into planks
pounded together nail by nail.
Carpenters sweated to cut those boards,

worked to build the frame tight
so the mill would stand through years
of hard storms and winter wind.

But the river had its own work to do,
its own craft of roaring and taking.
Here in the rip-saw crash of this water

I feel the grip of larger pattern,
how all things are shattered out
of themselves, broken and gathered up;

how one day rain was added to rain
until that whole ruined house
came showering out of the air.

The Narrator

All of a sudden you get tired of the story you've been telling yourself and decide to take a walk. You go to your front door, open it, and step out into the yard. A bird is singing in a nearby maple tree. You walk past without thinking of the arrowheads buried in the ground, without noticing the daylight-moon coasting far above your head. Now you are in a field where a gentle wind is blowing through long summer grass. But suddenly there is a roaring sound in the air, and a rope ladder unrolls from somewhere above you to come to an end at about the height of your shoulders. You take hold of the ladder with both hands and climb up it into an orange helicopter, which then turns and flies away until it can no longer be heard, until it can barely be seen, until it is just a small speck in the sky which then vanishes completely. Silence returns, and the birds start singing again in the empty field. A grasshopper jumps, a cricket rubs his legs together. The wind erases your steps, which for a short time the grass had kept. But I am still here. It seems that I have always been here. I go wherever the story goes, and without me many would say that there is no story. But that is a mistaken belief, a fiction, an error easily made by those desperate to believe in their own permanence. I am just a guest, the temporary voice of this house, as short-lived as the creaking of a roof beam in a summer storm. And when I depart as suddenly as you did—through this passage that has suddenly opened in the ground, along this glimmering tongue-colored trail which disappears into darkness—the story will remain like water under the earth, like buried granite, like the shape left in the air by an oak tree after it has been cut down. The wind blows through it. The wind blows through it all day long.

Tim McCoy

The Last Walk
Edward McCoy 1910-1980

He stood before the gate, already pale
in the falling light, a little breathless
and dust-stained from the road, smelling of leaves
before decay. He looked into the distance
and saw his death bloom in the falling sun,
as if it were already past, the pain and silence.
But then he trudged forward, and I followed
behind, through the gate that still hung crooked
on its one hinge, passing through the tall grass
beyond, passing the trunks that lay fallen
in their own leaves. And farther down we went,
raising the last dust from leaves underfoot,
farther into the trees, already dim.
Below we heard the creek falling lightly
over its stones, slipping quietly onward
into darkness. Here he stopped to listen
as he labored to breathe, and I could smell
the sickness sweating out of his skin. Deep
he listened, sifting through the water's sounds
as once he'd sifted through its sunken rocks
and silt, looking for arrowheads. He sought
something between the sounds, an assurance
of something I could not yet understand,
for he understood that silence deepens sound,
and that loss gives what is possessed its beauty
and strange worth, and that the place of assent
is silent and dark, littered with the pained
who, in their deprivation, live only
to praise. He understood what was coming,

standing here again by the water, hearing
its undercurrents speak. I turned to look
back up the hill and saw the day eclipsed,
and the darkness already pierced by stars.
I turned again, and he was gone. I stood
dumb on the bank, looking into the night,
listening. But I saw only shadows
deepening around the trees, and heard, always,
the creek falling lightly over its stones.

Wolfman

Daddy tied me to the tree before
he put on the mask, that old mask
I always called grandpa. He'd scared me with it
before. I hated those crooked eye holes
and that crooked mouth where I've seen teeth.
I hated the white mop-hair. He'd chased me around
the yard before, scaring me,
running. I can't forget that day in the yard,
wearing my big brother's big jeans and the t-shirt
Mama always said I should just throw out.
Daddy put on the old mask, just to chase me
I thought, but he tied me to the tree
I used to play around.
He stood in front of me and I saw
worn-out coins in his eye-holes
like what I'd find in gravel.
I heard the dogs in the pen chasing
back and forth and barking. They knew something
I knew but I didn't yell it.
The trees were bare and daddy kicked the leaves
on his way to pull the axe out of the stump.
He came towards me slow
and raised it up like to chop down
a tree. I saw the branches bare
and thought he'd stop. I couldn't get any more time,
I tried to put it off, I thought he'd stop.
Daddy split my head through. I saw it
split as my spirit got out.
I had some hope for that body.

Mike Petrik

Nordic (a biologist in winter)

I glide along beneath the haloed moon—
                rapid frozen upper-atmospheric ice crystals.
The wind cools me as I coast downhill—
                double-poling with knees bent and chin tucked.

I move across beluga-back hillocks—
                dips and rises of a golf course come Spring.
Pockets of trees stand like islands in the white sea—
                ecosystem fragmentation creates population isolates.

I follow paw prints that cloud the old snow—
                I have dissected them all,
                prodded and sliced their muscles,
                traced the veins that grant blood in the cold.
I can see how they move by the way their feet fall.

Below an elm, I find a mess of fur, blood, and quills—
                where a fisher has brought down a porcupine
                by worrying its face with sharp teeth
                until it fell from the tree, unconscious.
The murder shines black in the moonlight.

David Musselwhite

To a Dying Lover

Though no one could know it now,
I will watch your cheeks vacuum
into the hollows of your skull.

Though it is many years off,
your whitewashed skin will blotch and scab over,
and you will resemble nothing so much as
a bleeding elephant freshly-poached
eggs left uneaten on the ceramic plate
we will glaze on our honeymoon,
an artist colony set high in fog-shrouded hills.

Our own private Hiroshima
As the wave crushes the pier
And the crude smoke chokes the dogs
Under the approaching meteor
That'll get sucked up into the black hole right along with us.
The doctor makes his diagnosis.

But it is May, yet, and the sunlight dances
A two-step through your chocolate hair.
It is May and dandelions have taken over the yard,
So thick that I pretend with Aiden and Abigail
That I cannot see them, that they are the reincarnations
Of Vasco de Gama, that the stream
made by your gardening hose is the Great Fish River
and there, our southwest corner of pollen-yellow Earth,
Is Calcutta full of gold.

The Great Fish River, you know, my love,
Is where Dias turned back.
His crew would go no further,
fearing death in the Cape of Storms.

There is a monument to de Gama in Malindi, far north,
once rivaled only by Mombasa
For control of trade on Africa's eastern coast.
He built it himself, great coral phallus topped by a cross.
There is controversy now about how best to preserve the pillar,
Which threatens to crumble into the sea.

I cannot know if,
In ten or twenty years' time,
I will give in to the urge to mutiny.
But here, in the waxing months of summer,
Drift with me in our Cape of Good Hope.
Let our Junes and Julys keep me from falling over
the edge.

Margarita E. Pignataro

Speaking Spanish in Syracuse

El modo de hablar,
        The way to talk,
        You can tell the difference,
Se anota la diferencia.

Cuando hablo con mi Boricua del Bronx,
        When I speak with my Bronx Boricua,
Eh un español matao
como dice él,
        It's a Spanish that is murdered
        as he says.

Yo soy un camaleón cuando hablo el español,
        I am a chameleon when I speak Spanish,
Hablo un español mejor cuando no estoy con el boricua,
        I speak better Spanish when I am not with the Boricua,
        My accent is a Chilean accent,
Mi acento es un acento chileno,
Sin embargo, resulta ser más estándar que chileno,
        However, the result is more standard than Chilean,
La universidad taught me properly,
The university me enseño hablar en la manera apropiada.

        My Syracuse Spanish was once upon a time a Boricua Spanish,
        My Southwest Flare met an avalanche of a different Spanish here,
        In 'cuse.
Mi español de Siracusa era una vez un español boricua,
Mi brillo sudoeste encontró una avalancha de un español diferente aquí,
En 'cusa.
        But no more,
pero no más.

The sun has to shine
in order to melt away
the layers of linguistic ambivalence
I find myself in when around
The Syracuse Boricua.

I am back to standard Spanish,
Regreso al español estándar,
Porque no estoy con el Boricua,
Because I am not with the Boricua,
Quien siempre me decía que no me entendía,
Who always said to me that he didn't understand me.
Speak English!
¡Hable inglés!
Street English!
¡Inglés de la calle!

And so I attend Syracuse University,
Entonces asisto la Universidad de Siracusa,
Para practicar el español apropiado en mi clase de español,
To practice proper Spanish in my Spanish class.

Emily Pulfer-Terino

Fifth Cousins

With unfurled arms and a left hand gone,
enshrined in gladiolas, dirt and white washed brick,
the Virgin coaxed us down cement stairs

to the concrete room that blared with news
and harsh Italian slang under Albany.
Hunks of curing meat, deep, hunger pink,

hung from pipes that pulsed with condensation
in the basement where the cousins—having found us
in the phonebook once they immigrated—resurrected

what they meant to know of home here. John grew porcinis
on hay bales in the bathroom that housed heaped barrels
of Chianti and imposing jars of pitch dark olives.

Beyond, in what they called the parlor,
one blue cube of tube light filled the room,
reverberant as any of the several men there was.

At what point is a person part of a place, or
part of a place no longer? My family, with their deli
down the road, church clothes, their talk as taut

as tire rubber—how poor I always thought they were,
and strange. Upstairs, in the house they kept for holidays,
the kitchen fixtures glistered like so many phony coins

above the honey gleam of parquet floors. Overstuffed
recliners and a sofa were embalmed in see-through plastic.
A whole world they'd prepared, preserved, hung heavy overhead.

Downstairs on cousin Mimo's Casio, I tamped out
that one frail, exuberant tune he taught me. My uncle,
hunched over the table across the great, clay scented room,

made noodles. His marble hands would break eggs
into hills of flour; deep grooved nails, yellow globes
of yolk first pooling and then disappearing into dough.

Melissa Reider

I Dreamed Eaton Brook

I dreamed I was the old row boat
On Eaton Brook Lake,
Moored by thin ropes slung loose
Over the knotty post,

The battered cleat.
I dreamed the hollow sound
Of my wood plank sides
Thunking against the docks,

Softly, arrhythmically.
I dreamed the motion without rest,
The lift and lick of waves,
The ceaseless rippling of the lake.

I dreamed the utter emptiness
Of being tied and idle.
I dreamed the oars
Being fitted and pulled

And the rower's weight
Steadying my center
And the long silent glide
Across the green glass at night.

Kristian Rodriguez

Region

Even so
There are many
A poem
To be had
Up Here
In this
Region

In the middle of town
All around
On the porch
Of our old house
Growing along the
Side of the road
As we
Drive home

When you are
All ready
Sounding as cicadas
At sunset I am
Dreaming still
Of coastal plains in Georgia

I knew I'd leave
My love
I cannot bear
The Winter
My heart forever is
Humid

Mary McLaughlin Slechta

Disappearing Act
for Prudence Crandall and the little misses of color

If you put your hand
in the hat of the right person,
you might pull out a little girl.

Listen, before the windows blistered
and the flames licked through,
the sky was a hand-me-down dress

with the belt too high.
And the little girl was a nail,
back then, in a scratchy collar.

Some in tall hats liked to say "The Nail,"
in quotes, with the future of the school,
the whole United States, balanced on its head.

But she was only a simple nail,
kissed from the carpenter's lips
to make the worm work a little harder.

Only later, the books and maps
lighting up the ridge and the wolves
hollering for the little girl to come on out

and get eaten up this very second,
did that nail start to prove
the blacksmith false.

What, with Papa aiming at shadows
and Mama pointing them out,
nothing they threatened could keep the alloys

of metal and lace and book learning
and faith from de-evolving into fur
and teeth and claws and spit.

It took Mama and Papa, both pulling,
to trap that feral creature
between the flat iron of Nana's palsied arm

and the board of her chest.
And if there was any rocking,
you were seeing things,

for that good woman
hadn't lifted a bucket
or stirred a pot

or even had a decent conversation
in a score of years.
What you thought was rocking

was just a rock.
And what you thought was a child
was a rabbit in torn lace,

asleep in a hutch of stone.

Amber Christine Snider

On My Birthday

You lie in a prison bed,
you lie in that jailed bed,
me in my winter window seat
smoking your coveted cigarette
and drinking your breath.
I imagine us listening together
a song of sad city, you could not take
this place of poverty, pace, and demons.
I succeed where you could not.
Every year, on this day, I think of you—
the bloody day when I came into light,
this flaming orb, this wind of beauty.
Your creation of love from love, I am love.
I cannot promise I won't write bad poetry about you.
Make you want to cringe, sweat, smack
the face flesh you gave me.
I could write more, but this is a birthday song,
a thank you.
I am your product stored about the world,
a branded piece of furniture,
a laugh, a series of words.
It is raining now, cascades of verbs mean action.
Lack of lack of lack of lack of—
Tomorrow,
the still blue of this wretched beauty of earth
will find us both quiet in our sleep,
slaves to production, still slaves to ourselves.
Father, I don't write poetry as much as I should.
I need rain. I need silence. Like you.

Matthew J. Spireng

Vague Memories of Terrible Things

Which of us does not hold a memory
of a terrible thing, some discovery, usually
in childhood, that we knew at the time
was not right and swore then in silence
to never repeat, keeping our promise to ourselves,
keeping it so well we forget the terrible thing,
our brain altering it to the vaguest hint of what
occurred so that years later, memory stirred by some
stimulus we can't begin to connect in a
logical way, we remember something—the
room we were in, pattern of the wallpaper,
the painting hung by our kin—and though we
can't recall just what really occurred, we know
that that day we turned away from a path
some would call sin and embarked on a life
that led to this moment that lets bits of memory in?

Lou Ventura

Seams

It is the July after his operation,
the summer after my first glove.
We are in the basement

swinging a giveaway from Geneva's Shuron
Park, hopefully inscribed for the forgotten
Willie Brown.

But soon we move our play outdoors,
where hands that fashion works of wood
will teach me to practice

his other art, for my glove is still
too new, to delay a game of catch for lessons
in long odds and alchemy.

The line drive sent to my glove-side
I misjudge, deflect and chase. A fly
he manufactures,

lost in a haze of high sky,
smacks me in the forehead, square.
Rub? I don't dare.

Suddenly, he removes his shirt, and reveals his scar,
the back of his neck…under his arm…up his chest,
like the stitches on a baseball.

Later, on the couch, I hold our baseball; I finger
its seams; I fall asleep beside my Dad,
and try like hell

to feel that seam that runs the length
of his rhythmic beating and breathing,
his ticking and tocking.

Now when a west coast game is past the ninth
(oh the mercy of a game without a clock)
I, alone on the couch,

the entire house sleeping, except for me
and the TV, think of that inevitability
that went unspoken

but not unseen, taking the shape of bare chested
hugs along those seams that sealed and
separated him and me.

Charles Lupia

A Lawyer's Work

A lawyer packs his briefcase.
His files tell of his clients' lives
in crisis. He walks to courts
in large cities, and drives
to small jurisdictions on sun-tempting days.
But on nights, too, he drives when the snow
blocks him from seeing past his windshield.

After a while, his clients are replaced,
as is his car. The shoes he walks to court in
are as worn as the story-telling briefcase.
What is left after so many lives?

Andrew Martin

Everyday Engineering

Engineering is the application of science, technology, and mathematics to meet the needs of a certain situation. That situation could be something totally new, like modifying the genetic code of corn to make the corn more nutritious, or it could be a slight change to something old, like making a matchbox with a better striking surface. Some examples of engineering are so fantastic, so far removed from everyday life, that we are barely aware of their existence. They are the Mars Rovers and the terahertz processors; you might hear about them, but you will probably never use them. But most engineering involves things so mundane that we don't even notice them anymore, like the alarm clocks and light bulbs in your home. In my typical day, everything I do, besides breathing, involves engineering in some way. So I'd like to go through a typical morning and point out some of the subtle ways engineering affects our lives.

Let's start with the morning commute. Mine takes me from southeast Pennsylvania to central New Jersey. As the crow flies, my house and the office are about fifty miles apart. But the road winds around lakes, hills, and buildings that are in the way, so the trip is closer to seventy miles. If I were to travel on foot, it would take about fourteen hours of constant walking. To save time, I need to use a vehicle, one that engineering has improved upon for over a century: a car. Early cars had top speeds of forty or fifty miles per hour, meaning even they could make the trip much faster than I ever could on foot. But thanks to dozens of technological advances and refinements, I can make the trip in two hours, and it only takes that long if I obey the speed limit.

And that's just travel time. Over the years, engineers have come up with other ways to make the drive more pleasant. Say I'm traveling in the winter, when it's so cold outside that I could get frostbite. I'll want some heat. The engineers who developed the modern car's heating system could have installed a regular space heater and powered it from the battery, but that would be wasteful. Instead, the system uses the heat generated by the engine, heat which otherwise would have done nothing but leak into the outside air. The heat itself is just waste energy from inefficiencies in the engine. One of the features of good engineering is using an undesirable property for something beneficial.

My commute is twenty miles longer by road than it is by air. This is because the road must go around most obstacles, not through them. But some things, like rivers and valleys, are too big to go around. That's where bridges come in. The Delaware River lies across my route, and I'll need to get past it somehow. Without bridges, I see three options. I can go upriver until I can get around the source, or find a spot shallow enough to drive across. I can use my car to transport a boat, and use that boat to carry a smaller automobile that I can use on the other side. Or I can take a ferry. The first two options are incredibly inconvenient and impractical. The third would significantly increase the cost of the trip and the time it would take. A bridge will allow me to get across the Delaware quickly and safely.

When engineers design something, they ask three questions: What does it need to do? What could interfere with its ability to do it? How can I compensate for those problems? In the case of commuter bridges, their purpose is to provide a path for cars and trucks over some expanse. The most obvious problem with these structures is that they might get too heavy and collapse, and the most obvious way to compensate for that is to make them stronger. But exactly how to do that is up to the engineer. He must take many variables into account, like the length of the bridge, the nature of whatever it crosses, and the construction budget. Out of all the techniques and designs he knows, he must choose the one that best meets the needs of the current situation, or possibly develop a new idea specifically for that project. Having a large bank of relevant knowledge and knowing how and when to apply it is an important part of engineering.

Traffic congestion is another potential problem. The area I commute through has a large driving population, so congestion on the roads is a constant worry. When designing the road, the engineer must take such things into account. With tens of thousands of vehicles going between Philadelphia and New Jersey every day, one-lane bridges and highways would be worse than useless; the traffic would back up so far it would interfere with drivers on other routes. The simplest solution to traffic congestion, at least in concept, is to make the roads wider. However, it is much easier to design a bridge with many lanes from the start than it is to add more lanes after construction is finished. Knowing how the things you design will be used and being prepared for likely complications is also important in engineering.

When I arrive at work, I depend on the power grid in order to do my job. While there are occupations that do not use electricity at all, they are few and far between. Most people need power plants and wall outlets in order to perform the basic functions of their jobs. The power grid supplies electricity to nearly every office and factory in the nation. If something were to interrupt the supply, industry and finance would grind to a halt. However, the grid is built with backup systems. For example, if a tree falls onto a power line and breaks the line's connection to the rest of the network, the power that would normally go to that line must go somewhere else. If not controlled, the power might overload a second area, and damage would spread rapidly. Luckily, electric utility companies have software to figure out where a problem is and hardware to automatically isolate the area so the rest of the network doesn't suffer. Whenever practical, engineers like to build systems that are failsafe.

The power that comes out of the walls is in the form of alternating current, meaning that it quickly cycles on and off. Because of this, objects that need to run constantly will need some extra circuitry so the cycling doesn't affect them. Using this type of system seems needlessly complicated, but it is necessary to avoid a more difficult problem. Direct, or non-cycling current, loses voltage as it moves along the power line. Using such a system, a building more than a few thousand feet away from the power plant would not have enough power to do anything. Alternating current systems do not lose as much energy as direct current ones, and it is easier to control the level of voltage at various points in the network. Using this system forces some objects plugged into outlets to have more complex circuitry. But that is a small price to pay compared to the inconveniences associated with direct current systems. Part of engineering is foreseeing problems and developing ways around them. Sometimes the solutions create new problems, which in turn require their own solutions.

Even lunchtime depends on engineering. I bring my lunch from home, so I must store it somewhere. If I use Tupperware, then I owe thanks to petroleum engineers, who found a way to turn oil into a flexible, durable solid. If I use the refrigerator in the cafeteria, then I must give credit to mechanical engineers, who manipulate thermodynamics and fluid-flow principles just to keep things cold. And if I eat a frozen meal or drink canned soup, the convenience of my lunch is due to food engineers, who discovered ways to preserve food for unusually long periods of time at extreme temperatures, along with methods for restoring them to something resembling their tasty original forms.

As I said, a lot of engineering happens behind the scenes. We see the results of it every day, but those results are considered normal, so we barely notice them. Engineering involves constant improvements, making something just a little bit better each time. It involves using the right tool for the right job. It involves seeing a problem and fixing it, or making the best of a bad situation. And it involves doing things no one ever thought of, all with the goal of making life better.

Brian Rautio

Boffins, Tech, and RADAR, Oh My!

Our British friends across the pond would most certainly call me a "Boffin." I take an abundance of pride in that, even though the name isn't always glamorous. The precise origin of the term is a bit murky, but it rose to prominence at the beginning of the Second World War. A group of scientists, led by one Robert Watson-Watt, had just finished developing a system of tracking stations called *Chain Home,* which allowed the detection of incoming aircraft and missiles. Today, we would call that system RADAR, and it proved to be invaluable to the war effort. During the Battle of Britain, it gave British pilots the ability to precisely locate incoming attacks and intercept them, saving thousands and thousands of lives.

The heroics and bravery of the pilots and crews were nothing short of extraordinary, and the public commended them accordingly. However, a new set of heroes emerged from this battle, and they weren't all strong and brave. They were far from the front lines, residing in laboratories, wearing labs coats, and conducting experiments. The public welcomed their new heroes but didn't quite know what to call them. Somehow the term "Boffin" arose to adoringly refer to these brilliant backroom heroes—and it's likely that Robert Watson-Watt, by inventing RADAR, was the first.

Over time, however, the term lost prestige; in modern usage, its meaning is far closer to "nerd" than "hero." I believe this happened for several reasons. First, nowadays there are fewer clear examples of technology winning wars and saving lives. We still have great engineers and scientists backing up our armed forces in this time of conflict, but it's necessary to keep much of their work secret to protect us from those who would use such knowledge against us.

Secondly, there is an ever expanding "information barrier" between so-called "Boffins" and the general public. Take the weather report, for example. We can easily pull out our phone and check the weather, perhaps to see if it's going to rain. This is an instinctive use of technology that is a simple extension of our senses; humans have done this for thousands of years simply by looking at the sky. And yet, to actually learn what is really going on when you check the weather report—to understand the technology that allows us to find out if it will rain five days in advance instead of five minutes in advance—is often perceived as an unnecessarily difficult task.

Perhaps scientists and engineers complicate their work so as to appear more impressive, or perhaps there are too few of them trying to relay the information. Regardless of the cause, I feel strongly that the existing "information barrier" is detrimental to both technology and society as a whole. Because of its existence, "Boffins," originally perceived as great drivers of technology and innovation, are now perceived to be lost in a technical "never-never land" of jargon and equations.

This unfortunate perception couldn't be further from the truth, and the consequences go far beyond the meaning of clever nicknames. Without the general public understanding the contributions of scientists and engineers, they are less likely to support and fund the academic and commercial research that drives progress. To witness this, one need look no further than the radical funding cutbacks experienced by NASA, an organization responsible for many of humanity's greatest engineering and scientific achievements. In the 1960s, everyone understood that NASA was trying to put a man on the moon. NASA received 4.4 percent of the federal budget. Today, the layman is largely unaware of the details of NASA activities; consequently, NASA receives 0.6 percent of the federal budget. The average American may be thinking, *Why fund NASA if I don't understand what they're doing?*

Rather than continue my lament, I feel the need to take action. As a lowly graduate student, my say in the politics of the technical world is quite limited. Rather than engage in a futile effort to influence the course of technical fields by such mechanisms, I instead turn to a subtler but nonetheless useful approach. If I can explain a technical concept and its relation to society, and enhance the general public's understanding of one example of technical achievement, then I believe I have helped.

Let us turn our attention back to Robert Watson-Watt's invention of RADAR and how it works. Have you ever shouted in the direction of a barn, a cavern, or a stairwell? You hear an echo back. Sound is a wave of air pressure, and that wave bounces off the barn and comes back to be heard again shortly thereafter. RADAR works the same way, but instead of using sound waves, it uses faster and farther-traveling radio waves, much like an AM/FM radio broadcast station. RADAR sends out a wave, and then listens for echoes to come back from faraway objects like airplanes or raindrops. Then, based on how long it takes for the echo to come back, RADAR can determine the distance to detected objects.

This sounds readily applicable to the weather forecasting example I mentioned earlier, but how can we tell if we should expect a drizzle or a downpour? Fortunately, the density of the falling raindrops will actually determine how "loud" the returning radio wave will be. And that's not all, either! Have you ever heard a race car zoom down a straightaway? Even if the driver isn't accelerating, the pitch of the engine changes. This is called Doppler shift, and it happens with radio waves from RADARs just as it does with sound waves from race cars. Modern weather RADARs use this information to determine how fast rain is moving, not just how dense it is. While this might not sound important in its own right, the application of such knowledge has saved countless lives. When a tornado begins to form, the swirling winds can actually be seen by Doppler RADAR. Meteorologists use this information to predict the time and location of tornadoes at around fifteen minutes before they happen, providing a crucial window for those in danger to find safety.

The use of RADAR for weather prediction is just one example of the widespread benefits of science and engineering. At the time it was being researched, no one had any thoughts, hopes, or intentions of using RADAR to predict weather. Moreover, Robert Watson-Watt had not even been funded to design RADAR in the first place, but rather to build a "death-ray" to shoot down airplanes. As many research projects go, the intended result never materialized. Instead, something even more useful did. There are thousands more examples of the benefits of research innovations trickling out to shape our everyday lives, and we owe much of our standard of living to such accomplishments. Without the understanding of how such technical advances work and come to be, it's far more difficult for society to encourage the growth of new technology.

So it is my hope that by explaining an example of a technical achievement and how it came to exist, I can begin to bridge the "information barrier" mentioned earlier. I believe that the general public's understanding is critical to technical discovery and its associated integration into society. And whatever the connotation may be, I will always be proud to call myself a "Boffin."

Tom Moran

Pointing Toward the Moon: An Engineer's Path

Von Karman Auditorium sits on the edge of the sprawling campus that is home to the Jet Propulsion Laboratory, a NASA facility operated by the California Institute of Technology and best known by its initials, JPL. The auditorium's name honors Theodore Von Karman, a famed aerodynamicist who, during World War II, served as JPL's first director. On an early Tuesday evening, more than forty years ago, every seat in that auditorium was taken and nervous scientists, engineers, and technicians lined its walls. A voice boomed over the public address system, "Beginning retro descent," and the buzz of idle chatter instantly vanished. We all drew in our breath, apprehensive and hopeful.

More than 230,000 miles above Von Karman Auditorium a 3,000-pound spacecraft, Surveyor 7, was nearing the moon. With the exception of the press, everyone inside the building that evening had worked in some way on its mission. Relative to the moon's surface, the spacecraft was speeding downward at about 6,000 miles per hour. In the next few seconds, commands from the Space Flight Operations Center, only steps away across JPL's campus, would activate the onboard retrorockets and then a Vernier system to slow the craft so that it could safely land on the moon's surface. We all knew that the landing was far from a sure thing. Two of the six previous Surveyor crafts had failed. And, unlike prior missions that had been aimed at maria—relatively flat lunar surfaces—Surveyor 7 was headed for the rim of a crater. Its safe landing zone was only one third the size of the previous Surveyor targets. News media reports had been quite clear. The odds were heavily stacked against the spacecraft's survival.

Sitting in that auditorium that evening, waiting, I couldn't help but think of a humid summer night many years earlier, when my mother had extended her arm, her slim fingers pointing into the dark sky. Fireflies danced along the bushes bordering our yard. Far away I could hear the bell of an ice cream wagon. "Can you see him?" she had asked.

I squinted, my focus on a hazy white shape that gave off a soft radiant glow. Dark shadows spread over its surface, giving it a mottled complexion. "He's right there," my mother said, "the man in the moon."

I strained to make some sense of the patterns in the shadows on the moon's surface. Gradually I saw what could be, might be, a bulbous nose and long chin, dark eye sockets, hair brushed up into a pompadour. "I think

I see him," I replied excitedly and described what I took to be a face. "Is that him?"

My mother hugged me. "That's him. That's the man in the moon."

The concept of an actual man in the moon was elusive to my young mind. The figure I saw was vague, undefined, as illusory as the animals and monsters I had been able to discern in the shapes of clouds passing overhead. But what was truly intriguing was the moon itself: a huge glowing body floating above us, its surface unreachable and unknown. What was it? What was it doing there? What was it like out there in the heavens? The moon my mother had pointed toward was wrapped in mystery.

The Surveyor missions were designed to unravel some of that mystery and lay the groundwork for the Apollo projects that would take men to the moon. Out of college only a few years then, I was an engineer at JPL where I studied methods for protecting spacecraft from micrometeorite damage and the effects of heat sterilization cycles on spacecraft materials, designed a calorimeter for determining the heat transfer properties of spacecraft insulation, and was building a test facility for ablative materials that would be needed to protect a spacecraft as it entered the atmosphere of Mars. My contributions to the Surveyor program were miniscule, but all of us at JPL, or as we usually put it, "the Lab," had had some hand in sending that spacecraft on its path toward the moon. The engineers, scientists, technicians, and administrators gathered in Von Karman Auditorium were a team. Together, we had grappled with a gargantuan problem: how to get that spacecraft, with its cargo of complex scientific tools and cameras, safely onto the moon. Everyone had given their best to solve that problem. We all wanted the mission to be successful.

I had started my own mission, to become an engineer, when I was quite young, not very long after my mother had pointed out the man in the moon. I quickly discovered that I loved making things, using the thin open-end wrenches that came with Erector Sets to assemble bridges and windmills, coupling the notched ends of Lincoln Logs to construct cabins and forts, and customizing plastic models of biplanes and jet fighters. I built a balsa wood model rail dragster from plans I found on the pages of Hot Rod magazine and cobbled together a coaster from old wheelbarrow wheels and lumber scraps that made me feel as if I had been shot from a cannon whenever I rode it down the hill beside our house. In the fifth grade I pored over the schematic diagrams for a Heathkit short wave receiver, soldered the connections, hung an antenna wire between the house and a nearby tree, and tuned to transmissions from South America and Eastern Europe.

That same year I took apart and reassembled a one-cylinder lawn mower engine dozens of times, mostly for the thrill of hearing the ear-shattering roar as the engine leaped to life after being reconstituted from the greasy parts strewn over our garage floor. In high school I souped up a 1955 small block Chevy engine to the very edge of the limits that still allowed it to run in stock classes at the local drag strips; I also replaced the engine in a friend's old Jaguar, in exchange for lessons in the art of pocket billiards. When it came time to look at the long list of possible college majors, mechanical engineering was the obvious choice. I had no real idea what a mechanical engineer did, but I imagined it couldn't be much different from what I had already been doing with wrenches, wire cutters and a soldering iron, tweaking things to make them work better.

That summer I went to work at a small Santa Monica factory, doing minor repairs on huge injection molding machines. I also inspected the welds on gleaming, metal-cased lightning arrestors that kept America's Minuteman missiles, hidden deep underground, from being set off during a summer thunderstorm and inadvertently triggering global nuclear catastrophe. Much of it was boring, repetitive work, and the xylene bit into my throat and made me feel dizzy if I stood up too quickly. But I was learning things. A fellow in the machine shop showed me how to mill a few thousandths of an inch off the flat head of a motorcycle engine. The foreman taught me how to read an array of time-based logarithmic charts that recorded the heating cycles of the ovens used to bake on the resistors' coatings. From Floyd, a Kentucky mechanic, I learned how to methodically troubleshoot problems in the production equipment, eliminating suspects one by one until the source of the failure was staring me in the face. "Damn," he'd say, stretching that word out the way they do in southern Appalachia, so it doesn't seem a curse at all, just a state of heightened observation or perplexity. "It's the relief valve. Why didn't you tell me to test it right off? You're the one going to engineering school, ain't ya?"

I was. I had chosen California State Polytechnic College, a small agriculture and engineering school on the edge of the sleepy Central California town of San Luis Obispo, which had been rocked the year before I entered by a plane crash that had killed many of its football players. A sense of tragedy wrapped the school in mourning that freshman year. Cal Poly, as everyone called it, prided itself on a philosophy of learn-by-doing and, among other things, taught us how to fill boxes with punch cards that represented the Fortran programs we had written and prayed would work.

Cal Poly was and remains a good engineering school, and while I was there I learned that engineering came in many forms and shapes. I took classes, shared labs and studied with guys, and the tiniest sprinkling of girls, pursuing the aeronautical, industrial, electrical, electronic, air conditioning and refrigeration, metallurgical, and even agricultural varieties of engineering. It was, I discovered, a world of problem solving that would require creativity, innovation, and design; skills in research and analysis; an understanding of effective techniques for management and project control; and good, clear thinking based on a solid footing of engineering and scientific knowledge. A summer job crunching data and making charts for a scientist convinced me there was more to learn than the practical side stressed at Poly. I went on to earn a master's degree in mechanical engineering, relishing the theoretical aspects of engineering and filling blackboards with equations and calculations that solved fluid flow and heat transfer problems. Graduation took me to JPL, where the Surveyor missions were to be followed by the Mariner and Voyager programs that would probe the far reaches of our solar system. Those missions would be challenges that would require engineering at its best.

Back in Von Karman Auditorium, tension mounted as Surveyor 7 drew closer to the moon. Drawings displayed on closed circuit television screens at the front of the room depicted the spacecraft's journey, as retrorockets attempted to retard the craft's speed when it neared the lunar surface. The voice on the public address system gave us the details. When Surveyor 7 was 36,000 feet above the moon's surface, its speed decreased to 400 miles per hour. The retro sequence appeared to be working; soon the 1,400-pound rocket system would be cast off from the spacecraft and the Vernier engines ignited. Everything began happening very quickly. The next announcement reported that Surveyor 7 was only 500 feet from the moon's surface, traveling at a mere 20 miles per hour. Then 100 feet. Ten feet. Then impact.

The auditorium was silent as seconds ticked by. Had the craft slowed enough? Had it hit at the right angle? Had its three support arms, shock absorbers, and crushable pads been able to cushion the landing? More silence. Finally the voice returned to the PA system. "We have a signal." The presence of a signal meant that Surveyor 7 had landed successfully and was transmitting data back to earth. The auditorium erupted in wild applause and shouts of joy. We had done it.

After I left JPL, I worked for a number of aerospace companies. As I gained experience, I learned a lot of things not covered in engineering school. I designed and built some gadgets and systems that did what they were supposed to and a few others that never quite functioned as I had intended. Along the way I worked with engineers of every sort: researchers, designers, managers, innovators, pragmatists, dreamers, hands-on builders, number crunchers, field guys, by-the-handbook experts, salesmen, quality assurance and test specialists of every caliber. Some were good, some great, some, well...not so good.

Engineering, of course, takes many shapes and forms. More than one and a half million Americans work as engineers today, many of them in fields like environmental, biomedical, and software engineering that were practically unknown when I was in college. It is considered a practical profession, the application of mathematical and scientific principles to solve problems and, ideally, benefit society. Accreditation requirements for academic programs are rigorous, and students at most colleges and universities find engineering studies to be particularly demanding, often causing leisure time and social life to shrink, or even disappear. Graduates who wish to become consultants or take jobs with certain government agencies must take additional examinations to earn the designation "professional engineer." Engineering, whatever the specialty, can be a demanding career path, but it offers great opportunity for those who appreciate being able to apply their knowledge, innovative ideas, and hands-on expertise to projects that make a difference in our lives and our futures. Whether the end products are new communications devices, breakthrough medical test units, state-of-the-art bridges and storm drainage systems, or even exploratory trips to the moon or the far reaches of space, the engineers who contribute will have done something positive for their world. That is something not everyone can say.

Less than an hour after it had landed, Surveyor 7 began telecasting views of the moon's surface that appeared on closed circuit television screens around Von Karman Auditorium. We could see a crater's edge, rocks, and a far horizon. The black and white pictures were clear and sharply focused. It was incredible, seeing close-up images of what had been so vague and mysterious to me as a child, staring upward where my mother's finger had pointed. My role had been tiny but I had been part of the team that had made those photographs possible, and all of us sitting in that auditorium, cheering and clapping, had in our own way been a part of that journey to the moon. At no time before or since have I had a keener appreciation of what engineers can do and the importance of our work.

Robert F. Piwower

Lessons in Language

Incarceration has forced me to postpone my plans of traveling to the continents of Europe and Asia. Six years into a twenty-year sentence for manslaughter, watching Globe Trekker on PBS or flipping through vacation mags in the prison library is the closest I get. But I've learned something about foreign languages, nonetheless.

My travels to Quebec and Mexico taught me that every street sign, television or radio program, menu, and all product packaging provides a lesson in language. While you're simply going about a regular routine in a foreign land, the language teaches itself to you. This form of pedagogy may not be as effective as buying a Rosetta Stone DVD or enrolling in a Finnish 101 course, but it gets the job done. Infants learn to speak a language in a similar way, interacting with the people and world immediately around them. Every environment has its own lessons to teach.

My ideas about what constitutes language have changed greatly in the harsh spaces of a maximum security prison. Body language reveals mood and character more than the spoken word. It's important to observe and express yourself with care. Facial tics, clenched jaw or fists, a cold stare, even a wave of the hand can convey meanings that lead to violence. I've learned the art and science of reading people, how to listen intently even when not being addressed, how to discern silent tones of anger, fear.

Yet even behind thick, thirty-foot high concrete walls and razor-sharp concertina wire, foreign languages are available. Spanish novellas or variety shows on Univision provide daily opportunities to learn juicy phrases such as *Tenga cuidado!* (watch your step) or *buena suerte* (good luck) or *No hay vida sin fatigas* (there's no life without hardships).

For the truly motivated and fortunate enough to receive a call-out to the library—the equivalent of winning the daily lotto numbers—one can check out a beginner's Spanish or French textbook.

Speaking with my friend Max, who grew up in Colombia, has accelerated my understanding. Max is in his mid-fifties and enjoys a calm, friendly disposition. Gray hair and round frame glasses give him a scholarly look. He's been "down" (in prison) over twenty-two years. Young Latino prisoners address him as *"Viejo."*

I often engage him in Spanish while we sit in the dayroom, waiting to go to program or to the yard.

"Buenos dias, Max. Como esta?"

"Muy bien, Bobby. Esta bien?"

"Asi, asi, otro dia en la vecindad."

(So, so, another day in the neighborhood.)

We have acclimated ourselves to the neighborhood of prison. Prison has a language all its own. Correction Officers are referred to as "C.O.s," "hacks," or "police" when they're not present. A prisoner despises the term "inmate," preferring "convict" or "prisoner." A prison sentence is a "bid." Anything modeled into a weapon is a "shank" or "gun." A "bug" or "bug-out" is a crazy or insane person. A bug-out with a shank is a dangerous combination.

The dayroom we sit in is a 25-foot by 20-foot area at the front of two galleries in honor block. Furnished with black vinyl couches, overstuffed chairs, round formica tables, and a large color TV, it's a casual place to converse. The concrete floor is painted a rustic red hue.

About ten people sit waiting for the hall captain to call for honor block yard over the squawk box inside the C.O.'s bubble. Honor block is a small section of the prison reserved for those who have demonstrated a pattern of good behavior during their bid. It accommodates roughly seven percent of the population. Honor block affords us privileges: larger cells, more time out of our cells, unlimited showers, cooking facilities, refrigerators, and a private yard. The rest of the prison population get two showers a week, no access to cookware or refrigerators, and far less freedom of movement from their cramped cells.

Max is speaking to Shabib, a fortyish, balding man from Turkey. I've learned some Turkish and Arabic from him, but nothing of any consequence. I've found that unless I practice a language frequently, I tend to forget it. Shabib speaks in clipped, distorted English, often blurring pronunciations. He often asks me to help him.

"I have a new stragedy to work out," he says to me and Max.

"What's your new tragedy?" I ask.

Max laughs heartily.

Shabib says, "What, I say something wrong?" exchanging glances with us.

"The correct word," I say, "is strat-e-gy. So, what's your new workout plan?"

"Yes, yes, my plan. Thank you very much Bobby. Now I do light weight, many, many reps. No heavy, only light, much reps."

Our conversation is interrupted by two short rings of an alarm bell. A fight has broken out somewhere in the prison. We return to the gallery—a security routine that everyone knows. The rumor mill begins immediately. I hear someone say it's a fight in C-block, while another insists with vehemence that it's in D-block. I think about Seneca's essay, "On Noise," where he speaks about empty vessels and mindless chatter. From our vantage point in front of long windows and bars that border our gallery, I can see C.O.s moving quickly through the corridor toward A-block.

"They don't call A-block Afghanistan for nothin'," Panama says, "Shit's always poppin' off."

Panama is a short Spanish kid (under twenty-five) with spiked hair. He goes by "Panama" because he says he was born there, but he doesn't speak a lick of Spanish. Most of us doubt that he's from Panama. Prisons mirror society's deceits. Prisoners alter their history, pad their exploits, embellish stories, lie outright. We have our own language for this too. We call it freestyling, fronting, being stunters, truth-twister with lip blisters.

Everyone on our gallery is looking out the windows, trying to figure out what gallery on A-block the fight is on. Jorge, a rotund fellow, emerges from his cell. His bleary eyes tell us he just awoke. Bumping into Max in a groggy state he asks, "Que paso?"

"Tonterias!" Max snaps, *"Acuestate!"*

Laughter erupts.

"Yeah man, take yo' ass back to bed," his neighbor says.

A running commentary evolves around the bells breaking our routine.

"People be wilyin, son."

"Problee the po-lease beatin' on someone for nothin'."

"This shit is crazy."

"Another day in the neighborhood," I say.

Everything will be on hold until the "all clear" is given. This could be in as few as twenty minutes for a minor skirmish or as long as all morning in a rare major fight.

"Man, my stragedy is messed up," Shabib says.

Prison language transitions over time. Some terms endure while others fade away. Recently, I heard an antiquated yet accurate word to describe some prisoners. An old-timer told a friend, "That guy Sonny is really 'chateauing' up in honor block." Then he added, "Yeah, he's 'stretching out,' let me tell ya." Both terms mean someone who's relaxing during their bid, more concerned with personal comforts, food, and leisure than anything else.

The flip side of chateauing in honor block is the "box," officially known as special housing unit (SHU). Fighting with a weapon or getting a dirty urine test are the two most common routes to the box. There, nearly all privileges are stripped away, personal property is denied, any belongings confiscated. You spend twenty-three hours a day in a rancid cell, most likely next door to a bug-out. The incident we're waiting on is likely to send someone to the box.

Thirty minutes have passed since the bells tolled. A steady rain begins to fall from dark gray nimbostratus clouds. They nix my plans to work out in the yard. Seagulls cry out noisily while perched like sentinels on the A-block handball court wall. They're angered by the deluge as well.

I return to my cell, gathering clothes to wash and iron. I expect a visit tomorrow, so I select my best items: long sleeve, cotton Nautica button-down shirt, white Hanes tee, Nike socks, and standard issue green pants. The latter provided by the State.

While washing clothes in a five-gallon bucket in a slop sink on the backside of a prison gallery, I learn from the tag on my Nautica shirt how to say, "Machine wash, cold, gentle cycle, tumble dry, warm iron," in French. I can hear the mellifluous sound of a nylon-string acoustic guitar floating from Max's cell. He plays to relax. I imagine being on the Pacific shore of Colombia, watching cobalt blue waves gently blanket the white sand. The ocean is swallowing a burnt orange orb as I sip a mimosa.

A stream of people flowing off the gallery into the dayroom tell me that the "all clear" has been given. Routines begin anew. I can feel the tension and anxiety begin to subside. Pent-up tension will lead to bad things in prison.

Last week, while we were waiting in the humid corridor in two-by-two formation, a C.O. barked to the guy in front of me.

"Who you eyeballin', asshole?"

The guy kept staring, did not flinch. The C.O. stood there for a moment, then, obviously intimidated by the guy's stature, turned away. The line proceeded to the academic building. About thirty minutes later the C.O., accompanied by a sergeant and another C.O., stood outside the prisoner's classroom. From the office I work in I could see them take him out of class into the hallway staircase. Within five seconds I heard the thumping and pounding, before the bells chimed.

After washing and hanging my clothes to dry I return to my cell. I pick up a pen and notebook from my desk. Looking out past the windows and bars I write a Haiku:

Cold Steel Prison Bars
Twenty years to pass behind
Rain falls, Hope must rise.

I return the notebook and pen to their place on my desk. I take my silver and blue Bulova wristwatch off its clear plastic stand. It's a Rolex by prison standards. Miraculously, it slipped through property room scrutiny. According to written directives regulating property, watches are limited to a value of fifty dollars. The watch's instruction pages are written in four languages. I try to read how to set the stopwatch and activate split-time measurement in Korean, German, Chinese, and Norwegian.

If I had been born in Helsinki I would master at least three languages and serve only one-third of my sentence with good behavior. In the U.S., however, English remains the sole standard. Xenophobes view prisoners with the same disdain as immigrants. Learning foreign languages continues to be as eccentric as drinking absinthe or listening to a polonaise.

The following day I prepare early for my visit. On my thin mattress, I neatly lay out the clothes I will wear. My mood is happy, upbeat. A sonata plays quietly from my radio. When we were children, my brother and I would attempt to decipher the Polish that our parents sometimes spoke. They used it to veil their meaning. Our grandfather who was born in Krakow, Poland, had a Polish dictionary that we'd use in our investigation. When our translating hit a wall, we asked our grandfather directly.

"Dziadek (grandfather) what does *spokojnie* mean?"

"It means quiet."

"What about *Sobota*?"

"Saturday."

"How 'bout...."

"Dzieci, spokojnie." (Children, quiet). "Get the dictionary, I'm trying to read the paper."

The visiting room is vastly different from any other part of the prison. Brightly colored murals of Niagara Falls, downtown Buffalo, and lower Manhattan cover the walls. Women and children's voices are a welcome, pleasant change. Tall, clear windows allow natural light to fill the room. Walking through the entrance door after being pat-frisked, I quickly spot my brother Martin, his wife Kristen, and their two-year-old daughter Jenna. After checking in with the C.O. at the front desk, I approach their table with excitement. I embrace all of them individually. Sitting, talking with family during a visit is the closest to freedom a prisoner experiences. It's an escape, briefly, from confinement.

During our visit Martin brings up a phone call he was expecting from me last weekend that I didn't deliver on.

"Oh, we got burned on Saturday and stalled on Sunday," I say.

Kristen looks puzzled, "You got burned?"

"Yeah, that means the C.O. didn't let us out at night to use the phone. And he stalled us on Sunday, didn't let us out at the proper time."

I realize that I've learned a language from a foreign land, developed over years by the denizens of IncarcerNation.

As I hold Jenna on my knee, she smiles, places her tiny hand on my bearded chin and says, "Hi, Unka Bobby."

A lesson in language.

Michael M. Meguid

My First Appendectomy

It was an early evening in August 1969, and the family in Suite 2432 at the Grosvenor House telephoned for a doctor. The previous year, at the age of 24, I had finished a mandatory one-year hospital supervised house job, or internship, after completing four strenuous years as a medical student at University College Hospital Medical School, in Gower Street, London. This topped off my medical education and allowed me to become registered as a medical practitioner by the General Medical Council of the United Kingdom, following which one could become a general practitioner or embark on specialty training.

At that time of the telephone call from Grosvenor House, I was working days as a locum GP while studying for the qualifying exams given by the Royal College of Surgeons, at Lincoln's Inn Fields, in Holborn, London. Evenings and nights, as of 5 p.m. until 8 a.m., I was on call for emergencies at posh London hotels. The symptoms related to me by Mr. Erdman sounded ominous. His 15-year-old son Timothy's stomach ache had worsened over the last four hours. Would I come as soon as possible?

The old Morris station wagon, which belonged to the GP practice and which I used for morning and early afternoon house calls, took me from Camden Town to Hyde Park, in stop-and-go rush-hour traffic, a crawling ribbon of steel, plastic, and rubber in the feeble, late afternoon sunlight. When I arrived, Timothy lay on the bedspread, anxious parents hovering. His eyes apprehensively tracked me as his father ushered me into the suite. The family had driven down from Yorkshire earlier, starting shortly after an early breakfast. They'd planned a night at a West End theater—front row seats for *Hair,* followed by dinner at the Savoy.

"We thought we'd show him some of the finer side of life, now that he's becoming a man," Mrs. Erdman said. "Tomorrow both my men are heading to Savile Row." Mr. Erdman stood by her, wordless.

"Timmy didn't eat his lunch but drank a little Glucose-Aid, felt nauseated then lay in the backseat of the Bentley," she prattled on nervously.

As a medical student, I spent my free evenings in Casualty examining everyone with abdominal pain. I soon became quite good at distinguishing such diseases as pneumonia and cardiac failure that masquerade as abdominal pain from conditions needing urgent surgery, such as perforated stomach ulcers and acute gall bladder disease. In the latter conditions, I learned that severe abdominal pain lasting more than four hours was likely caused by a condition requiring an operation. Although acute appendicitis is the most common inflammatory condition, and common things occur commonly, it remains among the most challenging of diagnoses, primarily because it mimics almost every other inflammatory condition of the abdomen. It further lacks a definitive diagnostic test. Yet, over the course of my thirty-five year career—all the way up to the present X-ray, CAT-scan and even MRI era—I've occasionally delayed operating on patients, confident that their symptoms and signs were not sufficiently typical of appendicitis. And I have been mistaken. Further, I confess I have also operated on patients, convinced they had appendicitis, only to find they did not. In the latter cases, it often turned out that the patient suffered from acute pancreatitis, cocaine withdrawal, or even early pelvic inflammatory disease. Every error in diagnosis led to much soul-searching. I took comfort in knowing that a 5 percent rate of removing normal appendices meant that I was removing 100 percent of the diseased appendices I encountered. An accurate diagnosis is particularly important in young women, where a ruptured appendix spills pus into the pelvis, potentially scarring and blocking the Fallopian tubes and leading to infertility.

In Suite 2432, Mr. Erdman led me to the bathroom, where I washed my hands. My shoes sank into the deep pile carpet, a level of luxury I'd not seen in any hotel within my budget. Timmy's eyes were sunken and his face clammy. He recalled that he'd eaten breakfast—fried eggs, fried tomato, fried black pudding and fried bread—just to please his mum, even though it was tasteless, and he hadn't had his usual morning bowel movement. He said the pain had started in the pit of his stomach, and he pointed to the area about his umbilicus or belly button. He'd thought his nausea was due to car sickness because of his dad's new Bentley, but he'd never suffered from it before.

When his father had made a pit stop in Cambridge, he hadn't felt like getting out of the car to visit his uncle's college. Neither the chapel nor the stained glass windows nor the manicured gardens held any charm for him. He'd refused lunch, feeling certain he'd vomit.

Timothy had a temperature of 100 degrees Fahrenheit. After I examined his throat for tonsillitis then listened to his lungs and heart, he said softly, "The pain is now over here," pointing to the lower right-side of his belly.

I gently started to examine Timothy's abdomen, initially with my warmed hand, constantly talking to him, and asking him about school, his hobbies, and friends, while intently watching his face for signs of pain induced by my examination. Throughout, Mr. Erdman and his wife watched apprehensively some distance from the foot of the bed, occasionally exchanging a quiet word or two.

Using my stethoscope's diaphragm piece in my hand while the ear pieces were just placed on my neck to additionally distract him, I continued to examine Timothy's abdomen, allowing me to further examine more deeply his right lower quadrant, where his appendix lay. Palpating progressively deeper, I saw the pain reflected in Timothy's face, followed by a sharp "Ouch" as I suddenly released the pressure. I said I was sorry and meant it; I didn't add that I knew exactly how he felt.

Back in 1955, when I was roughly Timmy's age, or a little younger, my family lived in Cairo. One night, my parents were invited for dinner, leaving me and my older sister, Gulnar, without a babysitter for the first time. The late afternoon sun was setting, melting away the day's heat. Feeling unwell, I'd taken refuge in the cool Nile breeze on a chaise lounge on our second floor balcony overlooking the river; the Muezzin's call to the faithful for evening prayers wafted across the water from minarets on the opposite bank. My mother phoned often, concerned about having left us unattended. As the evening progressed, I vaguely remember the calls becoming more frequent, no doubt in response to Gulnar's concern about my worsening stomachache. Later that evening my mother appeared on the balcony where I slept in a fetal position. As I awoke, the balcony lights were glaring. I gazed up and saw a strange man standing next to her. He was elderly, balding, with gray-haired temples, and wore a dark suit. He ordered me to roll onto my back. Then he started to prod my bared abdomen.

I later learned that my parents' dinner host was a surgeon. He had accompanied them home to examine me. Proclaiming, "It is definitely appendicitis," he swept me up in his arms and carried me down to the back seat of his Ford. My father sat in front as the surgeon drove to Papaioannou Hospital. My next recollection was of lying on a gurney, being wheeled into a white-tiled, brightly lit operating room, and feeling lightheaded. The pre-med shot hurt and made me dizzy; noises echoed in my ears. The operating room smell had a sterile quality to it, a mixture of borax soap and anesthetics. I was moved from the gurney to the operating table. A black mask was placed over my nose and mouth. It smelled of rubber. I tried to fend it off. Then the overhead operating light started to sway as voices faded out.

When I came to, I smelled and tasted nothing but ether, which made me want to vomit. It was around 2 a.m., and a nurse was sitting at my bedside. Papaioannou Hospital was a private Greek establishment situated on the plains of Giza, at the fringe of Cairo, overlooking the Nile Valley. There I had been delivered by German Lutheran nuns, then circumcised by a Muslim cleric in the spring, when the apricot trees blossomed, at the height of the midmorning call for prayers. At the age of 11, I woke from anesthetized sleep to find, in a saline-filled glass bottle beside my bed, my gangrenous appendix.

The roar of traffic in Park Lane brought me back to the present moment. Standing up and covering Timmy with the bed sheet, I stretched my back. Turning to Timothy's parents, I said, "I suspect that your son has appendicitis. He will need an emergency operation. I recommend Mr. Rodney Maingot, the most eminent abdominal surgeon in London."

There's a reason why surgeons such as Rodney Maingot are called "Mister," not "Doctor" in the UK. The red-and-white-striped barber's pole historically signifies bloody and white bandages, emanating from medieval times when barbers doubled as surgeons. In 1540 England, the Fellowship of Surgeons represented a distinct profession. It then merged with the Company of Barbers to form the Company of Barber-Surgeons, all of them commonly addressed as "Mister." Instead of attaining a medical degree, they served a surgical apprenticeship. When summoned to a home on professional business, they used the tradesman's entrance. But physicians required university training to receive a medical degree, hence the title "Doctor." In 1745, the surgeons formed the Company of Surgeons, eventually becoming the Royal College of Surgeons in 1800. Surgeons, too, received university training before taking a surgical examination and being awarded a diploma but maintained their traditional title of "Mister."

I began at University Hospital Medical School, University College, London, in 1963, and obtained a qualifying degree in 1969, becoming "Doctor Meguid." To embark on a surgical career at that time, I had to pass the qualifying exams of the Royal College of Surgeons, which were held in two parts: a primary examination (anatomy, physiology, and surgical pathology), whose pass rate hovered around 22 percent. After that, I was required to undergo further surgical training via junior- and mid-level clinical posts before sitting for the final practical Fellowship exam of the Royal College of Surgeons to become "Mister." This would be followed by several more years of progressively more senior clinical experience that included the "BTA," or "Been To America," to pursue advanced specialty training and become eligible for a consultancy or professorship, similar to Mr. Maingot's. But back then, when I was a 24-year-old locum GP studying to be a surgeon, I had never actually taken up a scalpel and performed an appendectomy.

By now it was 6 p.m., the height of private surgical consultation hours. I phoned Mr. Maingot's Harley Street office, maneuvering past his protective office manager. Eventually, I was put through to the famous man himself. After briefly introducing myself, I related Timothy's history and the physical findings. Mr. Maingot agreed that the most likely diagnosis was appendicitis. His secretary would make arrangements to have Timothy admitted to St. George's Hospital, nearby at Hyde Park Corner. The secretary would also schedule his case with the operating theater, and Mr. Maingot would meet the patient and his parents around 8 p.m. In the meantime he would order blood tests.

"Would you like to assist me?" Mr. Maingot asked.

Jubilant, I headed to my flat near Regent's Park in the early dark of London's post-rush-hour traffic. I made a cup of tea, grabbed a scone, and pulled Mr. Maingot's well-worn book off the shelf. I started to reread Chapter 52, "The Treatment of Acute Appendicitis," with its step-by-step instructions and accompanying line diagrams of the operation.

I *had* once been on the verge of doing an appendectomy of sorts, some five years previously, during my first year in medical school. Back then, I was a naive 19-year-old. I'd traveled to Hamburg to spend Easter break with my sister Gulnar, her husband, and my 18-month-old niece. As a teacher, Gulnar also had Easter break. She'd invited a colleague, Ingrid, for Good Friday dinner.

In the tiny flat, the two women sat closely together, enveloped in the aroma of fresh coffee and the flickering light of a single candle. I sat nearby, preoccupied with a puzzle of King Tutankhamen's death mask. The women's murmured conversation revolved around the fate of Ingrid's husband. He'd been teaching at the Goethe Institute in Nairobi, Kenya. That morning, Ingrid had received a telegram informing her, regretfully, of her husband's sudden death and telling her when to expect the Lufthansa flight carrying his casket.

There was no information as to what caused the death of this otherwise healthy, thirty-something man, and no autopsy had been performed. Apparently, he'd developed a severe headache while teaching, and minutes later lapsed into a coma, then died. The two women wanted to know what "Herr Doktor" thought.

I moved to sit opposite Ingrid. In the fading light she looked older than my sister, probably in her early thirties, and she seemed incredibly sad. I said I was merely a first-year medical student, coming to the end of my initial year, but the symptoms sounded like a berry aneurism. These small balloon-like outpouchings of blood vessels of the brain are not uncommon in young males. They have the tendency to burst and bleed into the brain. Because of the closed-spaced bony skull, there is no room for leaking blood, which not only causes a wicked headache, but eventually coma and death. It seemed as if Ingrid was not listening to my explanation. I wondered if she was somewhere else, perhaps between Germany and Kenya.

Later, Gulnar read a bedtime story to her daughter, while my brother-in-law opened a bottle of wine and put on an LP of Mendelssohn's haunting violin concerto. Unaccustomed to alcohol, I sipped the wine. Ingrid drank freely, nibbling on crackers and artichoke cheese dip, and mulled over the situation with my brother-in-law. Finally, the lights were dimmed, additional candles lit, and dinner was served. My brother-in-law opened a second bottle of wine. The conversation ranged along a spectrum of political topics but invariably reverted to the incomprehensible death of Ingrid's husband.

Toward the end of dinner Ingrid left the table and went into the bathroom. After a while, we heard sobbing. In awkward silence, we exchanged glances. Gulnar rose and knocked on the bathroom door. "Ingrid... are you all right? Open the door." Gulnar slipped in. My brother-in-law and I cleared the table. The candles were extinguished, the LP stopped playing, and we started the washing-up.

Gulnar eventually joined us. "Ingrid is frightened of going home and being alone. I told her she could stay here." Turning to me, Gulnar continued, "Would you mind if she shared the sofa-bed with you?"

"It's pretty narrow... I mean, we could manage if we lay head-to-feet. Don't you have a spare mattress? I don't mind sleeping on the floor."

Gulnar shook her head, "It's only for tonight."

She and her husband went to bed. The living room lights were turned off. I slipped into my PJs and crawled under the duvet. There was barely enough room for one. I maneuvered onto my left side, my back against the wall. It was dark, although the curtains had not been drawn. My eyes adjusted. I saw Ingrid come toward me wearing a pale nightie. She slipped under the duvet; before I could object, she whispered, "My feet always smell terribly." A few millimeters separated us and I smelled alcohol mixed with toothpaste on her breath. She lay on her back, I on my side, gradually sensing her body heat creeping across the narrow divide. I found the prolonged silence reassuring, thinking it meant she was falling asleep. I too closed my eyes.

Suddenly she whispered, "Do you say a prayer at night?" In the dark, her voice sounded like that of a much younger woman, and certainly not one who had just been widowed.

"No. My mother used to say it for me."

"She did?"

"Yeah. She'd say, 'Thank God he's in bed.' "

Ingrid chuckled. Then, as if fearing what terrors and nightmares sleep might bring, she continued, "Have you ever done an operation?"

Did the dissection of Fred, my cadaver, count?

She shifted slightly, turning toward me, "Tell me of an operation you'd like to do."

I replied, "An appendectomy."

"Tell me about it," she asked, adding, "please."

"The appendix is like a worm. It's the underdeveloped end of the large bowel. Where it is attached to the large bowel is its base, which forms the landmark on the skin, known as McBurney's point," I whispered. "It lies on the skin, at the junction of the outer third with the inner two-thirds of an imaginary line joining the most prominent boney point of the hip bone and the belly button. That's usually the site of greatest tenderness in appendicitis." I paused. I couldn't hear her breathing.

"Are you asleep?" I whispered.

She nudged me with her ice-cold foot. I jumped. She murmured, "No, of course not. What do you mean by Mc... Mc-whatever point? Where exactly is that?"

"Shall I show you?"

"Yes," she said, shifting her weight onto her back, and swiftly hitching up her nightie. She took my right hand and placed it in the middle of her tummy. "OK, start again."

Her skin was warm and supple. Her belly flat, smooth and soft. It rose and fell with each breath. Where she had placed my hand, the tip of my little finger grazed her pubic hair. It felt coarse and rough, like steel wool. Using my index finger, I traced a line on her skin from her umbilicus to her anterior superior iliac crest, the most prominent bony protrusion of her iliac crest on the rim of her pelvic bone on the right side of her abdomen. Then I trisected it and indicated where her McBurney's point was, by pressing firmly to emphasize my point.

"Ouch, you're hurting me."

"Sorry." And, lifting my finger, I proceeded to make a horizontal skin incision with my finger nail, emphasizing that McBurney's point should be at about its mid-point.

"Oh, I see now," she said, but her breathing had become shallow and irregular. I then calmly described a grid-iron incision, whereby the surgeon bluntly splits the underlying three muscle layers in the direction of their muscle fibers, each layer running at a 90-degree angle to the next. As I wondered how to demonstrate this, she suddenly threw back the duvet, swung her legs over the edge of the narrow bed, stood up, whipped off her nightgown, slipped off her wedding ring, and then slid back into bed.

It was a night of firsts: the first time I was seduced by an older woman; the first time I witnessed an all-encompassing, shuddering orgasm that totally engulfed a woman and frightened the heck out of me; the first time I came uncontrollably in a welter of emotions. And the only time I ever aborted an appendectomy.

In London on another night of firsts a few years later, I reread Mr. Maingot's chapter, then left for St. George's Hospital. I met the great man himself in the surgeon's changing room. He was of medium height, with the paunch of prosperity, and spoke softly but authoritatively. He was probably in his early fifties. He thanked me for the referral and said he'd already met the Erdmans and examined Timothy. The boy's history and the physical findings were classic. We changed into green operating room shirt, pants, and shoe covers, and donned our caps.

As I stood in front of the scrub sink, I glanced through the glass window and observed that Timothy was already anesthetized on the operating table. Fluids were running through an intravenous drip into his veins, rehydrating him. They also filled his "tank," surgical-speak for the vast network of blood vessels now dilated by the inhaled anesthetic. The anesthetic's effects act as a narcotic to dull pain, as a relaxant of his abdominal muscles and the muscle fibers surrounding his vascular tree, dropping his blood pressure and reducing operative field bleeding. The anesthetist had given him an intravenous push of antibiotics to help his natural immune system kill off the bacteria infecting his appendix.

Not all patients are fortunate enough to be cared for in a top-notch hospital by a preeminent professor of surgery. A few months after I developed appendicitis in 1955, my sister too developed pain in her right side. Gulnar was fourteen, and my family was camping on the isolated coast of the Mediterranean near Balteem, a small Nile delta village, to escape Cairo's oppressive August heat and humidity. The scene: waves rolling onto a wide, yellow, sandy beach; huge army surplus tents erected along the beach and cooled by the constant breeze; a kitchen tent manned by university cooks; and a large mess tent with a flag pole, where each morning the green Egyptian flag was raised and communal information shared with the band of faculty and their families. Behind each family's tent, at some distance, was a long drop, protected for privacy by a screen of woven palm leaves. And about 50 yards beyond that were towering sand dunes, which hummed a precise C major chord as the breeze rose off them into a cloudless blue sky. On the other side of the dunes sprawled acres of vineyards and fig trees. There were no newspapers or radios. Only sun, sea, and sand. There was no electricity. Only communal life between sunrise and sunset, then campfires, storytelling, and the vastness of the Milky Way. The sole intrusion was the dawn and dusk coast guard camel patrol, materializing from one horizon and disappearing along the empty seashore into infinity.

Gulnar lay for two days in her camp bed. Finally, grasping the seriousness of the situation, the adults agonized over their options. Could she survive the fourteen-hour drive across rutted delta dirt roads and then onto single traffic asphalt roads into Cairo without pain medications or antibiotics? It was too risky. The next morning, my parents and Gulnar accompanied the morning camel patrol to the nearest delta clinic.

That afternoon, she was given sleeping pills and sedatives, and then held down on an operating table while local anesthesia was injected into the skin over McBurney's point. Then a newly minted young doctor, by Allah's will, operated on her. A screaming, terrified youngster clutched her mother's hand, her perceptions distorted by drugs. She felt the pain of the scalpel and the stretching of the abdominal muscles. She saw the reflections of the gloved surgeon's hands, the instruments that invaded her body, her exposed guts in the chrome reflector of the overhead operating room light. Her appendix lay behind her large bowel. It was smelly and gangrenous but intact. My parents had made the right decision: she would never have survived the longer ride to a hospital in Rosetta, Damietta, or Tanta, not to mention Cairo. Five days later, they brought her back with a surgical wound deliberately left open in order to heal from inside out and to minimize the chance of infection.

Unlike Gulnar, Timothy would have the luxury of general anesthesia. The scrub nurse at St. George's Hospital washed his lower abdomen, painted it with an antiseptic, and draped it off with sterile green towels, covering the rest of his body with sterile sheets. Mr. Maingot and I stood at the sink lathering up, now wearing masks. Suddenly he asked, "Would you like to take out the appendix?"

Holding the scalpel like the bow of a violin, I proceeded to make a 3-4 inch McBurney's skin incision. Using two retractors, Mr. Maingot retracted the skin and subcutaneous fat while simultaneously blotting the bleeders. Next, I incised the external oblique muscle, starting a gridiron incision. Mr. Maingot moved the retractors deeper, carefully stretching the dark red muscle fibers apart, widening the incision. As the deeper layers were incised, the retractors followed, placed deeper and stretching the tissues farther apart, like well-rehearsed dancers complementing each other's steps. We did not speak. I merely followed my mental map from Chapter 52, guided by the master surgeon.

As the whitish-gray glistening peritoneum was cut open, I stared at the abdominal contents, spellbound by the body's beauty...just a tad too long. I was nudged into action by the scrub nurse, who handed me gauze lap-pads to wall off the coils of the writhing pink and healthy looking small bowel, isolating the glistening beige colored caecum. I traced its dark brown cords of taenia coli muscles of the large bowel, to the point of confluence at the base of the caecum, and onto the appendix. Touching the tissues added to my sensory elation.

The scrub nurse nudged me out of my reverie by slapping a Babcock clamp into my palm. It was designed to encircle the appendix without crushing it, so as to serve as a means to hold it. I applied it about the appendix onto the mesoappendix—the curtain-like fold of fatty tissue containing the appendix's blood supply—avoiding injury to the acutely inflamed appendix. It was about five centimeters long. Its encapsulating tiny blood vessels were inflamed, the tissue infected, its necrotic tip looked bluish-green and smelling like ripe Gorgonzola. Even so, it was a thing of beauty. I applied a second Babcock clamp. Tugging slightly on both, I cautiously eased the appendix to the center of the operative field. I started to free it from its tethered mesoappendix by applying serial hemostat clamps across the mesoappendix.

"Would you know the eponym associated with the mesoappendix?" Mr. Maingot asked, breaking my concentration.

"No, sir."

"Does the name Frederick Treves ring a bell?"

"Ah, yes. Didn't he do an appendectomy on King Edward VII?"

"Well, not quite, but you are dissecting in what is called the ileocaecal fold, to which his name is attached. You may want to know this, just in case you're asked about this in your upcoming oral examination."

In May 1901, Frederick Treves, the sergeant surgeon to the Royal Household, was summoned to see the sixty-one-year-old King Edward VII shortly after his accession, because he had a two-week history of abdominal pain and nausea. He had no appetite, was feverish, and looked haggard from sleeplessness due to the increasingly intense pain over the past ten days.

The king feared surgery. He had reason to because at that time any major abdominal operation was a high-risk proposition with up to a 70 percent chance of death from infection or shock. In addition, an appendectomy was not yet a commonly performed procedure; the first-ever successful one had been done only sixteen years previously, on a twenty-two-year old, otherwise healthy woman. By the time Timothy underwent the same operation, antisepsis, the infection reducing techniques, effective anesthesia, cardiac monitoring, intravenous hydration, blood transfusion and antibiotics had been developed and were available for routine intraoperative patient care, reducing the odds of dying from appendicitis to less than one in ten thousand.

First, Mr. Treves needed to establish what was wrong with the king, whose coronation was two weeks hence. Though groaning with pain, King Edward ignored Mr. Treves's presence in his bedchamber. Per protocol, royalty had to speak first before being addressed. Mr. Treves paced the room, frustrated, itching to find out what ailed his monarch, who continued to ignore him, yet groaned with pain. It occurred to Mr. Treves that if he were to accidentally nudge the bed, the king would curse him, giving Treves the opening to speak. So it happened. Eventually, Mr. Treves diagnosed appendicitis, but the fearful king refused the operation. Treves is said to have remarked, as he walked out, "Instead of a Coronation, there will be a Royal Funeral." The king reluctantly consented to the operation and was moved to St. George's Hospital.

Recruiting Lord Lister from University College Hospital, who assisted by administering rudimentary anesthesia and ensuring an antiseptic operating environment with his carbolic acid, Mr. Treves prepared to operate. However, at the crucial moment when he was to make the McBurney's incision into his Royal Majesty's abdomen, Mr. Treves fainted. His humble house officer made the incision instead, drained an abscess because the appendix had burst, and performed an appendectomy. The next day, King Edward sat up in bed, smoking a cigar. He made a remarkably fast recovery; the press hailed Mr. Treves as a bold and skillful surgeon. The house officer became a mere historic footnote, but the appendectomy entered the medical mainstream, saving countless lives. The coronation took place as planned, and, in January 1902, Mr. Frederick Treves was knighted.

At St. George's Hospital, more than half a century later, I returned to the operation at hand. I was about to use Metzenbaum scissors to sever the tissue of the Treves ileocaecal mesoappendix fold below the serial hemostat clamps to liberate the appendix from its surrounding tissue attachments, when Mr. Maingot interceded.

"Give him a scalpel," he said to the scrub nurse. And to me: "You don't cut your steak with scissors, do you? Always use the knife…you're a surgeon." And so I have since always used a scalpel and, furthermore, I have taught generations of young surgeons in training with me: Use a knife! Use a knife! Use a knife!

I divided the tissue, thereby completely freeing up the appendix. The operation proceeded in silence save for the rhythmic beeping of the cardiac monitor. I then tied off the proximal cut margins of the mesoappendix with thin silk ligatures while Mr. Maingot released each clamp. The nurse placed in my hand a needle holder loaded with a black silk suture swedged onto a needle. I used it to place a purse-string suture in the caecum surrounding the appendix, and returned the needle holder with the needle in its jaws to the nurse.

Every choreographed move was designed to avoid an inadvertent stab or cut to a team member, thereby preventing the risk of transmitting hepatitis or other diseases. Keeping my vision focused on the structures, I merely held out my right hand and the scrub placed a knife into it. I cut between two hemostat clamps applied slightly apart at the base of the appendix, and excised it, handing the appendix off to her. Mr. Maingot grunted his approval. Using the electric-Bovie he coagulated the stump. Coagulation by heat to stop blood loss from a wound was introduced by the barber-surgeons on the Napoleonic battlefield. They were the first to apply hot pitch onto open wounds, which prevented death from exsanguination. The effects of Bovieing tissue bleeders leaves broiled, charcoal-looking tissue and rising white smoke smelling of burnt meat. This too is sucked up using the sump sucker to prevent it getting into one's clothes or worse, one's hair, including one's nasal hairs.

Using a forceps, Mr. Maingot dunked the stump into the base of the caecum as I snugged tight the purse-string and tied it off. I removed the lap-pads in the wound. The circulating nurse started to count them as well as the number of needles used to ensure none were left in the abdomen. But before I started to close the wound, Mr. Maingot placed his gloved hand over it, looked at me and said, "Remember you must see the caecum. Every so often," he continued, "only half of the appendix is unwittingly removed, because the confluence of the appendix base to the caecum is not visualized. And yet when the patient returns, several days, weeks or even months later with the classical symptoms of appendicitis, the diagnosis is frequently not considered, because of the patient's past history of an apparent appendectomy. Alas, the unsuspecting surgeon is blindsided by the telltale presence of a McBurney's scar. The consequences can be death from generalized sepsis caused by the infected hemi-appendix. But I am sure you won't make that mistake."

The anesthetist stared at us over the drape, as if to signal that we were wasting his time, so I proceeded to close the peritoneum. After I tied off the final stitch, Mr. Maingot indicated to the scrub by merely raising his right eyebrow that he wanted to irrigate the wound between each layer. She provided warm sterile saline in a small basin, which he poured into the wound. Bits of white fat and tissue debris floated to the surface. I sucked out the irrigation fluid and debris using a sump sucker. Mr. Maingot then sponged the wound, again using lap-pads; he was averse to using the traditionally provided 3x3 gauze sponges to avoid the unforgivable mistake of accidentally overlooking one inside the patient. I made another mental note: no 3x3s! A needle holder with a silk suture was placed in my hand, and Mr. Maingot whispered, "interrupted sutures," indicating that he wanted each layer of the gridiron incision to be closed with noncontinuous sutures. As I did this, Mr. Maingot cut on top of each knot, thus moving the operation along rapidly until I loosely closed the skin.

His anesthetic reduced, Timothy began to wake up. The anesthetist recorded wound closure time as 9:16 p.m., blood loss as minimal, and a correct sponge count. Mr. Maingot applied a dry sterile dressing to the skin incision, writing on it the date and time, and then proclaimed, "You did that with the alacrity of uprooting a turnip."

In the euphoria of my first appendectomy, I forgot to bill Mr. Erdman for the hotel visit and for an assistant's fee. No doubt, Mr. Maingot eventually collected a handsome fee for my first private patient. A few weeks later, a blue envelope floated through my mail-drop. "Dear Dr. Meguid," began the letter, "Just a note to say that I am very pleased Timothy Erdman has now settled down. Many thanks for asking me to see this case." Signed R. Maingot.

During the last week of June 1970, it rained steadily in London. I spent a grueling two days in the Russell Square examination hall, answering written, then oral questions. When I finished, I earned the right to be addressed not merely as "Dr. Meguid" but as "Mr. Meguid."

Tina Post

Fight and Flight: The Near Room

> *No other subject is, for the writer, so intensely personal as boxing. To write about boxing is to write about oneself—however elliptically, and unintentionally. And to write about boxing is to be forced to contemplate not only boxing, but the perimeters of civilization—what it is, or should be, to be "human."*
>
> —Joyce Carol Oates, *On Boxing*

I.

I did not see the airplanes hit the towers, although, like everyone, I can summon the newsreel with all the force of personal experience. And, though I will never shake the newspaper photograph of a jet engine on top of our crumpled street sign, I didn't actually see that either, for when we finally left our building, we went the other way—toward City Hall Park, toward sunlight and air.

I did see plenty of things that morning, but when it comes to my getting on a plane, I don't think that what I saw made much difference. I didn't like flying before, although it's possible that now I like it even less. There is, of course, the remote but real possibility of death. There are also the myriad small certainties: the white-knuckled moments of turbulence, the short-lived but stabbing pain in your ears—your body's ungentle reminder that what you are doing violates all nature and reason.

Some places you want to go, flying is the only way to get there.

II.

On September 25, 1962, Floyd Patterson and Sonny Liston met for the heavyweight championship of the world. The two men, in some ways, had a great deal in common. Both had been raised in large families in abject poverty and, by early adolescence, had gotten into trouble with the law. Both found a measure of redemption in the ring. But there the similarities ended.

Patterson, the reigning champion, was generally believed to be the nicest guy, and the least likely champion ever to set foot in the ring. He was small for a heavyweight. He was also gentle, considerate, and willing to speak about his occasionally overwhelming fears. Liston, on the other hand, was imposing in body, uneasy in spirit, and menacing in his carriage. Worse, for those in the boxing world, Liston, unlike Patterson, was deeply connected to, which is to say, owned by, the Mob—and by this point that was not very secret at all.

The two men seemed unequally matched, and no one anticipated a great title fight. Yet *Ebony* magazine's coverage of the bout says the $5-million draw, which included closed-circuit TV deals as well as earnings at the gate, bested the record, set in 1927, for the sport's largest take.

Never before in professional boxing had a fight between two black men been as lucrative as a fight between two white men or a fight between a black man and a white one. But something about the Patterson–Liston pairing compelled America to watch. Even President Kennedy weighed in, reportedly telling Floyd Patterson upon summoning him to the White House, "You've *got* to beat this guy."

What changed was not the talent or independence or showmanship or gameness of black fighters. Insofar as I can tell, America simply decided, seemingly for the first time, that it was invested in—and wanted to see staged—a battle between opposing versions of blackness.

• • •

Patterson and Liston fell quite neatly into America's classic "good Negro/bad Negro" opposition, and that is exactly what the press, for the most part, played up. In fairness, I don't think it was a contrivance, as "bad Negro" press was at other points in pugilistic history—most notably in the cynical, and lucrative, promotion of the Jack Johnson–Jim Jeffries fight. Most members of the press genuinely felt Floyd Patterson to be a good person and a good ambassador for the sport and for his race. Sonny Liston cut an ominous figure, and with good reason. Although I have a soft spot for Liston as a historical and sporting figure, his crimes, which were alleged to include assault and rape, seem often, if not always, to have been real.

Still, the press surrounding the fight doesn't, on its own, explain why the general public was suddenly interested in a "good vs. evil" contest between blacks when scores of other such matches had gone relatively unnoticed—including some far better pairings from a sporting point of view. I suspect it has something to do with the atmosphere of the early 1960s, when so many of America's racial structures were coming apart. It was suddenly possible that black men would become an actual *force* in American life.

Maybe at this point in our history, we needed to see forbearance and anger do battle, and to hope for the good to triumph, or to face the reality that the bad could instead. And, although everyone suspected Sonny Liston would win, hardly anybody—black or white—was rooting for him.

Sonny Liston demolished Floyd Patterson in two minutes and six seconds. It was the third-fastest knockout ever in a heavyweight title fight.

• • •

Oddly—fabulously—a men's magazine called *Nugget* sent James Baldwin to cover the match. To call Baldwin an unlikely fight reporter is to put it mildly. Aside from the obvious stereotypes associated with his sexuality and bookishness, Baldwin was, in his own words, "not an *aficionado* of the ring."

Here's a quote that seems illustrative of how *not* a fight reporter Baldwin was: "...no one agrees with me on this," he begins, "but, at one moment, when Floyd lunged for Liston's belly—looking, it must be said, like an amateur, wildly flailing—it seemed to me that some unbearable tension in him broke, that he lost his head. And, in fact, I nearly screamed, 'Keep your head, baby!' but it was really too late."

I have a good deal less stomach than your average boxing fan, and even I would never yell "Keep your head, baby!" Still, sending Baldwin to cover the match was a stroke of genius on the part of *Nugget*'s editor. Few writers were better equipped than Baldwin to understand the social complexities that underlay the fighters' psychologies or methodologies in the ring. Indeed, Baldwin began his *Nugget* piece with the admission, "I know nothing whatever about the Sweet Science or the Cruel Profession or the Poor Boy's Game. But I know a lot about pride, the poor boy's pride, since that's my story and will, in some way, probably, be my end."

I trust Baldwin to relate to me the truth of a sport he does not know well, because I trust him so implicitly with the truth that leads up to the first punch, and the last. I trust him to understand the ring and the fighters, for they are, in some way, nothing more or less than a distilled version of America and Americans. And here is what he had to say about the battle, translated into his eloquent prose style: "I felt terribly ambivalent, as many

Negroes do these days, since we are all trying to discover, in one way or another, which attitude, in our terrible American dilemma, is the more effective: the disciplined sweetness of Floyd, or the outspoken intransigence of Liston."

III.

Sonny Liston's life was overfull of heartbreaking, apocryphal tales. For example: upon being paroled from prison, a friend presented Liston, who'd been hungry for most of his life, with a celebratory chicken dinner. Sonny only stared at it before confessing he didn't know how to eat a chicken. Liston's age was unknown, because, he explained, the year of his birth had been recorded on a tree that someone then cut down. Throughout his adulthood, his back remained welted with scars that he accounted for by saying, simply, "I had bad dealins' with my father." In a life of such sadness, the story of Liston's homecoming as the newly crowned heavyweight champ might be the most awful of all, for, if his friend the sportswriter Jack McKinney is to be believed, it was the moment at which a door finally shut on—or in—the most powerful man in the ring.

The public's poor perception of Sonny consistently hurt the fighter, though few people took notice. Worse, he seems to have been compelled to reinforce the menacing impression himself, as though, having survived so many years on this persona, he was unable ever to put it down. McKinney, a white man and one of the few writers to become a friend to Liston, wrote in *Sports Illustrated* before the Patterson bout: "There is every evidence that Sonny Liston is operating under a self-imposed rule: that it is a confession of weakness to show his nice side to anyone outside the small circle of people who already know him. He seems hurt and bewildered by the wide publicity given to his police record. He seems to say to the world, O.K., you've got me typed as the bad guy, and I'll let you have it that way, and when I do anything nice at all, you'll never find out about it. Yet he does do, spontaneously, some kind and generous things."

In addition to those kind and generous acts—spotted easily by the few reporters who bothered to look—occasional pleas to the press slipped out of Sonny in spite of himself. "If I win the fight," he said, "you'll be able to see there's good and bad in everybody. Like the way things stand now, everybody thinks there's only bad in me."

When Sonny *did* win the fight, he sincerely believed that he had earned for himself a second chance. While that hope may strike us as naïve, it was a naïveté that was perfectly in line with the age. The era of Kennedy's presidency was associated with a new American liberalism that professed to believe in reform, even if its own record was less than perfect. Kennedy had developed a reputation for freeing blacks from jail, and in summoning Floyd Patterson to the White House, he elevated a black man who had served time in the Justice system—although Floyd was fortunate enough to have been sent, as a youth, to the Wiltwyck School for Boys, a bucolic Upstate New York reform school whose board was headed by Eleanor Roosevelt.

Liston received far less tender treatment from the St. Louis police department and the Missouri state prison system, but he nevertheless considered himself to be willing and able to live the example of a champion. But of course, it wasn't only up to him.

On the plane home to Philadelphia, where both men were living at the time of the title fight, Sonny practiced on McKinney all that he would say to the fans. "I want to reach my people," Sonny said while they were in the air. "I want to reach them and tell them, 'You don't have to worry about me disgracin' you. You won't have to worry about me stoppin' your progress.' [...] I know it was in the papers that the better class of colored people were hopin' I'd lose, even prayin' I'd lose, because they was afraid I wouldn't know how to act."

"I remember one thing so clear about listening to Joe Louis fight on the radio when I was a kid," he continued. "I never remember a fight the announcer didn't say about Louis, 'A great fighter and a credit to his race.' Remember? That used to make me feel real proud inside.... I want to go to a lot of places—like orphan homes and reform schools. I'll be able to say, 'Kid, I know it's tough for you and it might get even tougher. But don't give up on the world. Good things can happen if you let them.' "

I find this image so moving—the toughest man in the world, suspended in the air above everyone and everything else, floating so buoyantly on his own hopes, every bit as fragile as any man who, for any length of time, finds himself untethered in the frigid, unbreathable heavens.

McKinney, who knew very well what awaited Liston on the ground, was frustrated to the point of tears.

Finally, the plane touched down in Philly. As he approached the door and stairway, Sonny straightened his tie and fedora, preparing himself to emerge, forever changed, as the new world's heavyweight champ. McKinney watched Sonny as his eyes swept the scene. Only a few airline workers, reporters, photographers, and P.R. men were there. Philadelphia mayor James H.J. Tate had determined to freeze Liston out.

"He was extremely intelligent," McKinney later said, "and he understood immediately what it meant." Sonny's Adam's apple moved, and a silent shudder went through him.

"What happened in Philadelphia that day was a turning point in his life," remembered McKinney. "He was still the bad guy. He was the personification of evil. And that's the way it was going to remain. He was devastated. I knew from that point on that the world would never get to know the Sonny that I knew."

IV.

By third grade, gym class is, for me, its own special torture. I am the kind of kid whose head seems to magnetically draw poorly aimed missiles. I'm awkward and my glasses are thick. Compounding all this, I am small for my age, tiny in fact, the kind of smallness that others feel compelled to interact with—to slide encircled fingers up my arm, to try, unbidden, to pick me up. This makes me feel like an object of curiosity, although it will become worse, in a few years, when nobody wants to touch me at all. My discomfort is worst in gym class, where interactions are largely unmonitored.

On the sidelines on this particular day, we are discussing hair. As one of two non-whites in my school, it is a given that my hair is not good. This fact has been confirmed by my mother, who has forbidden me from taking my hair down, because to do so, in her words, makes me look like a witch. Today, we are discussing hair color. Blond hair is best, followed by dirty blond, followed by light brown, followed by red. The implication, though no one bothers to go this far, is that dark brown is next, followed by black. Black, obviously, is no good. I casually offer my relief that my hair is dark brown.

"No," the girl next to me offers. "Your hair is black." She, of course, is blond.

"It's not," I counter. "My hair is brown."

"It's black," she says again. "All black people have black hair."

Technically, I'm half black, although even this is confusing, as my mother has told me she is not black—she is, she asserts forcefully at any given opportunity, Hispanic. And while I know she means it, and while I would never dare to question it out loud, there are two main problems with this. First, Hispanic does me no good. From my Dominican cousins, I have some dim notion of what Hispanic means—enough to know it entails speaking Spanish and going to Catholic school and eating chicken and beans and about a million other things I don't do. This is not, in other words, a defensible position. But secondly, and more damningly, it seems perfectly clear to everyone who is not my mother that she is, in fact, black.

Black, obviously, is no good.

"I am not black," I say feebly.

"Your mom's black," the girl says, "I've seen her."

Instantly, I know I've chosen the wrong stance, although what the right one might have been, I have no idea.

V.

By the time of the first Liston fight, Floyd Patterson was acting as his own manager. The press corps was not accustomed to dealing with a fighter so directly, and, Baldwin reported, the fact that they had to in this case elicited a great deal of grumbling. "I think that part of the resentment he arouses," wrote Baldwin, "is due to the fact that he brings to what is thought of—quite erroneously—as a simple activity a terrible note of complexity. This is his personal style . . . and my own guess is that he is still relentlessly, painfully shy—he lives gallantly with his scars, but not all of them have healed—and while he has found a way to master this, he has found no way to hide it."

Floyd's former manager, Cus D'Amato, stayed on as a corner man despite feeling adamant that Floyd should not face Sonny Liston.

D'Amato, who suffered from extreme paranoia, cut an odd figure even in a sporting world full of exceedingly strange men. He also developed what may have been the most comprehensive training philosophy in the sport at the time—perhaps even to this day. D'Amato required a boxer to acknowledge his fears. "A boy comes to me and tells me he's not afraid," D'Amato would say, "if I believed him I'd say he's a liar or there's something wrong with him. I'd send him to a doctor to find out what the hell's the matter with him, because this is not a normal reaction. The fighter that's gone into the ring and hasn't experienced fear is either a liar or a psychopath."

Patterson thrived under this philosophy, for he was, perhaps more than anything else, a man who was intimately acquainted with fear.

As a child, Floyd was haunted by profound embarrassment and shame. From a very early age he believed himself to be stupid and burdensome. He had nightmares and sleepwalked. Avoiding school, he spent days in movie houses or yo-yoing the Eighth Avenue subway line, riding its length back and forth, over and over. By nine, he would jump off the subway platform at the High Street station and walk down the track to a little, dark, hole-in-the-wall room where track workers kept their tools. He'd lock himself in, spread newspapers on the floor, and go to sleep feeling hidden and safe.

He told his mother he didn't like the boy—himself at age two—in a family picture taken at the Bronx Zoo. She came home from work one night to find he'd scratched a line of x's over his image—one over his thighs, one over his chest, one over his face.

He rarely made eye contact, rarely smiled, never laughed.

Like many kids in his Bedford-Stuyvesant neighborhood, Floyd stole little things—never for himself, but for his family. He persisted in this though his mother told him it was wrong. He felt as though he was making some contribution to his family, and that they needed it. Picked up repeatedly for truancy and theft, Floyd found himself in front of a judge who declared that the boy was going from bad to worse. "The twig is bent early," his mother said. When the judge sent Floyd to Wiltwyck, she was overjoyed.

At the school, Floyd made huge strides in the transformation that continued at P.S. 614, and, later, in the boxing ring. He began to smile, to laugh, to look others in the eye, to make friends, to risk a wrong answer and, in so doing, to learn.

Floyd credited a range of factors in this success, including individual teachers, therapists, and friends who helped, in their own ways, to ameliorate his profound sense of inferiority. But he also singled out Wiltwyck's egalitarian philosophy, saying it provided the atmosphere that made such a transformation possible.

"For the first time in my life," he wrote in his 1962 autobiography *Victory Over Myself,* "perhaps the only time in my life, it seemed color didn't make any difference. In fact, that's what helped to bring me out of the shell in which I had been living and what helped me to make friends finally. I had always wanted to be friends with somebody, but I never knew how. Here, there was no difference. We dressed the same, did the same, ate the same."

His experience at Wiltwyck turned Floyd into a race man, albeit a quiet one. When his wife was refused an appointment with a Long Island masseuse, he sued. He bought a house in a white neighborhood in Yonkers, although, when his neighbors made his life miserable, he moved out. He was an articulate supporter of civil rights, and, together with Jackie Robinson, made a well-publicized visit to the bombed home of a pastor in Birmingham, Alabama. He remained a vocal and loyal supporter of the liberal establishments that he felt saved him, Wiltwyck and P.S. 614, one of New York City's "schools of opportunity."

When a young white reporter asked Sonny Liston why he wasn't fighting for civil rights in the South, his response was, "I ain't got no dog-proof ass."

• • •

Floyd was, then, a natural heir of Joe Louis—quiet, dignified, and accommodating. Cassius Clay, on the other hand, had yet to become Muhammad Ali. Louis and Clay were both ringside for the September 25 fight.

One writer has speculated that—excepting only Jack Johnson, whose heavyweight championship inspired America's quest for the "Great White Hope"—no fighter ever faced a more hostile crowd than Liston did that day. Yet, curiously, it was Patterson who suffered the greater disadvantage.

As footage shows, from the moment the bell rings, Liston is solidly in control. Patterson never hits his stride, and seems to spend the duration of the fight waiting to get hit. He bounces, ducks, and straightens, seemingly with no real strategy or presence of mind. The knockout punch, when it comes, is almost a relief.

The two men embrace after the fight. Baldwin leaves fighting back tears.

In their rematch some ten months later, Floyd would lose just as ignominiously, lasting four seconds longer than the first match, but with two additional counts of eight.

Once again, Clay and Louis were present to witness the alarming efficiency with which the "bad" could dispatch the "good." Within months, Clay would join the Nation of Islam. Louis and Liston would become very close friends.

• • •

After each of his losses to Liston, Patterson took flight. In 1962, he brought his passport and suitcase to New York's Idlewild Airport. After donning a false beard and mustache, he scanned the departure board, then got on a plane to Madrid. Once there, he wandered around poor sections of the city faking a limp.

Between the first fight and the second, Floyd, who was afraid of flying, bought a Cessna. After his second loss, he flew himself back to New York from Las Vegas. He kept losing himself in reverie, however, and his co-pilot had to repeatedly draw his attention back to the controls.

VI.

Ultimately, it might be that the root of the trouble Sonny and Floyd both faced was that so few people ever saw them as Baldwin was able to, as men caught in roles larger than they were. Each man, in his own way, collapsed under the weight of the expectations heaped upon him—expectations only tangentially related to the human being each of them actually was. As far as I can tell, neither man aspired to be the kind of superhuman legend that Jack Johnson or Muhammad Ali would yearn to be, making them doubly ill-suited for the roles they were handed in the great American narrative of the day.

"As many times as you see a fellow get tired in the course of a fight," D'Amato explained, "note that he gets tired when pressure builds up, after he gets hurt or he's been in some kind of doubtful situation, not being able to control the situation. That's when he starts getting tired."

When a fighter starts to weaken, D'Amato said, "it only means he's reached a point where he no longer can stand the pressure."

Floyd Patterson was exhausted before he'd even entered the ring. With everyone from the NAACP to John F. Kennedy telling him he had to win, it might be a wonder that he even lasted two minutes and six seconds.

"You're out there with all those people looking around you," he later told Gay Talese, the reporter to whom he was closest, "and those cameras, and the whole world looking in, and all that movement, that excitement, and 'The Star Spangled Banner,' and the whole nation hoping you'll win, including the president. And you know what all this does? It blinds you, just blinds you."

Sonny Liston was far less articulate, but no less poignant, in his rejection of his role. His gravestone in Las Vegas reads simply, "A MAN"—what should be, but isn't, the simplest declaration ever made.

VII.

In seventh grade, in a misguided effort to fit in, I join my school's field hockey team. It's not a bad sport for me as these things go; the ball is generally on the ground and I am fairly fast, and in my role as wing I can easily shift the ball—and the spotlight—back to the forward. But in all other ways, the venture is a failure. I have not succeeded in making myself any whiter or more popular. I do not belong any more than I ever did; I am just spending more time with people who know it.

One day in the locker room, messing around before practice, a girl whom I'm as much friends with as anyone, asks if I can fit into the tall, narrow gym lockers. I shrug and try, first testing the mechanism on the inside of the door that, by lifting, opens the door from inside. I slide sideways into the locker and shut it, then open it again. I fit, sure enough.

We finish dressing, and I'm about to head to the field when another, older player picks me up and shoves me into the locker. She is fast, and I am too surprised to fight. She shuts the door, then slides a lock into the handle. The lock is hanging open, I know, but it still prevents me from moving the long metal piece that would open the door. I am stuck. The team leaves. I try the door just to be sure.

I wait quietly, alone, declining to call for help, instead watching silently out the rows of squares that line the locker door. I wait for a few minutes. I wonder vaguely if I will sit out the entire practice in here. But eventually I hear the locker room door once more. The first girl comes and moves the lock. She cracks open the door and waits for me to come out. I do, and we head out to the field. I join the circle of girls in their pre-practice stretch, and the incident is never mentioned.

VIII.

Muhammad Ali offered a characteristically vivid description of a boxer's fear. As he described it to George Plimpton, his own place of reckoning, which he called "the Near Room," was "a place to which, when he got into trouble in the ring, he imagined the door swung half open and inside he could see neon, orange, and green lights blinking, and bats blowing trumpets and alligators playing trombones, and where he could hear snakes screaming. Weird masks and actors' clothes hung on the wall, and if he stepped across the sill and reached for them, he knew that he was committing himself to his own destruction."

D'Amato, too, believed that a boxer chooses his own destruction, that the boxer who is knocked out in some way wants to be. "When two men are fighting," he offered, "what you're watching is more a contest of wills than of skills, with the stronger will usually overcoming skill. The skill will prevail only when it is so superior to the other man's skill that the will is not tested."

I would be a terrible boxer. In a crisis, I do not keep my head.

I don't panic, exactly. In fact, it's quite the contrary. At the most horrific moments I turn downright Pollyannish.

On Murray Street, when the towers collapsed and the phones cut out, when the air turned pewter-gray, when our eyes stung and my lungs started to seize, I remember thinking, as I looked around the office at my co-workers and friends, that there couldn't be a nicer bunch of people with whom to die.

When the shell-shocked fireman who took shelter with us said it was time to make our break, and we did, and when I saw a reporter I knew on the corner of Murray and Broadway, I stopped to say hello, still clutching a wet scrap of T-shirt to my face. "Have you seen Gene? Is Gene okay?" the reporter asked after a well-connected co-worker of mine. "Yup," I replied with what I knew to be alarming cheerfulness. "He's on his way home now!"

My Near Room, in other words, has no bats and alligators. It has mid-century modern furniture and paintings by Rothko and a view of the East River and a fully stocked bar. If I ever found myself in trouble in the ring, there would be no blood lust, no tiger pounce. I'm quite certain I would look forward to being knocked out.

• • •

According to David Remnick, the conventional wisdom about boxing is that "only a fool or a desperate man gets hit in the head to earn a living." In fact, the biographies of many boxers do reveal foolishness, or desperation, or both—if not in their beginnings, which are usually full of privation and humiliation, then certainly by their mid-points, when, with mounting tension, all but the boxer in question can see that entering the ring is an increasingly dangerous and foolhardy act, one that sacrifices health and reputation and family life.

Some people on the "intellectual cult fringe" of the sport admire, in an aesthetic sort of way, this classic narrative arc and its tragic conclusion. I, however, take no pleasure in it. The story of being so thoroughly consumed by that which we love, human as it may be, is not, in fact, universal.

Instead, I'm drawn to the ways boxers take pride in their living, even if it happens to involve getting hit in the head. Whose living doesn't? But most of us stumble into our proving grounds by accident, and even if we come to be proud of the time we spent there—the fear we encountered, the bravery we mustered—few of us would choose to return. Boxers, on the other hand, enter the spaces of their doing, or undoing, open-eyed. No matter what impels them toward the ring, toward the knockout, through the door, into the air, there are lessons in the ways they go.

Dan Roche

Facilitating

A few years ago, I had a severely autistic student in my college literature class and, the next semester, in my nonfiction writing course. I would often be standing at the front of the room, talking about a short story or a poem, and he would rise up and walk from over by the door to over by the windows, then back again, sometimes stopping just inches from me, wringing his hands and staring intently into my face. I'd never had a student do anything like that. Usually I'd try to acknowledge him casually—"Hey, Chandi"—and go on teaching. But I also wondered: Should I lead him back to his seat? Call on him and try to help him into a more obvious engagement with the class? Make a joke to ease any tension the other students might have? Act as if he weren't there? I had no training in how to attend to special-needs students, and my assumption and hope, since I tend to run a pretty casual classroom, was simply that all of the students and I would adapt quickly and easily, which generally turned out to be the case.

If Chandi wandered around the room too much, his mother, Anoja, who always came to class with him, would gently call him back, or she'd lead him out into the hallway, where he could pace off his anxiety. Sometimes they'd return in a few minutes and Chandi would sit again for as long as he was able, and sometimes only Anoja would come back, to collect their belongings and signal that they'd see us next time. It helped, probably, that Chandi proved to the class early on that he was a better reader and smarter than most of them. He finished the semester with a high grade and, I think, a sense of satisfaction about having been a key part of an intellectual community, as well as a joy over being able to immerse himself in literary works he had not read before.

Chandi signed up for my nonfiction workshop because he desperately wanted to write, though his process was difficult and far from fluent. In fact, *fluency* is hardly a word that could be used to describe any aspect of Chandi's communication. He spent his entire childhood, until he was nineteen and got a facilitated-communication device to speak for him, not saying an intelligible word to anyone. Many people, including some of the psychologists and physicians who treated him, assumed he was, in the language of the day, severely retarded.

When he got that first FC device (it's a keyboard slightly smaller than a typical laptop; Chandi types into it and hits ENTER, and a computer-generated voice fills the air), Chandi proved all the dour diagnoses wrong. Far from retarded, he was in fact brimming with intelligence, with years of things he'd been waiting to say. He came out of his muteness having taught himself to read. And because he had been paying close attention when Anoja had been quizzing Chandi's older sister on vocabulary words for her SAT exam, Chandi's own vocabulary was adorned with *mellifluous* and *lackadaisical* and *prodigious* and *disapprobation*. "I so like to say them," he told me in regard to multisyllabic words. "Sounding them out in my head is fun. Inert, inside my head I spoke these words for so long."

Chandi's first literary genre had been poetry, because it allowed him to tap linguistically into his roiling emotions, and because he could write a poem during the scant moments he was able to force his body to stay in front of a computer. His poems were filled with the angst of the typical young poet, but they also, like this one, dealt powerfully with the depressing difference between his physical state and his intellectual one:

The Potter who spoiled
My poor body
Paused to pour
Poetry into my
Heart
I pour it out

The essays Chandi wrote in my nonfiction class were almost exclusively about his attempts to break out of what he called either "the cave" or, more sarcastically, his "gilded cage." (Anoja, who is both tender and lovingly stern with Chandi, once told him: "Be thankful it's gilded.") It had been about fourteen years since he'd begun to communicate with FC (Chandi was thirty-three when I met him), and that previous long experience of entrapment seemed horrifyingly fresh to him. I had almost no concept of what that experience might have been like. So I learned about Chandi's life as he turned in his essays, each a few pages of lively personal experience or explanation of his own desires for normality. I didn't really know how to match up the smoothly controlled sentences and paragraphs, the conversational and occasionally self-deprecating voice, and the relative calmness on the page with the man who paced back and forth, his fingers weaving in and out of each other, his arms frequently moving outward and then back in like the wings of a bird considering and then deciding not to fly. Or the man who grunted, growled, occasionally wailed.

"Speakers open their mouths and words pour out," he wrote in an essay called "On Speaking." "I open my mouth and scream. My spastic body imagines that a speaker only needs to get a thought into his mind for his mouth to express it. Your sounds emerge modulated, shaped into words. Mine emerge unmodulated, ununderstandable squeals. The reality is that I sound like an animal. It is an awful thought."

My comments on Chandi's essays were hesitant attempts to avoid sounding paternalistic or dishonest. I didn't write, "No, you don't" next to the harsh self-description, not only because I didn't think he sounded anything like an animal, but also because I wasn't sure where to walk on that thin line between responding to the writing and responding to the content. I'd had plenty of students write about personal miseries—depression, suicide attempts, hopelessness—but I'd always tried, as much as possible while still remaining an empathetic human being, to be the writing teacher rather than the counselor.

Still, I couldn't help wanting to help Chandi personally, because the physical and emotional challenges of his life were more entwined with his writing than I'd ever seen with a student. He struggled so hard to communicate. And I saw how exhausting it could be for him to confront the subject of his own life. Once, when I asked him outside of class about his childhood, he immediately became so anxious and upset that after several minutes of extra-intense pacing and hand-wringing and shouting, he had to lie down on a couch and take a nap.

Even with that, though, it didn't really get into my head that Chandi might not have a writer's appreciation of having such a rich and natural subject as autism. I'd always envied writers who had large subjects handed to them. In some ways, I plugged Chandi into the model of Nancy Mairs, who has written extensively and poetically about her multiple sclerosis, even while making it very clear how much she hates the disease. (Then again, Mairs wrote her most well-known essay on the subject, "On Being a Cripple," after her early years of "grief and fury and terror.") Also, I had assumed—without asking Chandi whether I was right—that his essays were heavily therapeutic. The least I could do, I thought, was encourage him to write them.

I spoke with Anoja now and then about how I could be most helpful to Chandi. She was so good at facilitating for him—sitting next to him to help steady his arm when necessary as he typed, holding his hand or touching his leg to help him, as Chandi wrote in one essay, know where his own body was. She thought I was doing what I needed to. But she also suggested I talk with two other people who might help me understand my work with Chandi more, or at least know that my uncertainties were not unique.

The first was a writing tutor that Chandi had worked with for three years in Maryland, where his family lived before moving to Syracuse. Her name is Leslie Lass, and she had no more disability training than I did. One of the first things she told me when I called was that when Anoja asked her to tutor, she wanted to say no because she couldn't imagine how she could do anything but fail. She took the job, though, and described those three years as mysterious, frustrating, and—as she discovered Chandi's "brilliance" and "acute sensitivity"—filled with deep, surprising joy.

"I never knew what he was going to be able to bear," she told me of how Chandi would respond to her teaching. "At times he didn't talk. Other times, a word, a phrase, or something in the way his mother moved, or something about the way his autism intervened—got in the way of—his creative expression. It was always an adventure."

It took Lass a couple of years to move Chandi from brief poetic images to sentences strung together. With her, as with me, Chandi wrote only about his autism.

"At times I thought it was stubbornness," Lass said, "but I came to see that he had to write about those things. There was such a press of need in him. His creativity couldn't go in any other direction."

The other person I talked with—Chandi's speech therapist—told me in the same vein, "There were so many walls that had to be dealt with," by which she meant the emotional and psychological effects of Chandi's having been mute for nearly two decades. In her early sessions with him, Marilyn Chadwick said, she never really knew what they were going to be doing. Her goal, though, was much the same as mine: to bring Chandi "into voice," to act as a facilitator of sort, trying to help the words and sentences form more smoothly and copiously. (She recalled with affection what Chandi's initial goal had been: "He wanted to go right to talking with girls on the quad," she said.)

Chadwick had a much broader scope of approaches she could bring to her work with Chandi than I did—and a great deal more training. She was, when I met her, the assistant director of the Facilitated Communication Institute at Syracuse University. She understood much better than I could that what Chandi needed as a communicator—whether in speech or in writing—was to separate into his own indviduality.

"He hides in Anoja's mental and emotional sphere," she explained. She theorized that evidence of his growth as a writer—"when he decides that he wants to write about something other than himself"—would also signal a healthy separation from his mother.

Chandi finished my class and thought about writing a memoir. He'd been encouraged to do so by many people who knew his story—people, I imagined, who were not only sincerely curious but also assumed that telling the story would be good for him. Then he and his family moved back to their native Sri Lanka. The book, I know from e-mails, is still of interest to Chandi, even though one of the things he told me the last time I saw him was, "Apart from my autism I have nothing to write about. But I don't want to write about autism."

His lament made me wonder how well I had actually served him, and I had his words in mind the following summer, when I received an e-mail from Chadwick asking me to teach a personal-essay writing workshop for a whole class of FC users. It would be part of a four-day gathering at Syracuse University, with people coming in from around the country. The theme would be "Communication Through the Arts," and there would be other workshops on sculpture, drumming, mask-making, poetry, and dance.

I was only barely more qualified to teach this workshop than I had been to begin teaching Chandi in the first place, and so my acceptance of Chadwick's offer was filled with trepidation. Partly that was because she described the group's writing abilities as "anything from being able to write a few paragraphs to barely being able to write a sentence." And even more so, it was because of what Chadwick advised me when I asked for suggestions on what I could have them write about.

"I've always found," she said, "that if you go deeper you'll get better results."

When I showed up for the first day (it would be only two days, ninety minutes each time), there were ten students, ranging in age from thirteen to about forty. Some students had come with one facilitator, others with small entourages. One student had five people with him, and when he was settled into a seat, his cohorts took up most of the rest of that row. Most of the students could not speak without aid, or could do so with little range or articulation. One teenage boy spoke with frequency, strength, and clarity, but only in the phrases, his dad told me, that he uses all the time.

The room's entropy of movement and voices (some human, many computer-generated) made me skeptical not only of being able to "go deep," but even of adequately leading everyone through the exercise I'd designed. It was much more disorienting than having just Chandi pace between desk and window.

On the other hand, the room was incredibly loose, and I try to teach all of my students to be loose in their process of writing. To shake them out of routine and limiting expectations, I have, for instance, at times required classes to write first drafts on anything *except* 8-1/2 x 11 sheets of white paper. My favorite was a draft written on the metallic-blue hood of a 1968 VW Bug. (That student brought only the hood, not the full car, on the day the draft was due.) In this room, I hoped the looseness involved not only behavior but also imagination—and that I would be able to simultaneously energize and corral it.

And I wanted, in the short time we had, to give everyone a sense of accomplishment. We had to produce something tangible, something with a little artistic heft to it, something that took the students into the essence of what it means to write a personal essay: articulating the inner workings of the writer's mind. I'd decided upon a group project, so that even if a student was able to produce only one written word, it would be a part of something larger.

I explained to the class that we'd be writing a collage. It's a form I've used in many creative writing classes, with almost unshakable success. The "artistic" students like it because it allows freedom, and even the uptight students come to appreciate how it is so forgiving, simply because it has no beginning, middle, or end, no transitions. It can hold a multitude of voices, be messy and abrupt and contradictory and unfinished. I told the class that a written collage is just like the ones you make on posterboard, with pictures and words cut from magazines, all held together by a theme—sports, friendship, fashion—or even something as intangible as a single consciousness choosing its many parts. As a group, I told them, we would be that consciousness.

People fidgeted, squealed, moaned, hummed. Some rose and paced, and facilitators tried to ease them back to their seats. I remembered how Chandi heard everything I was saying in class even when he seemed to be in his own world, and I hoped these students were catching half of what he would catch.

"You can contribute one word," I explained. "You can write a paragraph, or a page. You can tell stories, quote books or song lyrics or friends, describe objects, be opinionated. What is in your mind will work because it will be true and it will be yours. We'll put everything together and let it talk. Whatever we come up with," I proposed with some optimism, "we will have something."

It had not been easy to act on Chadwick's advice about a topic. Chandi's frustration still resonated for me, and I didn't feel a lot of authority to be a non-autistic person telling a group of autistic people, "Write about your autism." So I decided to come at the common reality of these students' lives not through condition but through effect. I wrote our subject on the whiteboard: "Independence/Dependence." Happy stuff, sad stuff. I hoped it would take us deeply enough to satisfy the student I'd chatted with before class, who told me how much she loved poetry. She was maybe twenty, almost immobilized in a wheelchair, but with a sharp sarcasm that came through her eyes and her slowly formed words, like someone who doesn't have patience for inanities. I really didn't want to look frivolous to her.

"What I'm going to do," I explained to the class, "is give you a series of prompts, and then let you write in response to each one. Some of them may interest you more than others. Feel free to skip any."

I wanted to begin with something specific and positive, but something that would also invite an emotional reaction. "Describe," I said to begin, "a physical object that makes you feel independent."

Immediately, facilitators around the room repeated and rephrased my prompt and began transcribing the students' words to paper. I walked over to see how the poetry-loving young woman was doing.

She'd already dictated this to her dad: "Holding my bottle I can sip my drink, and when it falls I can wait independently for someone to pick it up."

"All right," I said, smiling at her.

To get them thinking in terms of action, I said, "Write about one moment when you felt most independent." A few minutes later, I asked the same thing about feeling dependent. And then I wanted to turn around their conceptions about what roles they inhabited in their relationships, and I said, "Describe a way in which another person is dependent on you." We worked onward, with some students shooting out responses quickly, and others struggling through layers of hesitation, translation, confusion, and the ever-constant movement in the room.

"What activity would you most want to do independently that you haven't been able to do so far?" I asked.

"Finish this sentence with a good feeling: To be dependent feels like...."

"Now finish it with a bad feeling."

"What's the wisest thing anyone has ever said to you about being independent?"

"What's the dumbest?"

By the end of the hour and a half, we had a mess. The energy had been high, the output impressive—facilitators delivered dozens of sheets of paper to me—but I'm sure no one, including me, yet felt much coherence to our activity. I did feel something else, though, different from what I had ever seen in any other writing class: a collaboration that was necessary—writers and facilitators working together intimately—and vivifying. The process felt alive and, as Chandi might have said, prodigious.

"We'll bring it all together at our next meeting," I promised.

During the time between sessions, I wondered about revising. There was a lot of smoothness to many sentences, but also a fair amount of roughness, both mechanical and logical. I recalled how Chandi had held tightly to the words that came so laboriously. "He doesn't like to be edited," Anoja had told me. I thought too of the Zen philosophy of "first thought, best thought," and the surrealists and their automatic writing, and poets who liked their poetry raw, electrostatic, succinct, off the top of the head. I suspected that for artistic reasons as well as for pragmatic ones, we would have to—and should—value outpouring of emotion over refinement. I had to trust what I'd assured the students: that resonance would arise on its own.

The second session did not have the same high energy as the first, but it was productive in a different way. Students came ready to add statements and images beyond the new prompts I offered. We quickly got to a feeling of fullness, a communal sense that the first thoughts and best thoughts were now in our hands, to be caressed and palpated, to be held out for others. Based mostly on gut feelings, I suggested an order for the pieces, and people approved it. We called it "Voices on (In)Dependence."

A few hours later, we met all the other students, facilitators, and families from the week's gathering in the auditorium for the "Grand Finale," the presentation of the creations from each of the various sessions. There would be dancing, poetry, drumming. The presentation of our essay was last. Since the writers themselves could not read aloud what they created, I and two of the facilitators did so. We cycled through the entries, halting as the language dictated in the bumpy parts, aiming for mellifluousness when the prose guided us that way. The three of us read the voices of ten others, and from my vantage point on the stage, even with the grunts and shufflings and squeals throughout the room, even before the loud applause at the end and the smiles and tears, the voices seemed to have a rhythm and a pulse and a resonance that made them all one.

Here are some:

If I had complete independence, I would... eat all the time and be with everyone that realizes that I am intelligent.

Someone told me that life is not that a person is dependent or independent but that he lists himself as a loving person.

To be dependent is like riding a tandem bike with two flat tires.

To be independent is like riding in a balloon with plenty of helium.

Free. Popular. To. Happy. Lover. Independent is testing.

I feel independent when I can typing with you and the dear deep connection that we have—vast. Dear, you are the best mother in the world.

To be dependent is lousy. I know nothing positive about that.

I never had someone dependent on me. It would feel different. I do not feel independent when someone is dependent on me.

When I was on vacation I was very bored. And I wanted to go for a ride. My helper was lazy, so when she left the room I ran away and got in the car.

I can see that other people enjoy helping me, but it doesn't make me feel better.

"Who is dependent on you?" A soldier in Iraq who hopes that I might find time to vote on the first Tuesday in November.

If we abolish the customs house of normalcy, help will abound and fear will be the discarder. Or, let's abolish customs altogether!

Green. Weightless. Certain. Unencumbered. Responsible. Satisfied.

I felt more independent... when I learned to type and you are the sweet person that taught me to write treasure to me.

Great. Try. Eat whenever I wanted to.

If I were independent I would be able to make friends.

I would write full-time with a mountain view.

I feel dependent on you for everything, and I often think that you are tired and I greatly feel breathless.

If I had complete independence right now I would get up.

Freedom. Gallant. Realization. Festive. Satisfaction. Amazing. Happy. Beautiful.

What does this have to do with FC?

Can we talk about something else?

Natalia Rachel Singer

Found Art, New York City: Midterm Election Day, 2010

At a rain-drenched crosswalk en route to the French Consulate, where I am pursuing my current exit strategy, sewer steam rises and engulfs us, the street a stage set for Heathcliff crying "Cathy!" or Shakespearian gravediggers reminding us we'll soon be gnawed on by worms. I stare at this cloud of mist rising over traffic, beguiled and oddly serene. Are the others clumped beside me under the same spell?

9 a.m.: two men getting out of a cab, Fifth Avenue and 80th, near an election day sale window: "The Democrats need...The Democrats...The Democrats...."

My childhood friend, John, has left a message from the West Coast city where he's mayor. "This is Blank-Blank-Blank (fill in name of your favorite caustic, racist, misogynistic, paranoid bully.) Why are you saying all those terrible things about me?"

I call back, forgetting the three-hour time difference. "Hi, this is Blank-Blank-Blank (fill in name here of your favorite caustic, racist, misogynistic, female bully.) People are talking. I think they know we're seeing each other!"

Man passing me as I line up with fellow visa seekers on East 75th and Fifth Avenue in the now torrential rain: "Wow, I've never seen an umbrella so perfectly turned inside out. It's a work of art."

Inside, I discover I have filled up all my passport pages with other exit strategies and three years to go, a visa to get, and nowhere to put it. I am almost turned away, until the man behind the counter agrees to use the page with the faintest stamps: a get-out-of-Dodge palimpsest.

To celebrate I go to his favorite French restaurant. He says it is *"pas mal,"* not bad, which is French for awesome and amazing.

I am the only one eating lunch alone at Café Boulard, but I don't mind. I am a middle-aged woman enjoying butternut squash soup and chicken stuffed with cabbage and wrapped in bacon with chestnut gnocchi, and writing about it in her journal. This is a very good situation.

Once, I was the hungry person peering into windows where prosperous people left good food on their plates, distracted and bored. Once, I counted coins to get inside art museums. These days, I savor each bite, walk around, sniff out beauty, and write in my journal. Last night it was Korean squid and vegetables, glass noodles and gnocchi-like lumps of goodness, searing hot, and the tattoo of the coiled scorpion on the arm of the only other non-Korean, one table over. It was the lurid green of alien blood and from where I sat the ink looked wet, like he'd just rolled in his favorite cartoon. I wanted to go over and touch it.

I am too full for dessert, but the waiter brings madeleines in a to-go bag: "My colleague, the maître d', likes you so much. He said you're a very, very nice lady and I have to do everything for you." After all these years on the planet, I have discovered, by accident, the way to get impeccable service: go alone and write. Dress like you're trying to trick the French Consulate into letting you in. A maître d' might mistake you for a restaurant critic.

Proust should be so lucky to have free madeleines, still warm from the oven, in a recycled brown box to swing while walking along the wet pavement.

Around the corner on Madison Avenue I blink at a tall, thin woman in a moss-colored fleece coat on a bike twirling jewel-colored pinwheels in the spokes, with Easter basket grass lining the two baskets in back. Was there ever anything as lovely as those twirling colors, the moss coat and green grass, fall leaves flying behind them on a street cleaned by a morning's heavy rain? This is a woman who can't see the beauty she makes: who does it for us, strangers on the street. Who could not feel gratitude and love for someone who so understands the need for us to stalk fugitive beauty in a world of grit and gray?

Men and I walk past more steam, the red hand of the stop light like someone waving "hey" from deep inside a bubble bath.

A man washes the windows of a Fendi store making the luxe objects he cannot afford more visible to passersby. I want to give him the madeleines, but I would have to go in there. I want to give the madeleines to the people working in the French Consulate when I come back for my visa, but there is no private, discreet way to do this without making it look like a bribe.

To celebrate getting my visa, I go to the Whitney, which is just around the block. I check the madeleines in the coatroom along with my raincoat and the wrecked umbrella that now looks like roadkill, a run-over bat.

These are the things that will stay with me from the museum:
1. Louise Bourgeois's pink coat on a hanger, lace chemise on bone, child-size, haunted. How long has the child who wore it been dead?

(Louise Bourgeois died this year. Did she have any intimation, when she saw the number tick over on the calendar, that 2010 would be the right-side bookmark on her tombstone?)

2. *Portrait of Allen Ginsberg* by Bruce Connor: burnt gray candle wax on scaffold and some droopy bags that look more like udders than testicles. Did the poet drink a lot of milk?

3. Julian Schnabel's "Hope," circa 1982, and David Salle's "Sextant in Dogtown," a snarl of yarn afghans and black-eyed raccoons. I am glad the Eighties are long gone. Ronald Reagan may have been the emperor of free market ice cream, but I don't remember those neon-lit years as a good decade for sniffing out beauty. But I do remember dogs playing poker on dark velvet in loud rooms. I always have time for the dogs.

4. Duane Hanson, 1977: a woman with a dog. A dummy—not even a mannequin. A person who has been embalmed sitting up, with her little dog too. I keep expecting her to come to life, to blink off the fly resting on her gray hair, to awaken the snoozing poodle at her feet, and head out to look for pigeons to feed in the park.

5. A display (1978-88) by Paul Thek, who writes: "Design something to sell on the street corner. Design something to sell to the government. Design something to put on an altar. Design something to put over a child's bed. Design something to put over your bed when you make love. Make a monkey out of clay."

And later: "It delighted me that bodies could be used to decorate a room, like flowers. We accept our thing-ness intellectually but the emotional acceptance of it can be a joy."

Today's thing-ness has put me in my happy place. Ugly, caustic people may be poised to take over the land, but I am still a thing surrounded by other things, some of them pink, and all with reassuring edges to remind us that the world is solid and enduring, although I continue to be bewitched by the texture of manhole vapors.

6. *Now is the time for good folks to come to party.* Moet champagne flutes float above this installation. What will I have reason to celebrate next?

7. Edward Hopper's "Night Windows, 1928": a red rump behind blue curtains, bending forward on green carpet and rumpled bedspread: a painting that makes us into voyeurs. We watch life swirl around us thinking we are alone, until we realize we too are part of the scenery, bodies decorating a room—someone else's found art.

Overheard, a very old woman and slightly younger man at the Lee Friedlander "America by Car" exhibit:

Woman: "My grandparents, with the consideration they showed each other, their relationship, I don't know if they were in love, but they certainly understood each other. And in their own way, they were modern people. I don't know, I really don't know, how they, in such a small household, could have produced three sons like that. Those brothers, the uncles, well, they were handsome, but they showed no consideration to anyone but themselves. Uncle Max, he could be very cruel. He was so very handsome, but he was the worst of the three."

Man: "You know my mother, Carol, she hadn't been feeling well, and when she went to the doctor and he told her, thyroid, it's your thyroid, you have two or three months, she just went home and sat in front of the TV and waited to die. We visited, we brought food, we tried to get her out, but she was waiting to die. And the thyroid got bigger until she couldn't swallow, not even liquids, and she died."

I stop for a very long time in front of a Biennial Collectible, "Girl Looking at Landscape, 1957," and think that could be it, the title of my next collection of essays, so I buy the postcard in the shop upstairs along with an Edward Hopper bookmark.

Then I think, *Isn't that kind of literal?*

And, then, *Do I really need to advertise my age?*

Out on the street behind the Dolce & Gabbana window, Madonna smiles beside four pretty Italian boys. She looks ageless and lovely, an American classic, her hair the blond of Marilyn's, her brows as black as her lashes, which curl up like centipedes. I didn't like her in our youth, I found her crass and fetishistic in a menacing, cold, not-fun way, but she's growing on me. Has time mellowed us both, or is it all the yoga?

"She's starting to show her age, don't you think?" says a man behind me.

I thought I was alone, but now I see the man's reflection in the window, his face under a baseball cap obscured by shadow.

"I disagree," I say. "She looks as good as she ever has. Maybe, better."

"It's starting to show around her eyes," he says. "Look. Considering all the oxygen she takes... you'd think she'd get them done."

I look at him. He's an American classic himself: grumpy old man in sportswear.

I wish he would explain. Are people staying young by shooting oxygen into their skin? Is this something everyone knows, except me? Even grumpy men in their seventies posing as beauty critics? Our man slumps beside me in sweatpants and a windbreaker, with a bag labeled "Oxygen" strapped to his back.

"Well, for 50, I think she looks amazing."

"Fifty was last year's news! The year before that, even. She must be 52."

I have just turned 53, but my face is hidden beneath my raincoat hood. I wait for him to walk away so I can escape his merciless scrutiny.

At dinner with a friend I met when we were 17: "So I put him on a train today." Her older son is starting to look at colleges and my friend's a little blue. I remind her of the time she visited me upstate and left early because her boy was a baby and she ached to have him in her arms. They had never been apart.

"I'm not sure if I like our age," she continues. "I'm starting to lose people." She asks if I remember one of her former colleagues from a famous magazine catering to the young. They met now and then for lunch over the last twenty-five years until one day her friend stood her up. "She was gone," she says. "Dead. And I didn't know."

"Cancer?" I ask tentatively.

"No," she says. "She jumped."

"The fifties..." I start to say after a respectful pause, then another that allows me to swallow the kim chee and dried anchovy, bok choy and tofu, pork dumplings, and rice balanced on my chopsticks. I am thinking of menopause and depression, but I don't want to talk about anything so clinical when I am with my good friend who is so smart and kind and lovely and stylish and youthful, and my mouth is so nicely on fire, and I am still high from the eternal thing-ness of the world.

I say, "In the bathroom I just read the Wordsworth poem on rainbows translated in Korean. 'The child is father to the man.' So did we know how we were going to turn out, when we were kids? At the cellular level, were we prepared for all this?"

"The fifties..." she says soulfully, "it's a sober age, isn't it?"

The next morning, someone is inside the Election Day sale window moving mannequins around, their sweaters and coats. No sale today. No one gets out of a cab here or says anything about the Democrats.

John, my friend the mayor, finally catches me on the phone. He says, "The tea party is the party of Tim McVeigh. No government, guns everywhere. That's the country they want. That's where it's going, unless we stop them. You can use that in one of your essays."

I consider this. Will guns be sold as accessories, along with the purses and scarves and shoes, in display windows along Fifth Avenue? Will they go on sale on Election Day? Will they come in pink?

And how will we know the difference between fanatics yelling caustic things, street people without a filter, or performance artists? Will a lot of us, the still wistful types, unabashedly sensitive souls... will we jump?

A woman around my age on Madison Avenue with a severe, top-of-the-head bleached blond ponytail, drawn-on brows, red lips, and a prim tweed skirt grins broadly at passing truckers and passersby, including me. "Have a good day," she cries. It's a command and kind of a come-on. Is she a street person, a performance artist, a fanatic, or a little of each?

Inside the Pierpont Morgan, Thomas Jefferson's letter to his daughter, Martha, from Aix-en-Provence, March 25, 1787:

"It is a part of the American character to consider nothing as desperate, to surmount every difficulty by resolution and contrivance. In Europe there are shops for every want. Its inhabitants therefore have no idea that their wants can be furnished otherwise remote from all other aid. We are obliged to rent and execute, to find meaning within ourselves, not to lean on others."

Anne Morgan, daughter of Pierpont, went to France after World War I and documented a country devastated by war and hunger. I stare at the bleak black and white photographs, then watch a bleak film. Ransacked villages. Hungry, gaunt people, so skeletal the hard bones cut through the glass, the grainy film. I imagine someone coming to America to document us now, circa 2010: fat and thin, well-dressed or shlumpy, journal-toting or heat-packing, some of us tattooed, with not enough oxygen, not enough of whatever it is or was we missed today, and yesterday, obscured by sewer steam and hunched under our big bent inside-out umbrellas.

I think of all the art and all the shops and all the wants I have seen on display in this celebrated American city. Why does nothing, not even that ghostly dress on the hanger by Louise Bourgeois, seem as beautiful to me as the display window I just came upon at Louis Vuitton: a woman in a pink Chinese dress surrounded by paper lanterns in the shape of steamer trunks, stacks and stacks of them piled to the ceiling, a lone figure in a window devoted to *Le Voyage,* dusty rose and ghostly, a dream of a dream of escape inside a dream?

I will leave this country, for a time, when I can find more pages for my passport for the customs officials to stamp. I will eat madeleines again, although they are not really my favorite. They are nice, though, for breakfast in a New York hotel room when you are talking to a good friend on your cell phone about how it's all going to hell in a handbag.

What will America look like when I come back?

Renate Wildermuth

The King of Crumbs

Because his eyesight had always been as poor as his paychecks, my father never drove a car. He relied on my mother to take him back and forth to his job in the pantry of the Woodloch Pines Resort. Without a license he had learned patience. My mother, with three young kids to look after and a job of her own, had learned to drive really fast.

Sometimes if I had a doctor's appointment after elementary school, I'd be with her as she flew along those country roads straightening curves and leaving potholes gasping for breath. She'd pull up in front of Dad, sighing when she saw the bags and boxes surrounding him like beggars. They bulged with day-old bread, or cakes, or singed chicken thighs, or tubs of leftover ice cream and sometimes a chipped dish. "If you bring home one more box, I'll divorce you," Mom would say as she got out to open the trunk. My parents were like World War I pilots, flying without parachutes. Bailing wasn't an option.

Dad would load up the trunk, spot my form and smile. "Free at last, free at last," he'd say throwing his fist up in the air. His pants were a little short with black and white checks that turned gray in the distance. His shirts were never white again after one day on the job. When he opened the car door to get in, a familiar smell would squeeze in after him like another passenger. It was more a color than a smell. Not even a color really, just drab, like worn-out socks. It came from the eggs he scraped off breakfast plates, or the chemicals the big industrial dishwasher used. It came from the food in those bags and boxes, not stale, but not exactly fresh either. It smelled like routine.

Sometimes, he wouldn't be outside when we arrived. Mom would pull all the way into the lot, back to the service entrance. "You know where to go?" she'd ask, but I was out of the car already, moving past garbage cans taller than I was, past crates of bulk food and into the stainless steel big kitchen. And still farther back.

"Hey, Eddie! You've got a visitor," someone would yell, and there was Dad, looking like a stranger but still kind of familiar, like a distant relative maybe. I recognized his stocky build, his barrel chest. But his face was pulled down, and he looked worried about the trays of juice glasses the machine was spitting out fast, racing him to the finish, except there was never a finish.

He'd look up, a little wary at first. He'd squint and see me and turn all familiar again. It was like taking a black and white film and turning it Technicolor. But there was nothing fake about his smile. It made me feel like I was the best thing someone could have done for him that day.

"Hiya!" he'd say. Then he'd motion me over behind the machine after he had turned it off. "Look at these fish buckets. I ran 'em through the machine." And he'd pick one up and turn it over so I could see how there was nothing wrong with them. They still smelled a little like fillet of sole, and Mom was going to kill him for bringing them home, but I just nodded, and watched him put them in a box.

Sometimes a manager would come by and hand Dad a crumb cake. They'd stand inspecting it, heads bowed a little, nodding at the quality, even though the topping had gone on unevenly, and it couldn't be given to paying guests.

Then Dad would put on his jacket, hoist a box onto one shoulder, take a bag in the other hand, and we'd start walking out. We'd pass the waitresses and the waiters, and Dad would say, "I'm goin' over the wall," or, if it was a Friday, "I got time off for good behavior." I'd watch the smiles flare on their faces, igniting their eyes like a clear blue flame. He was a lamplighter, and I was his assistant.

Then we were out again in the ordinary light, and Mom was getting out of the car shaking the keys at Dad in empty threat. He was already sticking up for the crumb cake like it was a friend with nowhere else to go.

She'd sigh, thinking of our freezer filled up with tubs of whipped cream, bags of shrimp that could only be fed to cats, and boxes of mud pie with the layers melted together. And she knew there were all those stops to make. There was a widower whose trailer leaned a little like the Napoleons he liked so much. Or the woman with three kids whose house sagged a bit in the middle like the apple pie we'd drop off.

"It's either me or the crumb cake," Mom would say as she was opening the trunk and taking a bag from Dad's hand. He'd pretend to think about her ultimatum; she'd pretend to be mad. Out of habit she'd tell him the box wasn't going to fit, and as usual Dad would make room. Even if it meant filling up the whole back seat.

Then Dad would insist I sit up front, and he'd squeeze into the back, hugging a box like it was a plush armrest instead of plain old cardboard. Mom wasn't in such a hurry now. She'd drive slowly enough to let the potholes catch their breath, while we chauffeured Dad home like he was the richest man in town.

Mykolaj Suchý

UKRAINE

About twenty years ago, my mother worked as a photographer in a very small, remote and unusual village. The name of the village was Kryvorivnya, which means something like "crooked straight" in Ukrainian. The village has a population of under 2,000 if you count just the people; if you count the cows, geese, sheep, and goats, it would be much, much higher.

My mother lived in this village on and off for about a year, so she has some good friends and memories from there. Since we were already in Europe (in the Slovak Republic) and relatively close to Ukraine, my mother decided to take us all to this village last year.

The road from Slovakia's capital, Bratislava (my father's home town), to Ukraine is an arduous one. Although Ukraine and Slovakia share a border, it's a short one, and it's on the other end of the country. We decided to take the highway through Hungary, which would lead us to Ukraine faster. We drove for what seemed forever. We passed through the Hungarian capital, Budapest, and continued east to the Ukrainian border.

Ukraine is not part of the European Union (EU), while Hungary and Slovakia are. Boarder crossings between non-EU and EU countries are closely monitored by police and soldiers. As we came closer to the border, our nerves were on edge. Being in Hungary with a borrowed car from Slovakia with three American passports and one Slovak passport trying to cross the border into Ukraine is not very typical. We thought it very possible we could have some problems with the border police.

My parents have many painful memories of the "Iron Curtain." In my father's bedroom there is a small rectangular turquoise box. Inside the box is a strand of barbed wire. This barbed wire came from the fence that separated Bratislava from Austria and the rest of the free world. It came from the Iron Curtain. Today in Bratislava there is a monument where the Iron Curtain used to stand. The monument is in the shape of a massive concrete doorway riddled with bullet holes. Inside the pillars of the doorway are the names of those who were slain while attempting to cross the border. Above the names twisted metal pieces extend from the concrete, the original metal of the Iron Curtain.

We came to the border checkpoint and everyone went silent except my father. Using all his linguistic skills—he grew up in Slovakia, learned some Russian in school and understands a little Ukrainian along with "sign language"—he was able to communicate with the guard enough to get us through the checkpoint. We congratulated ourselves and rejoiced. Moments later our good feelings evaporated as we realized that we had only gone through the Hungarian part of the border crossing and now the Ukrainian part was coming up. We were only halfway through.

After a few minutes that seemed like hours, we rolled up to the second checkpoint. All was not as we expected. Instead of the typically gruff "tough guys" guarding the border, the guards we talked with were very amiable. As we waited for the guards to return our documents, we realized it was almost midnight and we needed to call an acquaintance in the nearby town of Uzhorod, who had set up our sleeping arrangements for that night. Our cell phones didn't work in Ukraine, so we were unable to call. One of the guards offered us his cell phone. A border guard lent us his phone!

Our acquaintance was waiting for us at the first gas station in Uzhorod. He climbed into our car and navigated us back to the outskirts of town. It was very dark. We came to a large gate where a dog started to bark. He opened the gate and beckoned us to drive into the courtyard. We pulled into a school for young men studying to become priests, complete with a church and several other buildings. The seminary was named after a priest murdered by the KGB during the Stalinist era. My brother and I were shown to one dorm room by a future priest, while my mother and father where shown to another dorm room by another future priest. I woke up the next morning well rested. Since we had stayed with religion students, we found it was not exactly possible to refuse an invitation to early morning mass on Saturday. My brother and I showered and dressed, then went down to our parents' room.

Soon we all shuffled into church. The only people there were seminary students in dark robes. It was slightly odd coming into church and seeing only young men dressed like priests in the pews. We were acknowledged by the priest, I mean the one who was conducting the service, as special guests from France. I still have no idea why he thought we were French. The mass was in Ukrainian and almost all of it was sung. It was very peculiar for me. After mass ended, we had breakfast with all the future and present priests. The breakfast was simple but good: bread with cheese and ham.

We still had a long day of driving ahead. We continued on our way. The countryside slowly transformed before us. The flat land changed into steep mountains, the clear sky into mist-shrouded mountain peaks. Farms, fields, cows, and the occasional fruit stand all flashed by the car window. Although everything was a blur from the car, I was amazed at the beauty of the Ukrainian countryside. I began to see why my grandparents missed their country so much.

My grandparents were both born in Ukraine and both were well educated; my grandmother was a pharmacist and my grandfather, a veterinary doctor. Both lived through World War II. In the midst of the war the Nazi-Soviet front came closer and closer to Ukraine until finally it was in Ukraine. Everyone knows about the terrible genocide committed by the Nazis but few know that the Soviets did almost the same thing. As my grandmother puts it, "What the Nazis did during the day for the whole world to see the Soviets did secretly during the night while everyone was asleep." My grandparents fled their homeland on the last train leaving Ukraine. They hoped they would return "home" soon. They never did.

As we peacefully continued on our way, we were suddenly attacked without warning by a huge swarm of cows. Well, I guess it wasn't so much attacked but more enveloped. All we could see through the windows were cows. The cows had been out grazing all day in a meadow and were being herded back to their rightful owners.

Traffic both ways slowed almost to a halt. Honking and mooing were constantly heard. Then the semi trucks came. Now there were two or three semi trucks freely blasting away on their horns and many more cars, also blasting away on their horns, and all the cows mooing. All this commotion didn't in the least bother the two or three cow drivers. This was an everyday happening for them, as I was later informed.

Slowly but steadily, the mass of black, white and brown thinned and eventually dispersed, leaving the road clear of all except the occasional cow dropping. Soon we were well on our way to the mountains.

After a while of driving we came to a small town called Tiachiv, where a woman named Kalynka who had been my mother's "assistant" in Kryvorivnya now lives. She had agreed to guide us to Kryvorivnya.

We traveled up small winding roads into the high peaks of the Carpathian Mountains in two cars: Kalynka, with my mother, brother and father; I in the second car with Kalynka's husband and son. Kalynka spoke some English, which was good for me. Unfortunately, Kalynka's husband didn't speak any English at all. It's insanely hard to communicate with someone who does not share a common language with you. Luckily, Kalynka's husband spoke some Czech, which was similar to Slovak, and with a combination of Czech, Slovak, and Ukrainian, and a great many hand signals, we managed to have a "conversation" about Ukraine, the mountains and other things.

Traveling in Ukraine, all my attempts to read the road signs were futile for a long time. However, I took it upon myself to learn to read the Ukrainian alphabet, which is called Cyrillic and is somewhat similar to the Greek alphabet. Eventually, after much pain and struggle, I learned to decipher it. I can also write my name in it—Микола Сухі.

Time passed, and we made our way farther into the mountains. The forest we had been driving through suddenly broke to reveal a beautiful clearing with an extraordinary view of Mt. Hoverla, at 6,762 feet the highest peak in Ukraine. We could not see the top because it was covered by clouds.

The road was more or less a pothole minefield. Somehow both cars came out in one piece. By now we had arrived in the village. I mean the one I've been talking about all along, the one with the long complicated name. It was after nightfall. All we did was unload the car and go to sleep.

This region has a good number of mountains and since we were in them, we figured that we might as well climb one. We were invited to hike up the mountain and sleep in a shepherd's hut (it belonged to Kalynka's mother and father). My dad, my brother and I hiked up with eleven-year-old Andrej (the mayor's son). After navigating through many cow cakes, a stream or two, and climbing many feet in altitude, we had a delicious and not at all nutritious meal of mac and cheese, bread and salo, prepared by Kalynka's mother, who had been taking care of the cattle and staying in the hut. Salo is a Ukrainian food that consists of fat. It is straight fat that you eat on bread. Although this food is extremely unhealthy it is incredibly delicious, especially after a lot of physical activity. We also picked wild strawberries and ate them with this amazing cream that the Hutsuls (the people of the Carpathian Mountains) make. We slept in the hut. We could hear the pigs, cows, and sheep through the thin walls of the hut in the barn next door as we tried to sleep. When we woke the next day it was raining. We hiked down in the rain, returning to the village tired and wet.

"Futbal" (what we call soccer) is extremely popular throughout Europe and is played pretty much everywhere. As the village is in the mountains, there is not very much flat ground to play soccer. However, this doesn't stop kids from playing. They play on a flat but narrow grass path that runs horizontally along the mountains through the village. To play, we set up some empty beer bottles for goals. Then I got scraped in soccer, scraped real bad.

Pictograph is the name of the film my father made from the photographs my mother made 15 years ago in this village. I'd seen this movie many times and just as many times I'd been told that someday I would go to the place in the movie. The film is black and white; thankfully, my visit was in color. It was very interesting to finally get there and to meet the people the film was about. We screened the movie in the village museum for all to see.

Not too long after we arrived, it was time to leave the village, but our trip to Ukraine was not at a close yet. After Kryvorivnya, we visited a larger Ukrainian city, Lviv, often referred to as the capital of western Ukraine. My grandmother went to college there.

In Lviv we met an old friend of my mother's who grew up in Syracuse and is now the head of the Ukrainian Catholic University there and also a priest. Their university has one of the very few chapels in Eastern Europe that has a ramp and is wheelchair accessible. Father Boris insisted that the chapel be open to all. He called me and my brother "gentleman" and explained lots about Ukraine's history, culture, alphabet, and current political situation, which is more precarious then you might think. This was extremely interesting and eye-opening.

On the way back, we stopped to find the grave of my great-great grandfather. Somehow, we found it. We took a pinch of earth from the grave and put it into a little bag to bring home with us and put in our garden. The inscription on the tombstone of my great-great-grandfather was carved in Cyrillic. He had the same first name as I.

We also visited my grandmother's village called Pomorjany. The house she was born in and lived in was still standing, but only barely. It is no longer inhabitable and is starting to fall in on itself. There was a very old church, a very special church for my grandmother. While the Germans or the Soviets were bombarding, she came into the church and prayed to a special icon hanging on one of the walls. We saw this icon and got pictures of it for my grandmother. We did not give her the photos of her home, because they could make her feel distressed. We only spent half a day in Pomorjany, but it was an important half-day.

The trip back was just as long as the trip there. Actually, that isn't true. The way back was about five hours longer. At the border, we passed the Ukrainian checkpoint without incident. Then, we came into the mile-long line for the Slovak side of the border. To re-enter the European Union we waited in line for five hours. The problem on the Slovak side wasn't with anyone's paperwork. It didn't have much to do with the few cars being completely unpacked. It wasn't even because there was too few staff. It was simply because almost all the patrollers there weren't doing anything; they were all just sitting around. Finally, we made it through and were back in Slovakia.

Just before I traveled overseas, I had dinner with my grandmother (she is more than 90 years old). The simple advice she gave me was "see good things." She had to leave her home in Ukraine when she was 23 and was never able to return. I was able to visit her home for her. My eyes were opened to a world that I was previously oblivious to.

This world is a part of me now.

D.S. Sulaitis

DEVIL'S PATH MOUNTAIN RANGE

It's really dark inside our house, a one-room house, and our bed is in front of the massive stone fireplace. It's night, a late summer night. A hand holds on to my leg, tightly, and I try to kick it off, but it's hard going, since the hand is under the blanket, the force of fingers pushing into my calves, and my heart is somewhere in my throat, like in some horror thing on TV. Why can't I reach Morton? He's right on the bed beside me, and my arm is outstretched, my hand trying to wake him, my free leg trying to get the icy-cold grasp off my other leg. It goes on forever, and the dogs are asleep, and I think I'm calling out to one of them, but my voice is gone, sound OFF. By the time my heart is back in my rib cage, my breathing steadies, and Morton is stirring, asking, "What's going on with you?" I have absolutely nothing to say.

There is in fact nothing going on with me. It's going on in the house. It's been going on for a while, since the day we moved in. But it's happening to *me*. Someone, something is living in our house, appearing at night, but it's nothing I can see; by appearing I mean it takes hold of me, my leg or arm. I once felt breathing, a slightly warm breath on my cheek. I can't see it, I can't kick it away, can't push it away. It's like if you were standing next to two mirrors: images going on and on and on, and you can't reach in, can't touch one. The reflection is there, but it's not.

In the morning when I get up there are marks: red marks on my leg, the size of fingerprints, stains like deep red wine. "Look," I frantically showed Morton one morning, the first time it happened. "Bruises, fucking bruises!" I screamed, rubbing at them, poking at them. He looked, got dressed and said, "You're nuts. They're bug bites."

I pulled at his sleeve, following him, my leg up, showing him, dancing to keep up and stop him. "Someone's trying to get me. I'm never coming back here. I hate this house."

He shucked me off, he had work to do, and dry wall was going up in the breezeway. "The problem with you, D., you make stuff up."

The house is small, it's just one room now, everything blasted out—inside walls, ugly past-owners' furniture dumped, cabinets pulled out and smashed, carpeting peeled out—a war zone. When we first bought the house, which is really a cottage, there were four rooms, equally cut: living room, kitchen, one bedroom, another bedroom, a bathroom in the middle. The ceiling was low, for short people in olden times, the walls covered in wallpaper that was peeling, the kind we liked with rope patterns and dusty pink roses, except that on the other side were holes, and mice, and nests and dead mice, and the smell of it all made me gag. But all that's gone, everything gutted to only the wood posts, new walls are up, the ceiling raised like a church—high up, really high. Now it's like living in our city loft, except we're in the mountains, hours north of Manhattan, and even though the house is drafty, really cold, and always really dark, well, I guess it is like being back in our city apartment. Morton, who's an interior designer and builder in the city—the artist type with one pencil behind an ear, pens that leak in his shirt pockets, gooney eyeglasses, and industrial hip work boots with rolled-up jeans and red socks sticking out and drawings under an arm—tells me *this* is his dream house, and even though I don't see it that way, because it's dark and cold inside, I like that he's happy. He hasn't been happy for a long time. But like a shadow tagging along behind him, I'm not so happy. Our weekend getaway, our country cottage is a place of terror for me. We've been here since the end of May, which makes it three months. All week long in the city, and then when we get here, I'm carrying the terror in my gut like you would a recent death of someone, a feeling that haunts you, you can't shake, can't do anything normal without feeling that dread, that sickening cloud all around you and inside you.

There were things that happened our first day in the house. I'll get to that later.

But the real trouble began once we pushed our bed in front of the fireplace. The hearth and mantle has stone around it all, like something in a lodge, so big that it almost takes up the side of the house. Morton built the bed from cherry wood boards he found in the attic, found them and yelped like he won the lottery, and he was running his hands down those wide boards, crazy-smiling, and he built this modern bed, and we put a futon on it, then our sleeping bags and a sheet and blanket over it. We moved the bed to the front of the fireplace because the rest of the house was all crowded with saws, ladders, and scaffolds. The dogs sometimes like to go into the cave of the cleaned-out fireplace which is big enough for all three of them: two fat pit bulls (mine) and one loud tall mutt named Neptune (his). All are rescued from shelters, and they like to huddle in a heap either in the fireplace or on the bed.

That first night in front of that fireplace Morton fell asleep fast, as he usually does. I'll watch his lips go slack, and his breathing gets slow and he begins to make a soft *puff-puff* sound. He's older than me and gets tired fast, and likes to warn me, "Just wait until you hit fifty." I'm thirty-five and he's fifty, which to him means going to bed around eight o'clock and crunching on a handful of Tums before he falls asleep. We have no TV upstate and that first night in our new bed, our heads under the thick wood ledge of the fireplace mantel, I sat up with the dogs, just sitting, watching the sky outside the windows turn from lavender, to teal, to black. It was a really warm night. The windows were all open and there was no breeze, just humid heaviness, the silence ear-ringing, except for sometimes I'd hear coyotes screaming after a kill, or the sudden scary shrill of a screech-owl, or the distant barking of someone's dog. Around midnight I'd dozed off. A sound woke me, a clinking sound. It was glass clicking against glass, as if a phantom tremor had passed through the earth. The sound came from downstairs, from the cellar, directly beneath our bed, in that one spot of the basement that scares me, and I listened for a long time as the sound would start up, stop, start again, then stop. The clinking defined the phrase *chill up my spine,* and at one point I remembered thinking: I am in a restaurant, before it opens, someone making their way through with a tray of empty clean glasses. I shook Morton awake and he said, "What?" but after I told him and he listened, the glass clinking stopped. "Are you making it up?" Morton asked, and I told him no, I heard it. Someone's down there. He picked up the flashlight he always keeps by his side and turned it on, shining it on my face. "You're serious," he said and I told him again, I heard it. He shut off the flashlight and thought about it. "Were you dreaming?" he asked. "I heard something," I said. "Mice," he said. "It's probably just mice. We need to clean things out down there."

Later that night, much later, the wind began. At first it was soft, a balmy breeze, which within seconds turned colder and colder. Slowly an icy wind began moving through the house, the sting of cold crawling over my face and through me. Strands of my hair lifted, moving over my cheek. Wind blew in gusts as if we were outside in a winter storm. Morton slept. I kept still, terrified, trying to figure out if windows or the door had been blown off, or the roof gone. My mind tried to pinpoint a logical reason for the wind inside our house. Did the person carrying the glasses on the tray downstairs open all the windows? Was someone trying to get in the house, or in the house already, opening windows, doors? But of course there was no logical reason. As quickly as the wind started, it suddenly stopped.

I sit on the bed, my bad leg up and I look closely at the bruises, my reading glasses on, my messy hair pulled up into a ponytail, looking closely at my skin. I'm not making this up because I see the marks, roundish and purple-red. They don't itch, they aren't raised. They're all identical in size: five marks. *Could* these be from bugs? It is late summer and the mountains and woods are filled with bugs and birds and snakes. We've only been here a few months and only on weekends, so I'm not all that up on the spiders and things that might bite. But I know these aren't bites, I know because it's happened before. It happened that night in July, and it happened again another night, then again and again. Something takes hold of my leg, and once my arm, and those purple-red finger marks will fade within a few days, turning the mottled yellow of old healing bruises. *Am* I imagining these episodes? I say *episodes* because I don't know what to call them. Am I just in bed thrashing about even though I'm awake? *There are no ghosts.* I don't believe in that, and, besides, our tiny house is so ordinary. So, nothing. That paranormal stuff happens in big houses with shutters and porches and staircases that lead to endless upstairs bedrooms, houses you'd look at and think: haunted.

Our house looks like it belongs in a beach-side town: a Cape Cod style with shingles, a steep roof, stone chimney, breezeway, and attached garage. If you saw this house you'd think it was a happy cottage. That's what we thought, other than the feeling that came over me the first time I stepped inside and felt the freezing air, wrapped a scarf over my head, held my elbows, old-woman-style, so cold, and the darkness, even though it was sunny that day, hearing the eerie pine boughs over the rooftop, shooshing as they moved madly in the spring wind, a sound that's so lonely. I hear those pine branches now, it's getting windy again, the branches thumping and smacking at the roof. A storm must be coming.

After inspecting my leg, putting peroxide and aloe on the bruises, I get dressed fast because I want to go outside and start digging in the garden, because that's where I like to be, where I feel safest up here in the mountains. I think of calling my mother, calling her for comfort and telling her about my night here, so many nights up here, maybe start with telling her about the wind that enters the house at night. She probably won't believe me because she is a woman of science, but she'll listen and will sense my terror and her voice will soothe me, because sometimes just hearing her voice gives me the feeling that I'm OK. I pick up the phone. The line is dead. Wind, rain, anything knocks it out: gone, dead, nothing on the line. Our neighbor who lives down the road, closest house to our house, comes over a lot, comes over in his stinky shirt, his bad teeth, but weirdly sexy dark beard, worn bandana, and likes to tell me, "Wait until winter. You'll lose electricity. You city people will never survive that."

Hate comes over me fast. I hate winter threats.

You want winter? I am winter. I want to yell out. You will never survive that. I hate him when he says that. Yet I'm drawn to him in a way I can't describe, won't dare to even explore. I don't yell, instead I stare at him maybe a bit too long, and pull my sleeves, all stretched out, a habit I have, pull them over my hands, fabric in tiny clumps in my palms.

Here, have tea, and I begin to go about the routine, and I will give him, our neighbor, a cup of tea, because he'll show up every Friday night, no matter what time we pull into our driveway, and there he is with his flashlight and wearing clog slippers, following us into the house as we lug in coolers with weekend food and tools and clothes. Here, have your tea, and I'll make one for myself, and he calls my tea STICKS because herbs are floating around, and I push the bowl of sugar we keep just for him and give him a spoon and watch him: one, two, three, four spoons of sugar, mixing it up, then glancing at me amused, like I am pure city and as good as dead come winter. I want to slap him and tell him: I am winter. Look at my face: pale as a baby blanket, my eerie so-blue eyes, yolk-blonde hair—I am of winter. I have parents who are from the Baltic Sea, across from Sweden, parents from tiny, cold Lithuania. Lithuania is pure winter. I know winters of frozen sea, snow so deep, so thick, that when we visit graves of our ancestors in Dew Cemetery, we shovel and dig to get to the surface of tombstones, and the candles we place to burn, burn in icy snow, our breaths curling in wind gusts like arctic squalls, burn bright, fantastic. The flames. The flames!

"Just wait until winter," he snickers, loves saying this, can't say it enough, as if this will scare us. Can't use his real name so I'll call him Hud, a name I made up and like and secretly call him when I think of him at night in our city bed.

As we drink our sticks I hear Morton banging around in the garage. He hates Hud, says you can't trust him because we know he's been in our house during the week when we're not here. He's left the light on. He's left the basement door unlocked.

I'm nice and patient with Hud, and wait for him to finish his tea. He's really slow, and even though I'm tired from the office, the work week, I don't rush him, and I pull out my two stumpy braids, blonde braids which I'll sometimes pin up, because that's my office look, but now, at our round butcher-block table, I know my eyes dance their blue mesmerizing color into people's blabbering, talking at me, telling me things. There are things I want to know:

Tell me if the man who built this house, died in this house.

Tell me if he died a horrible death.

I don't ask, but I hope Hud's gabbing leads me to these answers, because Morton says I scare people the way I ask so many questions and that I put people on the defensive. So I hope my patient eyes are asking Hud these things, hoping he gets off winter, and snow, and a hiker who was found dead—stepped right off a cliff holding his sandwich bag.

Hud can talk late into the night and Morton stays in the garage working, that's where he's set up the shop: table saw, big things like that, since the garage is huge, has the look of a mausoleum attached to our breezeway. Built of cinderblock with a door almost on the road, big enough for a truck to pull in. Hud did tell me the old man fixed cars here, told me the man once lived in California and left there to come here, to this cliff, and built this house by hand, by himself.

Who leaves California for these dark mountains?

Until now I didn't give much thought to the name of this mountain range. Actually, we are at the base of Pine Island Mountain, and that's the way I've thought about exactly where we are. But Devil's Path range is named for the early settlers that came here who believed these cliffs were built by the devil. It's so remote that this was a place for the devil to retreat.

The phone must be out from the wind and there are things to do to get my mind going and off my bad night, my leg, and the bruises. The garden to the side of the house, near the stone chimney, is my ongoing project and once I get outside, where I feel safe, I am reminded of how much I love nature, thick old trees, endless state forest, wild waterfalls, the river with glacial rocks that tumble in storms making a crashing noise like earthquakes, and why I said OK to buying this house. I could live outside: we are on a cliff overlooking the river, and mountains steep as walls in a climbing gym that rise at the front and back of the house. Way up over our mossy roof and through the pine branches that loom over it, you can see the sky. Clouds are coming in, wind bringing them fast, the field to one side of the house in shadows from the clouds, then not.

What I'm doing today, looking over my project as I drink coffee, strong and black, is planting Siberian sage and hoping it takes root and survives the winter. It's an experiment. I love sage.

I've already pulled up the last of the endless invasive lilies, transplanted them down the hill. The garden is next to the basement window, a dirty small window which rests on the ground, its glass slightly open. It's always been like that, propped open, ever since we bought the house, and if you stand there, you can smell something rotting from down below. The stench is like when newspapers get wet, or when cats pee on fabric, or like if there is a dead mouse decomposing, or like the time Neptune licked human shit he found in Washington Square Park, his breath a cave of rancid fatty feces as he later tried to kiss me.

I'm digging holes and sweating and my bruised leg hurts when I use it to force the edge of the shovel into the ground. It's hard work. Over in the field, on a hammock attached to a turquoise painted frame, something we found in our attic, Morton's resting, his arms bent, hands under his head. Did I mention we've only been married for one year? We met and married fast, within a couple of weeks. Maybe I *am* losing it and maybe after marrying is when I started losing it—discovering someone after marriage is a head-fuck, and you feel trapped because you find out things you hate, but you're already married, that license rolled up with a ribbon, next to the dog veterinary files and passports, and other things you'd rather not stir. Keep it all in place or you'll never find it when you really need it.

I dig. It's nice to have a long weekend, and it's Friday, and I'll have all weekend to water the sage once it's planted. Maybe it'll take away from the rotting smell coming up from the basement. I've tied a bandana over my nose and mouth. I smell the rot through the fabric. Digging the holes I hit a lot of rocks and pull them out, and everything's going pretty normal, until something weird happens. My shovel hits something mushy: a black plastic bag, really old, the plastic thinned, almost rust-black in color, and I work at digging around it, until I can get it out of the ground. The bag is big, knotted at the end. Something's inside. I open it and pull out a bone. The bone is odd shaped, like a handle to a suitcase, arched and smooth, the color of an old marble statue.

I use my gloves to brush off dirt and I'm thinking this must be an animal bone, deer or coyote. I call out to Morton and see only his one leg moving, the leg hanging over the edge of the hammock, swaying him. Nothing like a nap for him, staring up into the sky which still has sun, clouds coming in fast and thick. "Come here," I now shout louder, which I hate doing outside among trees, because shouting doesn't belong in the wilderness, unless an animal is doing it. My one dog responds to COME HERE and she's making her way over to me, her skinny pit tail wagging.

"Hey, Morton!"

"What? What are you yelling about?"

"Come over here. Look what I found."

"What is it?"

"Come here."

Morton slowly sits up, pulls on his beat-up hiking boots, stands, stretches, pets the two dogs under the hammock, making his way over, his wild curls like springs, his eyes squinting, his sanguine cheeks always so red, gnome-like. Slow, plodding along like an elephant, stopping to look up at the sky, then glancing down to ground, something interests him and he bends down to inspect something: a weed, which he picks and will give me, tucking the frail wispy purple blossom in my hair. Never in a rush, he likes to tell me that the slower you are, the faster you can get things done.

I show him the bone and ask him what he thinks, and he says he needs his good eyeglasses, and disappears into the house for a long time, because he forgets where he puts things. He finally comes back outside wearing big magnifying eyeglasses, the ones with thick black frames which practically cover his whole face. He studies the bone. "It's a foot," he says. "I'm pretty sure it's a foot."

"What foot? A human foot?"

"Probably."

We pass the bone back and forth between us, turning it over, holding it up high to the sun, then in the shade when a cloud passes over us. We stand like that for a long time because it's both scary and surreal to hold someone's foot.

"It's really a foot?" I ask again.

"I think so."

"What should we do with it?" I ask.

"I don't know. Keep it, I guess."

"I'm going to wash it," I tell him and get the hose. The post office will still be open, so after I wash the bone, I put it in a bucket, which makes it look sad. The post office will have an official person, and I should report the find. When I get to the small P.O. building with its cute flower boxes, a tiny bell rings over the door as I enter, and I place the bucket with the foot bone on the counter. The foot looks strange on the official counter where people put letters and postcards, and the woman behind it asks, "What have you got there?" There's a tone of familiarity in her voice and I can tell she knows of me, of us. The word's probably out: we don't shoot squirrels and don't eat meat and don't go to hog roasts. We are the new city people.

"It's a foot. I found it buried next to our house," I tell her, breathless, the way I get when nervous, like my words and breathing don't work at the same time, and I take out the foot, now trying to get control of my words, breath. Staying back, she looks, not touching it, but definitely looking and interested. She fixes her wig. I'm pretty sure it's a wig because I see it move slightly, and wigs are big around here. Everyone's always selling them at garage sales: ugly brown ones. The postmistress wears a straight piece with bangs, flipped up at the shoulders. "This is no place for such things," she tells me.

I tell her that maybe we should call the police or something, but she tells me there's no police here. We have a sheriff, but he's busy right now. Then she explains in a tone like I'm stupid, because of course I'm from the city—I've heard a neighbor click her tongue while shaking her head, seeing me in the tiny town cemetery just sitting on grass, resting after a long walk one day: *city people,* she said in that same tone, placing flowers on a grave—"People dumped a lot, back in the day. Backyards were for dumping." Then maybe because the post office is empty or maybe because she's suddenly thinking good things about her past, she sighs, seems to relax, the way I've seen my mother do, about to slip back in time, decades back, dreamy almost, ready to tell a story. There's a glass jar of candy on the counter and the postmistress pushes it toward me, just a little, and I politely take one, and we both unwrap the clear plastic which makes a whole lot of crinkling noise in the quiet place. We put the candies in our mouths, almost at the same time, and the tangy mint is weird because there is also a gooey taste, as if at some point the candy had melted, a coating now over it, which is both slimy and mealy.

"Did you know that the *famous* Robert Modes built your house?" she asks.

"I've heard."

"He was quite the man. He was a storyteller, you know."

"I've heard that, too." I'd heard this from the realtor who sold us the house, the lawyer at the bank for our mortgage, heard it from the owners who'd had the house briefly, just before us, heard it from Hud.

"Doesn't surprise me that you've heard of him. He was famous. Everyone's heard of him." Then, like some big secret she adds coyly, *"And I personally knew him."* Quickly working the ages out, like Hud, I figure she probably knew him as a child or a teenager, so maybe she'd have more information.

"How was he famous?" I ask, because so far I can't get more out of anyone.

"He was a storyteller," she says again, in case I didn't get it.

"A writer?" I ask, adding that I write short stories, and that I'm a kind of writer, and now she looks at me suspiciously, head cocked slightly, eyes almost to a squint.

"Are you a newspaper writer?"

"No," I say, and stop, deciding not to tell her anything else because explaining that my short stories have been published in literary journals will involve telling her where to buy them, find them, neither of which is possible, and the fact that I don't write for a newspaper seems disappointing, so we eat our mints. I chew up mine, she sucks on hers, and for a few seconds neither of us says anything and I'm looking over at a wall with flyers and I can feel her staring at my face, and I hope she tells me more about Robert Modes because I'm getting the feeling people aren't telling me things, and whatever they are telling me, they've all decided to say the exact same thing.

Someone walks into the post office: a man wearing a straw hat, with a big hump back, stooped, shuffling like his shoes don't fit. The postmistress starts in about the weather, winter is coming, and it'll be here before you know it. Just wait until winter. Winter is the worst. You haven't lived here if you haven't lived through a winter. The man leans, elbows on the counter, hunches over and sighs as if it was hard getting here and now he's ready to chat, probably assumed this same position, slack and comfy, his entire life. I want to shove winter in their faces, take them to my house and show them my 40-below jacket, thermal undershirt, faux fur and fleece hat with ear flaps, and my knitted scarf from Lithuania, made from big warm sheep.

I say nothing. The man adjusts himself—sighing, shifting, elbows holding his weight against the counter where I'd had the foot, the bucket now in my hand hanging at my side, and as I head out I swear I hear the postmistress quietly tell the man that I'm in the old Modes house, and he says something back to her and then she says something. When I get to our car and glance back they're both at the window, looking at me, just staring. If people dumped back then, they buried too, and this couldn't be Robert Mode's foot because I'd found old-fashioned, homemade wooden shoe stretches, marked LEFT, RIGHT. So I know Modes had two feet. Had he chopped someone else's foot off? Were there more body parts somewhere outside our house? Who did he kill? I know he was married and had a wife named Edith. But I heard he really loved her. Did he cut off her foot? But why would he do that? To keep her as his possession? Maybe he'd tortured her, cut off her foot?

Any which way I look at this, it's like some fucked-up puzzle, those large ones with a million pieces which I could never do. I'd get like two pieces to fit, always edges, and I'm thinking that this could be like those puzzles. Getting nowhere fast, and the only thing I'm thinking is: I need to figure it out, or I'll never sit still in this house, never feel at home, because isn't paranormal activity from unsettled, unreleased spirits, and if I don't figure it out, I'll never be able to close my eyes, because whatever is pulling me, whatever hates me, yanks my legs, leaves bruises, isn't going to stop.

The next morning is cold, fall arrives overnight and I have coffee, black, and put on the following in this order: undershirt, long sleeve T-shirt, crappy long button-down shirt, sweatshirt with long stretched-out sleeves, big cotton underwear, jeans, knit cap, woolen socks with prints of snowflakes, and my big hiking boots.

When I get outside I'm surprised it's warmer outside than inside the house. Inside, it's cold, the cold of an open fridge. I test it: in and out, dogs following, because with rescue dogs, they're like shadows, devoted saints with tails.

"I'm going down the road," I tell Morton. He's in the garage, wearing his plastic goggles, cutting wood on the table saw. He stops running the saw, which is loud and spitting sawdust all over.

"I'm going down the road," I tell him again.

"Where?" he asks, kind of annoyed because I've interrupted his work.

"To Hud's."

"He's a fucker, stay away."

"I'm going."

"What for?"

"I want to talk to him about the foot."

"What does he know? He's a liar. Stop with all your questions."

"I'm going. Bye."

"Take the dogs."

I always take the dogs. In the breezeway I put on their leashes even though I don't really need leashes because the dogs walk so close to my legs. Velcro style, leash-less, they're like a fur hoop skirt around me, but to be safe I put on the leashes. The breezeway is small, with a door to the garage and a door to the main house, a door to the outside, and then the opening down to the basement. The steps down are steep and narrow like for a dwarf and Morton, who is tall, has to duck to get down there. As a reminder he's put a toy duck above the first step: it's yellow, rubber, from when his daughter (from his first marriage) was a baby. Now the little breezeway is crowded by swirling dogs and before we go, Morton comes out and asks me, "Why are you always running off and leaving me?" He's got his wild dark curls pulled back with an elastic band. Is that *my* hair band? His red checks are sweaty, redder now than usual, and there's sawdust all over his shirt and in his scruffy beard. He's morphed into part mountain man, with a gritty sweaty smell and a new, tired slump in his shoulders.

"I could use some help," he tells me in a nasty voice, a tone I've noticed surfacing on weekends. He always wants me to help with dry wall and heavy lifting and building.

"Later," I tell him. "I'm going to see Hud."

I have my questions and rehearse them out loud while walking down the quiet road, questions Hud might either A) not know the answer to, or B) lie about. But I have to believe he can tell me things. Hud's told me he's lived in this town since he was twelve years old. He knew old man Modes. Tea time late Friday nights isn't cutting it, as Hud seems to be fixated on reporting roadwork, mountain lion sightings, old Sitzer's cancer, the next pancake supper over at the church.

I'm ready. I've found a foot.

Hud's house is set off our road. It's a log style, painted yellow, with a C-shaped driveway. By the time I get there, the dogs are panting hard, and I'm glad to have a bottle of water to dab their noses, ears, and big tongues.

Hud's standing on his porch, as if he'd sensed me approaching, and he's watching as I make my way toward him. He's holding something. When I get closer I see it's his dog, a Maltese. Hud looks at me as if I'm from outer space: stunned, suspicious, guarded. His dark eyes are like bullets. I love dark eyes. I hated growing up around blue-eyed people: parents, friends, and everyone in the entire country I visited summers, with those exact same ocean-blue eyes.

"What kind of dogs are those again?" Hud asks when I get to the porch steps.

"City dogs," I tell him and he opens the screen door, puts his dog inside the house, gently, and then closes the door. We talk while standing, even though two rocking chairs look good about now and a bowl for water for my dogs would be nice, but he's all business. He tells me he'll come over and visit with us later, he's got work to do at old Sitzer's house, cleaning out the chimney.

"I need to ask you some questions," I tell him and lose my breath and feel my heart pounding. "Did Robert Modes die in our house?"

"No," he says. "He got sick and went to a nursing home. He died there."

"Which nursing home?"

Hud doesn't answer, looks off at his view of a northern mountain, then he's back to talking about the hiker who stepped off the cliff last week, can you believe he didn't eat his lunch? There it was, right next to his body.

It's something I think could happen to me: anxious to eat, doing one thing, looking elsewhere, then down, down, down.

Hud's eyes intrigue me and hold me—black, reflectionless, the kind that won't meet my own. I want the truth if he knows it, maybe be does, but I don't believe the old man died in a nursing home. I know he died in our house, and I know something horrible happened, but what, I don't know, people aren't telling me.

Then out of nowhere Hud says, "Modes was in prison."

"Prison? Why?"

"He never talked about it, I'm not sure." He snickers. "But you should have heard that submarine story he used to tell."

I know that story, a boring story about a submarine Modes saw coming down our river, a story without any punch. I listen to Hud tell the submarine story, again, and before I leave Hud says, "I saw you at the post office yesterday."

"Yeah, that was me."

"I passed by and saw you in there."

I nod and tell him I have to get going. I'm being watched. Everywhere I go, I'm being watched.

When I get back to the house Morton's got a red painted wood box on the bed—dirty and dusty with cobwebs—and he says maybe it's a treasure chest. He found it in the attic above the garage, sort of a secret-style attic, but the tiny latch of the box is stuck and too hard to open, so I set it aside. Besides, I'm tired and need a nap, so I wrap myself in the folds of my sleeping bag, carry it outside, and lie down on Morton's mother's old lawn chair. This was her chair which she kept in the Bronx, where Morton grew up. Here, imagining how this pale green lawn chair would be set out on a city sidewalk, I can rest, sleep, here, under branches of poplars, their leaves like tiny hands, dogs around me like sheep.

I don't look inside that wood box for a long time.

As for the foot, it disappears. I'll ask Morton again and again: Where's the damn foot, where'd you put it? When I brought it back from the post office I'd given Morton the bucket, and we'd planned to bury the bone properly with a marker. But the foot is gone, and for weeks after that I'm crying. It was my clue, *my bone,* my real connection to someone.

"It's gone, forget the foot," Morton kept saying.

"Where is it? Try to remember where you put it!" I screamed, my braids swinging back and forth over the top of my shoulders as I'd grab Morton's arm, his sleeve, my friend, his sleeve: cotton long sleeve tee fabric so familiar in my hand. My fingers, as I pull at it, pull at him for answers, pull at him, trying to get him closer to me.

"I'll be in the garage working," he'd say.

"Where's the foot?"

Then one day he'd had enough. We were in the breezeway, and he was ignoring me, heading into the garage, when I grabbed his sleeve, starting in about the bone. He slowly turned, looking at me, his eyes dead-like, glazed, and he breathed in and out and in and out, like he was going to let me have it. His sleeve was tight in my hand. I was holding on. But there was something in Morton: a distance, as if a blank space was opening up between us. It was that mirror upon mirror, the image so far away.

I let go of the sleeve.

"Grow up," he said. "You're such a fucking kid."

I'll never see the foot again. In time Morton is baffled at the way I'll bring it up out of nowhere, like while watching TV in the city, or having pizza on University. "Where's the foot?" I'll ask, because I know this: the truth is not always coaxed out by my urging, water-blue eyes. I know that sometimes surprise questions can bring answers.

Visiting Editors

Kyle Bass is a New York Foundation for the Arts (NYFA) Fellow in both fiction and playwriting, and a finalist for the Princess Grace Playwriting Award. His plays have been produced by several regional theatres and his work has appeared in the journals *Stone Canoe, Folio,* and *Callaloo,* among other publications. Kyle teaches at both Goddard College and at Syracuse University, and is Resident Dramaturg at Syracuse Stage. Kyle holds an M.F.A. in creative writing from Goddard College.

Jennifer Brice has taught creative nonfiction and literature at Colgate University since 2003, and once worked as a newspaper reporter. She is the author of *The Last Settlers,* a work of literary journalism, and *Unlearning to Fly,* a memoir, and has had her work published in a variety of magazines. A native of Alaska, she graduated from Smith College and University of Alaska Fairbanks.

Yvonne Buchanan is a professor of art and design at Syracuse University who is best known for her prizewinning illustrations for children's books and for her cartoons and illustrations in major publications such as *The Wall Street Journal, The Nation, The Los Angeles Times,* and *The New York Times.* She is a winner of the Parents' Choice Silver Award, and has been nominated for the NAACP Image Award, for her work with children's literature. Lately, she has focused on experimental video.

Paul Cody, a resident of Ithaca, New York, and a graduate of the Cornell M.F.A. program, is the author of four critically acclaimed novels, including *Shooting the Heart,* as well as a number of shorter articles and stories for major magazines. He has taught at Cornell University and Ithaca College, and also has served as associate editor and award-winning writer of *Cornell Magazine.* He has also taught at a maximum security penitentiary.

Megan Davidson, former editor-in-chief of Lee Shore Agency and Sterling House Publishers, has edited hundreds of books, including two Pulitzer Prize-nominated novels, and has ghostwritten half a dozen books. She is the author of three historical romances and coauthor of two nonfiction books on writing. She has an M.F.A. in writing from the University of Pittsburgh. She currently does freelance consulting and teaches at the Downtown Writer's Center in Syracuse.

Dr. Jerrold Heller, a member of the Board of Trustees at Syracuse University, is renowned for his contributions to the field of digital technology, particularly digital television, and has been awarded two Emmys for outstanding achievement in engineering development. He has held senior executive positions in several corporations, has several patents, and has authored many technical papers on various subjects of digital communications. Dr. Heller has a B.S. from Syracuse University and an M.S. and Ph.D. from M.I.T.

Neva Pilgrim teaches at Colgate University and is the artistic director for the Society of New Music, now in its 39th season. She also hosts and produces *Fresh Ink,* a classical music program now in its 15th year on NPR. Ms. Pilgrim, a well-known soprano, has performed in orchestral and opera settings throughout the world with a host of distinguished musicians and orchestras, and has recorded extensively with several music labels.

Minnie Bruce Pratt recently completed *Inside the Money Machine,* a book of poems about living under capitalism. Her last book of poetry, *The Dirt She Ate: Selected and New Poems,* received a 2003 Lambda Literary Award for Lesbian Poetry. Previous books include *Walking Back Up Depot Street,* named Best Lesbian/Gay Book of the Year by *ForeWord: The Magazine of Independent Bookstores and Booksellers,* and *Crime Against Nature,* the Lamont Poetry Selection of the Academy of American Poets. She is professor of writing and rhetoric, and women's and gender studies at Syracuse University.

Dorene Quinn is a multimedia artist and professor of three-dimensional design and sculpture at the Pratt/Munson-Williams-Proctor Arts Institute in Utica, New York, and also teaches at SUNY Oswego. She has exhibited in solo and group shows throughout the Upstate New York region, as well as in California and New York City. She has degrees from the Pacific Northwest College of Art and Alfred University. Most recently, Dorene has partnered with Yvonne Buchanan on the development of innovative art programs for Syracuse's Near West Side Initiative.

Nancy Keefe Rhodes Nancy Keefe Rhodes is a writer, editor and curator whose work covers film, photo and visual arts. She is a member of Syracuse's Public Arts Commission, teaches film theory and criticism in Transmedia/College ofVisual and Performing Arts at Syracuse University, and in 2011 was founding editor of the Moving Images section.

Bruce Smith is an English professor at Syracuse University and author of six named volumes of poetry. The latest, *Devotions,* was a finalist for the 2011 National Book Award in poetry, and was named by Publishers Weekly as one of the best books of 2011. Another of his books, *"The Other Lover,"* was finalist for both the NBA and the Pulitzer Prize. A native of Philadelphia, Bruce has held faculty positions at several universities, and has also taught in a maximum security prison.

Steven Stucky, widely recognized as one of today's leading classical composers, is the Given Foundation Professor of Composition at Cornell University and president of the American Music Center. He won the Pulitzer Prize for his *Second Concerto for Orchestra* in 2005, and has had his works performed by leading orchestras throughout the world. He is currently Consulting Composer for New Music for the Los Angeles Philharmonic, and is serving as composer-in-residence for the Pittsburgh Symphony for the 2011-12 season. He has degrees from Baylor University and Columbia University.

CONTRIBUTORS

The following contributors appear in the print edition. See p. 400 for a list of contributors to *Stone Canoe 6 Online.*

JENNIFER R. ADAMS, a former journalist and ESL teacher, is currently a lecturer in English at Cornell and is working on a novel.

KAZIM ALI, author of many books of poetry and prose, teaches at Oberlin College and is the founding editor of Nightboat Books.

BETSY ANDREWS is the author of *New Jersey,* recipient of the 2007 Brittingham Prize in Poetry, and deputy editor of *Saveur,* a food magazine.

AIMÉE BAKER is a fiction writer and poet who grew up in Upstate New York and returned to the North Country after completing her M.F.A. at Arizona State University.

BARTOW + METZGAR began their collaborative practice in 1999, and have had their projects exhibited throughout the U.S. and in Quebec, Canada. More on B+M's collaborative work can be found at *bartowmetzgar.wordpress.com.*

CARROLL BEAUVAIS, former Editor-in-Chief of *Salt Hill Journal* and winner of the Hayden Carruth Poetry Prize, currently serves as interim associate director of the Creative Writing Program at Syracuse University.

MARNA BELL, a New York State Council of the Arts grant recipient, participated in the 2008 Everson Museum Biennial, and has had numerous solo shows throughout the Upstate New York region.

BRUCE BENNETT, author of nine books of poetry, is professor and chair of English at Wells College.

* **PETER T. BENNETT** is an artist living in Maine whose current projects involve explorations of the artistic and symbolic possibilities of aluminum.

ALEX BIEGLER, a native Texan, recently graduated from Syracuse University with a degree in painting.

DIANN BLAKELY, an acclaimed poet and arts journalist currently living in Savannah, Georgia, is at work on a book-length series of poetic duets with Robert Johnson.

JOHN BLANDLY is a fiction writer living in Albany, New York.

Asterisked authors appear in both the print issue and *Stone Canoe 6 Online.*
See *www.stonecanoejournal.org* for more detailed information on our contributors and their connections to the Upstate New York region.

Karen M. Brummund is an Ithaca artist whose public installations of architectural and environmental structures have been shown worldwide.

Molly Burdick is a junior at Nottingham High School in Syracuse.

John Colasacco lives and writes in Syracuse; he has degrees in advertising and creative writing from Syracuse University.

Elinor Cramer, whose first book of poems was published in 2011, practices psychotherapy in Syracuse.

Jessica Cuello teaches French at Marcellus High School in Upstate New York. Her poetry won the 2010Vivienne Haigh-Wood Poetry Prize from the online journal *Melusine.*

Juan Cruz is a Puerto Rican-born painter and community activist whose current project involves the redevelopment of the Near West Side neighborhood in Syracuse.

Num Cung, a native of Burma and now a senior at Nottingham High School in Syracuse, enjoys writing poetry and music lyrics.

Susan D'Amato, associate professor of drawing at Syracuse University, has exhibited and published extensively throughout the United States and abroad.

Angela DeSantis Dailey is a poet and English teacher who also owned and operated Inkblotz Studio and Gallery in Geneva, New York.

Francis DiClemente is a poet, photographer, and video producer in Syracuse.

George Drew, author of four collections of poetry, won the 2009 Adirondack Literary Award for his book *American Cool.*

Gregory Donovan is a poet and fiction writer who teaches in the graduate creative writing program at Virginia Commonwealth University and is the senior editor of the online journal *Blackbird.*

Stephen Dunn, a Pulitzer Prize-winning poet and author of fifteen books, has a master's degree from Syracuse University.

Jimmy Ellerbe is a community artist and a senior at Corcoran High School in Syracuse.

Myron Ernst, a poet from Vestal, New York, formerly taught French and Italian at SUNY Plattsburgh, and was co-owner/director of a Montessori preschool.

Lisa Feinstein lives in Rochester, New York. Her work has appeared in many journals and literary reviews.

Eliot Fisk, a Syracuse native, is a world-renowned classical guitar virtuoso and the last student of Andrés Segovia.

Kit Frick, a poet and associate editor for Black Lawrence Press, is currently studying in the M.F.A. Program in Creative Writing at Syracuse University.

Eric Geissinger lives in Watkins Glen, New York, and works as a technical writer. He has published short fiction in several journals.

* **Mary Gilliland,** recently retired from teaching poetry at Cornell University, has numerous publications to her credit, and has recently won awards in such journals as *AGNI, Notre Dame Review,* and *Stand.*

Beckian Fritz Goldberg's most recent volume of poems is *Reliquary Fever: New and Selected Poems* (New Issues, 2010). She teaches in the M.F.A. program at Arizona State University.

Christine Hamm, a native of Endicott, New York, currently teaches English at CUNY. She is a widely published poet, poetry editor of the literary journal, *Ping Pong*, and founder and editor of the Fat Gold Watch Press.

Edward Hardy, an Ithaca, New York, native currently living in Rhode Island, is the author of three novels. The piece included in this issue is an excerpt from a novel-in-progress, *The Return of the Lovely Wrecks.*

Tara Helfman is an assistant professor at Syracuse University College of Law.

Cliff Henderson has lived in Upstate New York for twenty years. Having written travel, art, and entertainment articles for years, he is experiencing a late vocation as a poet.

Akua Lezli Hope is a writer and visual artist living in the Finger Lakes region whose work has appeared in a number of magazines and anthologies.

Anya Maria Johnson is a December 2011 graduate of Syracuse University who has won awards for both her fiction and her poetry.

Anna Journey, a poet and essayist whose book *If Birds Gather Your Hair for Nesting* was selected for the National Poetry Series in 2009, recently received a poetry fellowship from the National Endowment for the Arts.

Mike Jurkovic is co-director of Calling All Poets and vice-president of the Howland Cultural Center in Beacon, New York. He is also a music producer and writes reviews for music magazines.

* **Nancy Kang** teaches writing and literature at Syracuse University.

★ **Gina Keicher** is an M.F.A. candidate at Syracuse University.

Ivy Kleinbart teaches academic writing and creative nonfiction at Syracuse University.

Chrissy Kolaya's poetry and fiction have appeared in many magazines and anthologies, and she has received several grants and fellowships from both private and public foundations.

Ilyse Kusnetz teaches English and creative writing at Valencia College. Her manuscript, *Tips From the Underworld,* was a finalist for two poetry prizes in 2009.

Charlene Langfur is a teacher and writer, a graduate of the Syracuse creative writing program, and a grateful student of the late W.D. Snodgrass and Philip Booth.

John A. Lauricella is an Ithaca-based fiction writer and author of *Home Games: Essays on Baseball Fiction.* The piece included here is the first chapter of a book-length manuscript.

Jude Lewis is a sculptor and custom furniture builder who lives in Jamesville, New York.

Tatianna Lebron is a junior at George Fowler High School in Syracuse.

Jay Leeming is a poet from Ithaca, New York, who has taught at Butler University and SUNY Plattsburgh and was a past Poet Laureate of Tompkins County.

Naton Leslie teaches at Siena College in Loudenville, New York. He is the author of seven volumes of poetry and a prizewinning collection of short fiction.

Lyn Lifshin has published over 120 books and chapbooks, edited four anthologies, and was the subject of the award-winning documentary film *Not Made of Glass.*

Kenneth Lin, a Cornell graduate, is an award-winning playwright and screenwriter whose plays have been commissioned and staged throughout the country. *Fallow,* excerpted here, is scheduled to premiere in January 2012 at People's Light & Theatre in the Philadelphia area.

David Lloyd is a widely published fiction writer and poet who directs the Creative Writing Program at Le Moyne College in Syracuse.

Stephanie Loveless is a Montréal-born media artist who lives and works in Brooklyn and Montréal. Her work has been presented widely in North America, South America, Europe, and the Middle East.

★ **Charles Lupia,** a graduate of Syracuse University, is the author of many plays and a children's musical, *The Ugly Duckling,* that was produced by the Society for New Music in Syracuse.

Stephen Marion is a fiction writer and Cornell University alumnus currently living in East Tennessee.

Andrew Martin is a student at Syracuse University, where he is pursuing a master's degree in Electrical Engineering.

Tim McCoy has an M.F.A. from Syracuse University and teaches at several regional colleges.

Christopher McEvoy is currently an assistant professor of art at the State University of New York at Oswego, where he is also the painting coordinator. He lives and works in Oswego, New York.

* **Thomas McGraw** grew up in Weedsport, New York, and is now teaching at Phillips Academy in Andover, Massachusetts.

* **Bridget Meeds** was born in Fairmount, New York, and lives and writes in Ithaca, New York.

Michael M. Meguid has retired from an active life as an operating surgeon and research scientist at Upstate Medical University in Syracuse, and now divides his writing time between Upstate New York and Marco Island, Florida.

* **Philip Memmer** is the author of three books of poetry and founder of the Downtown Writer's Center at the YMCA of Greater Syracuse.

* **Devon J. Moore** is a Buffalo native and an M.F.A. candidate at Syracuse University.

Tom Moran is a professor in the Center for Multidisciplinary Studies at Rochester Institute of Technology (RIT) and a widely published author.

Nicola Morris teaches in the English Department at SUNY Cortland and in the Goddard College M.F.A. in Creative Writing Program.

David Musselwhite is a recent graduate of Cornell, where he studied contemporary poetry with Alice Fulton. He currently teaches social studies in Detroit, through AmeriCorps' Teach for America program.

Jeanie Nguyen is a poet and senior at Nottingham High School in Syracuse.

Jesse Nissim is an award-winning poet who currently serves as Faculty Writing Fellow in The College of Arts and Sciences at Syracuse University.

Lori Nix, a former visiting artist at Pratt/Munson-Williams Proctor, lives and works in Brooklyn, creating model landscapes and complex dioramas for the camera.

Steve Pearlman, a widely published photographer and Maxwell School graduate, is a career administrator for nonprofit organizations serving the disadvantaged.

Mike Petrik is a native Central New Yorker now pursuing his Ph.D. in fiction writing at the University of Missouri.

Margarita E. Pignataro is a visiting assistant professor at Syracuse University. She is a U.S. Latina of Chilean descent.

Robert F. Piwowar is an inmate at Attica Correctional Facility.

Marc-Anthony Polizzi's art is heavily influenced by his experiences growing up in the post-industrial city of Utica, New York. He currently lives and works in Kansas City, Missouri, and exhibits throughout the United States.

Tina Post lives with her husband and two sons in a ramshackle farmhouse in Upstate New York. She is currently writing creative nonfiction on the themes of boxing and race in America.

Michele Poulos is a poet, fiction writer, and screenwriter currently studying in the M.F.A. program at Arizona State University.

Nate Pritts, the author of five collections of poetry, is founder of *H_NGM_N,* an online journal and small press. He teaches at Bryant & Stratton College and the Downtown Writer's Center in Syracuse.

Emily Pulfer-Terino, a native of Syracuse and recent recipient of an M.F.A. from Syracuse University, currently teaches at a boarding school in Western Massachusetts.

Brian Rautio is studying for a Ph.D. degree at Syracuse University, majoring in electrical engineering.

Melissa Reider has been writing—and publishing—since the third grade, and describes Central New York, with its "unapologetic ruralness," as her "situating place." She currently works at Upstate Medical University.

Ann Reichlin is an artist based in Ithaca, New York.

Dan Roche is the author of the memoirs *Great Expectation: A Father's Diary,* and *Love's Labors.* He teaches nonfiction and journalism at Le Moyne College in Syracuse.

Wilka Roig, a native Puerto Rican based in Ithaca, New York, and San Miguel de Allende, México, works in photography, performance, and installation. Wilka earned an M.F.A. in 2005 from Cornell University, where she lectured until 2009, receiving the Merrill Outstanding Educator Award.

Kristian Rodriguez was raised in a Puerto Rican household in Atlanta, Georgia. He recently completed his degree in drama at Syracuse University, where he was appointed an Engagement Fellow, and serves as an artistic associate at the Red House Arts Center.

Edward Ruchalski, a musician and composer with nine studio recordings and numerous commissions, is currently visiting assistant professor of music at Le Moyne College in Syracuse.

Natalia Rachel Singer, author of *Scraping By in the Big Eighties,* a memoir, and co-editor of *Living North Country,* teaches English at St. Lawrence University.

Mary McLaughlin Slechta is a poet and fiction writer who moved to Syracuse from rural Connecticut to attend graduate school and never returned, feeling "seriously at home here."

Alexandria Smith is a Syracuse alum who lives and teaches in Brooklyn, and has participated in various exhibitions throughout New York City, including "The Gentrification of Brooklyn: The Pink Elephant Speaks" at MoCADA.

Amber Christine Snider taught poetry in the New York City Schools before relocating to Syracuse to enroll in the English literature Ph.D. program.

Matthew J. Spireng, lives in Lomontville in Ulster County. His book *What Focus Is* was published in 2011 by Word Press and his book *Out of Body* won the 2004 Bluestem Poetry Award. He is also the author of five chapbooks.

Ruth Sproul, a NYFA MARK artist who teaches at Cornell University, has exhibited in over 25 national and international group shows.

Barbara Stout, an internationally renowned artist and NYFA MARK Fellow, recently joined the art faculty at the State University of New York, Oswego.

Mykolaj Suchý is a ninth grade student at Nottingham High School in Syracuse.

D.S. Sulaitis is a prizewinning writer from West Kill, New York, who has received New York Foundation for the Arts fellowships for both her fiction and nonfiction work.

Ed Tato, a Buffalo native and the author of two books of poetry, is currently an M.F.A. student at Syracuse.

Tony Trischka, a Syracuse native, is considered by many to be the most important banjo player of his generation.

Lou Ventura was raised in Geneva, New York, and attended St. Bonaventure University in Olean, where he now lives. His poems are often grounded in Upstate New York experience.

James Bradley Wells teaches Classics at Hamilton College in Clinton, New York. He has written one poetry collection, which has been a finalist in multiple book competitions, and will soon complete a second.

Renate Wildermuth is based in North Creek, New York, and is a poet and freelance writer for various newspapers and magazines, and a commentator for North Country Public Radio.

Jerome Wilson is a former New York State Senator now living in Essex, Connecticut, who likes to experiment with the sonnet form and also translates from the German the poems of Rainer Maria Rilke.

Brianne Wood is a junior at Nottingham High School in Syracuse.

Elizabeth Wyckoff grew up in Canton, New York, and now lives in Austin, Texas, where she hosts author readings at BookPeople—Texas's largest independent bookstore—and works as the Outreach Coordinator for American Short Fiction.

Christian Zwahlen is a fiction writer from Rochester, New York, whose work focuses on the neighborhoods of his native city.

• • •

The following contributors are featured in the **SC 6 Online** section at *www.stonecanoejournal.org.*

Nicolae Babuts taught French language and literature at Syracuse University for three decades and served as the director for the SU Abroad program in Poitiers, France.

Robert Bilheimer is an Academy Award-winning documentary filmmaker based near Geneva, New York. His latest film, *Not My Life,* about global human trafficking, premiered on CNN in October 2011.

Michelle Bonczek teaches literature and creative writing at Lebanon Valley College in Pennsylvania. Originally from the Binghamton area, her first two degrees were from SUNY Brockport.

Haim Bouzaglo is an Israeli filmmaker who has had two films in the Syracuse International Film Festival, and shot his recent film, *Session,* in Upstate New York when he was a visiting professor in Syracuse University's Transmedia program.

Willa Carroll, originally from Rochester, New York, currently lives in New York City, where she maintained an active career in theatre and dance through 2005. She has a B.A. and an M.F.A. from Bennington College.

Patricia Clark teaches English and creative writing and is director of African and African-American Studies at SUNY Oswego. Her forthcoming book is about food and black female identity.

Terese Coe recently completed her M.F.A. at Cornell University, where she served as assistant editor of *Epoch*. She is currently teaching at the New York Institute of Technology in Manhattan.

William Cordeiro has an M.F.A. in poetry from Cornell University, where he is currently a Ph.D. candidate studying 18th century British literature. His work has been published or is forthcoming in several literary journals.

Deborah Diemont lives in Syracuse and has had poems published in several journals. Her chapbook *Wanderer* was published in 2009.

Paul Doty is a reference librarian at St. Lawrence University, and has resided in St. Lawrence county for fourteen years, after careening Kerouac-like around New England and the Midwest.

George Drew, originally from Mississippi, is an Upstate New York resident and the author of five poetry collections, the most recent of which won the X.J. Kennedy Prize in 2010.

Sharon Greytak is an awarding-winning experimental filmmaker whose latest film, *Archeology of a Woman,* stars Sally Kirkland. She divides her time between New York City and Syracuse, where she teaches in the Transmedia program.

Colin D. Halloran is a former infantryman and public school teacher from Albany, New York, who is currently an M.F.A. candidate at Fairfield University and editor-in-chief of *Mason's Road* literary journal.

Gayle Elen Harvey, author of eight collections of poetry and winner of a number of literary prizes, lives in Utica, New York. Eating barracuda for lunch and taming Catskill rattlesnakes, she says, has prepared her for life as a poet.

Andrew Johnson, founder of Film Geek Radio, is a veteran videographer who has lived in China and Latin America, and is currently in the Goldring Arts Journalism master's program at Syracuse University.

Kerry Kennedy is a writer and career arts administrator now working with the Downtown YMCA Arts Branch in Syracuse.

Kevin Martin Kern a Syracuse graduate, is currently based in North Hollywood, working as an archivist for a major Hollywood studio. His passions include classic animation, film archiving, and film restoration.

Kiki Koroshetz is a graduate of Colgate University who worked in rural poverty programs in Upstate New York before moving to New York City, where she is an editorial assistant at Hyperion Books.

Doran Larson is a English professor at Hamilton College and has been both a contributor and guest editor for several issues of *Stone Canoe.*

Mike Levin, a native of Rochester, New York, is currently the creative writing/theatre arts chair at Flagstaff Arts and Leadership Academy, a performing arts high school in Arizona.

Milcho Manchevski is a Macedonian filmmaker who has screened four films at the Syracuse International Film Festival. He teaches in New York University's Tisch School of the Arts.

Jeffrey H. MacLachlan is a poet who grew up in the Finger Lakes Region and currently resides in Skaneateles, New York.

Becca McArthur, originally from Denver, Colorado, is a writer of nonfiction and recent graduate of Colgate University.

L. Noelle McLaughlin is a poet and fiction writer who currently resides in New Paltz, New York.

Dan Menkin is an Israeli filmmaker who taught screenwriting at Syracuse University in the fall of 2011. He has had three films screened in the Syracuse International Film Festival.

Lisa Mullenneaux was born and raised in Albany, New York, and is now a medical writer/editor in Manhattan. Her poetry has appeared in several literary journals.

Rob Nilsson is a leading independent filmmaker and teacher based in San Francisco who participated last fall, for the third time, in the Syracuse International Film Festival.

Karl Parker teaches contemporary poetry/poetics at Hobart & William Smith Colleges in Geneva, New York, and is poetry editor for *Seneca Review.* He has published three chapbooks and served as assistant editor for Best American Poetry (2004) and the Oxford Book of American Poetry (2006).

Mary Elizabeth Parker, currently living in Greensboro, North Carolina, is the author of three poetry collections. She was born in Schenectady and visits family as often as possible in Syracuse.

Elizabeth Preston, (a recent Williams College graduate) grew up in Syracuse and currently lives in Chicago, where she is editor of the children's science magazine *Muse.*

William Preston, a science fiction writer and winner of the Zoetrope All-Story Short Fiction Contest, teaches English and creative writing at the Manlius Pebble Hill School in DeWitt, New York.

TANIA PRYPUTNIEWICZ is a poet, photographer, blogger and poetry editor at *The Fertile Source*. Born and raised in Utica, she currently lives with her family in Sonoma County, California.

FRANK READY is a film and television enthusiast currently enrolled in the Goldring Arts Journalism masters program at Syracuse University.

BUSHRA REHMAN is co-editor of *Colonize This!: Young Women of Color on Today's Feminism*. Her writing has been featured in numerous magazines and on numerous radio shows, and her first novel is forthcoming from Upset Press. She lives in West Skokan, New York.

RYAN SKRABALAK was born in Binghamton, "The Parlor City," raised in Delmar, and resides now in Brooklyn, New York. Like many up-to-downstate transplants, he believes his spirit-heart still wanders about the Hudson Valley and the Adirondack Mountains. His most recent work is published in the *Brooklyn Review*.

JAY ROGOFF, the author of four books of poems, teaches at Skidmore College in Saratoga Springs, New York.

PAUL B. ROTH, founder and editor of the award-winning The Bitter Oleander Press, based in Fayetteville, New York, has published six collections of poetry.

CHARLOTTE ZOË WALKER, a prizewinning short story writer, novelist, and editor, and professor emerita at SUNY Oswego, is nearing completion of her latest novel, *Gray Face and Eve,* about a twelfth century sculptor. Walker earned her Ph.D. in English literature from Syracuse University.

THOM WARD resides in Rochester, New York, and is the author of five poetry collections.

The Syracuse University Humanities Center, founded in 2008, fosters public engagement in the Humanities, and is home to the Syracuse Symposium™, the Central New York Humanities Corridor, the Jeanette K. Watson Distinguished Visiting Professorship and Visiting Collaborator programs, the HC Mini-Seminar and Symposium Seminar series, the Perpetual Peace Project, and other major initiatives, fellowships and public programming.

Working Toward a World Where Every Person is Valued

The Burton Blatt Institute was established to open the world to the enormous potential of people with disabilities. It starts with building an understanding of the challenges they face each and every day.

Our mission is to build upon that understanding—creating inclusive environments in schools, the workplace, and the community—through research, education, training, policy, technical assistance, outreach, and fundraising. Our ultimate goal: To create a world where every person is valued.

"We can change the world. The first step is to change ourselves!"
–Burton Blatt

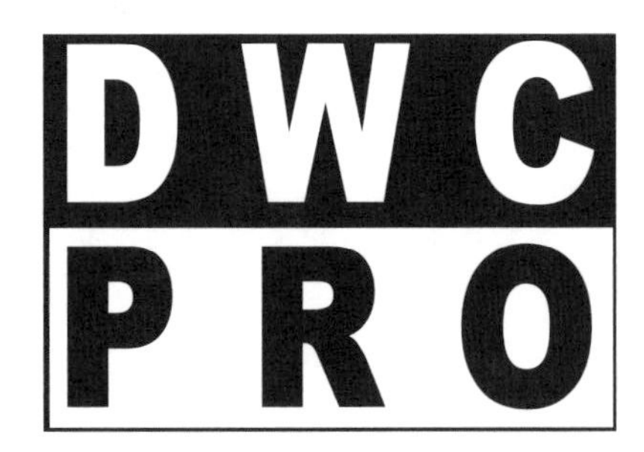
DWC
PRO

The YMCA's
Downtown
Writer's
Center

the
YMCA

www.communigration.com
Sean Branagan
President/Founder
communigration
technology marketing
315-579-4323

stressdesign
WWW.STRESSDESIGN.COM

2011-2012 season

SOCIETY *for* NEW MUSIC

Music from the Heart of New York

5pm Sept. 17 Steve Reich *Music for 18 Musicians* - Everson (where the Society began)
In conjunction w/ David MacDonald's African inspired *Power of Pattern* exhibit– 4pm

7pm Oct. 14 premiere Philip Rothman's† score for D.W. Griffith's 1920 film *Way Down East* - Palace Theater (w/ Syracuse International Film Festival & LeMoyne C.)

4pm Oct. 23 *The Geography of the Imagination* premiere of Greg Wanamaker* & Carrie Mae Weems commissioned "A Story Within A Story" (music with visuals)
Hendricks Chapel (w/S.U. Humanities C.) - addressing the poetics of identity & historical memory.
Also music by **David Feurzeig, Kevin Puts, Anna Weesner† & Nicholas Omiccioli†**

8pm Nov. 9 Kronos Quartet premiere of Douglas Quin's *Polar Suite*
(in partnership w/ S.U. ArtsEngage) - **Setnor Aud, Crouse**

2:30pm Feb. 26 Brian Israel tribute - Everson Museum
Music by Brian Israel*, for whom the Israel prize was named 25 years ago. Guest composer **Derek Bermel†, Rob Paterson† & 2011 Israel winnersThomas Healy & Bret Bohman**

4pm March 25 *Vision of Sound* (live new music with dance) - **Carrier Theater, Civic Center**
Music by **Paola Marquez (premiere), Roberto Sierra*, Diane Jones (premiere), Carlos Sanchez-Gutierrez*, David Hanner, Mark Olivieri*,** choreographed by **Melanie Aceto, Candy Aguilera, Michelle Pritchard, Cheryl Wilkins-Mitchell, Sarah Zehnder** & dancers from across Upstate NY.

What the critics say:

"powerfully moving work" ArtsVoice, Buffalo

"enormous success" Rochester

"sounded sensational" New Times

"high-quality entertainment" Post Standard

Sept. 16 OCC Arts Across Campus, Reich *Music for 18*
Nov. 30 Utica College LunchHour Series, Music by **Mellits*, Sierra* & Jin Ping***
Jan. 27 OCC Arts Across Campus, Music by **Wanamaker*, Jeleniauskas, Puts & Bacon**
Feb. 1 Wed. Morning Club, Rome, NY Music by **Ascioti, Sierra*, Mellits***
Feb. 5 Arts Alive, Liverpool Library, *Two by Two, Too* - Puts, Morrill*, Farr, Jeleniauskas
Feb. 12 Hamilton College, Clinton, NY *Eleanor Roosevelt* (fully staged opera w/ chamber orchestra) by **Persis Parshall Vehar,** based on **Rhoda Lerman's book & play Eleanor: Her Secret Journey**

***FRESH INK* Sundays at 2pm WCNY-FM, WJNY-FM, WUNY-FM www.WCNY.org**

***SNM commissioned composer www.societyfornewmusic.org †Israel winner**

MIX
From responsible sources
FSC
www.fsc.org
FSC® C018421